The Dynamic Cosmos

Bloomsbury Advances in Religious Studies

Series Editors: Bettina E. Schmidt, Steven Sutcliffe and Will Sweetman
Founding Editors: James Cox and Peggy Morgan

Bloomsbury Advances in Religious Studies publishes cutting-edge research in the Study of Religion/s. The series draws on anthropological, ethnographical, historical, sociological, and textual methods amongst others. Topics are diverse, but each publication integrates theoretical analysis with empirical data. The series aims to refresh the interdisciplinary agenda in new evidence-based studies of "religion."

Religion and the Inculturation of Human Rights in Ghana
Abamfo Ofori Atiemo

Religion as a Conversation Starter
Ina Merdjanova and Patrice Brodeur

Religion, Material Culture and Archaeology
Julian Droogan

Rethinking "Classical Yoga" and Buddhism
Karen O'Brien Kop

Secular Assemblages
Marek Sullivan

Spirits and Trance in Brazil
Bettina E. Schmidt

Spirit Possession and Trance
edited by Bettina E. Schmidt and Lucy Huskinson

Spiritual Tourism
Alex Norman

Theology and Religious Studies in Higher Education
edited by D. L. Bird and Simon G. Smith

The Critical Study of Non-Religion
Christopher R. Cotter

The Problem with Interreligious Dialogue
Muthuraj Swamy

UFOs, Conspiracy Theories and the New Age
David G. Robertson

The Dynamic Cosmos

Movement, Paradox, and Experimentation in the Anthropology of Spirit Possession

Diana Espírito Santo and Matan Shapiro

BLOOMSBURY ACADEMIC
LONDON • NEW YORK • OXFORD • NEW DELHI • SYDNEY

BLOOMSBURY ACADEMIC
Bloomsbury Publishing Plc
50 Bedford Square, London, WC1B 3DP, UK
1385 Broadway, New York, NY 10018, USA
29 Earlsfort Terrace, Dublin 2, Ireland

BLOOMSBURY, BLOOMSBURY ACADEMIC and the Diana logo are
trademarks of Bloomsbury Publishing Plc

First published in Great Britain 2022
This paperback edition published 2024

A catalogue record for this book is available from the British Library.

Library of Congress Control Number: 2021952915

ISBN: HB: 978-1-3502-9885-9
        PB: 978-13-502-9936-8
      ePDF: 978-1-3502-9933-7
     eBook: 978-1-3502-9934-4

Series: Bloomsbury Advances in Religious Studies

Typeset by Integra Software Services Pvt. Ltd.

To find out more about our authors and books visit www.bloomsbury.com
and sign up for our newsletters

Contents

Contributors

Diego Maria Malara is an Assistant Professor of Social Anthropology at the University of Glasgow, whose research to date has mostly focused on Ethiopian Orthodox Christianity. He has recently published on topics such as exorcism, secularity, and religious pluralism; fasting, ethics, and urban temporalities; discipline and lenience; hierarchy, intercession, and love; and secrecy, magic, and transgression.

Anastasios Panagiotopoulos' research focuses on Afro-Cuban religiosity, divination, spirit possession, death, secularism, and the historical imagination. He has published articles in peer-reviewed journals and is the co-editor, with Diana Espírito Santo, of the edited volume: *Articulate Necrographies: Comparative Perspectives on the Voices and Silences of the Dead* (2019).

J. Brent Crosson is Associate Professor at the University of Texas. His book *Experiments with Power: Obeah and the Remaking of Religion in Trinidad* was published in 2020 and won the 2021 Clifford Geertz Award from the American Anthropological Association.

Miho Ishii is an associate professor at Kyoto University, Japan. Her current research focus is on the relationship between spirit worship and environmental movements in South India.

Diana Espírito Santo is Associate Professor at the Escuela de Antropología, Pontificia Universidad Católica de Chile. She has researched Cuban espiritismo and the dead in Afro-Cuban religion, cosmological plasticity in Brazilian Umbanda, and more recently, technologies, historicity, and the paranormal in Chile.

Bruno Reinhardt (PhD, Anthropology, UC Berkeley, 2013) is an anthropology professor at the Federal University of Santa Catarina, Brazil. His published research has focused mainly on religious conflict and pluralism in Salvador, Brazil, and religious pedagogy, power, and authority among Pentecostal Christians in Ghana.

Matan Shapiro (PhD 2013, UCL) is Research Associate at King's College London. He is the author of multiple publications on religiosity, cosmology, kinship, ritual, play, and politics in Maranhão, Northeast Brazil.

Katherine Swancutt is Reader in Social Anthropology, Director of the Religious and Ethnic Diversity in China and Asia Research Unit, and Project Lead of the ERC synergy grant "Cosmological Visionaries" (grant agreement no. 856543) at King's College

London. For more than two decades, she has conducted fieldwork on shamanic and animistic religion in Inner Asia. She is the author of *Fortune and the Cursed: The Sliding Scale of Time in Mongolian Divination* (2012), co-editor of *Animism beyond the Soul: Ontology, Reflexivity, and the Making of Anthropological Knowledge* (2018), and editor of *Crafting Chinese Memories: The Art and Materiality of Storytelling* (2021).

Jon Bialecki is the author of *Machines for Making Gods: Mormonism, Transhumanism, and Worlds Without End*, and of *A Diagram for Fire: Miracles and Variation in an American Charismatic Movement*. His work focuses on Transhumanism, Mormonism, Charismatic and Pentecostal Christianity, and the anthropology of Christianity.

Marcio Goldman is Professor at the Post-Graduate Program in Social Anthropology, National Museum, Federal University of Rio de Janeiro. He is Researcher at CNPq, CAPES, and FAPERJ, and the author of *Razão e Diferença: Afetividade, Racionalidade e Relativismo no Pensamento de Lévy-Bruhl*; *How Democracy Works: An Ethnographic Theory of Politics*.

Michael Lambek is Professor Emeritus of Anthropology and the previous holder of a Canada Research Chair at the University of Toronto Scarborough. He has written a number of books and essays on spirit possession among people in Mayotte and Madagascar as well as on religion, memory, historicity, and ethical life. Recent books include *The Ethical Condition: Essays on Action, Person and Value* (2015); *Island in the Stream: An Ethnographic History of Mayotte* (2018); and *Concepts and Persons: The Tanner Lecture* (2021).

Introduction: Possession and Paradox

Matan Shapiro and Diana Espírito Santo

Statement of Purpose

When actor Jim Carrey received the news that he was hired to play the role of Andy Kaufman in Milos Forman's 1999 film *Man on the Moon*, he was absolutely flabbergasted. He had admired Andy Kaufman since he was a teenager, and being able to actually act out Andy's life was a dream come true. To digest this fact, Jim Carrey went for a long walk on the beach. He looked at the ocean, "and then Andy came," as he put it in an interview recorded in 2017.[1] The sudden arrival of Kaufman—who died in 1984, fifteen years before Forman's feature was shot—became a prologue to what would be a thoroughly deceptive environment on the *Man on the Moon* film set, one characterized by the constant breaching of boundaries between people, temporalities, and relationships. In part, this was because Carrey "remained in the character" most of the time, which means that he did not only "play" Kaufman in front of the camera but also quite literally remained united with him for the duration of the entire production. For example, while embodying Kaufman backstage, Jim Carrey continuously tricked and harassed Milos Forman—the renowned director who had initially insisted on the casting of Jim Carey in the lead role—occasionally causing the latter to lose his temper and once even shout ferociously at Carrey. While "in character" behind the scenes, Carrey also harassed Andy's old-time friend, actor-wrestler Jerry Lawler, who took part in the 1999 movie (playing himself). On one occasion, shown in the 2017 documentary *Jim & Andy*, Lawler appears perplexed as he shares his amazement with other people on the set, saying that he and Andy had been such good friends before he died. On a different occasion, Lawler physically assaulted Carrey, who was still embodying Kaufman backstage. Other events that took place on the set of the 1999 film had a cosmological or spiritual edge to them. For example, Carrey once spoke for many hours with Andy Kaufman's real-life daughter as if he were the *real* Kaufman. Carrey described that conversation in the 2017 documentary as a heartfelt communication between Andy and his daughter, which he (Carrey) facilitated.

In sum, as the shooting of the film continued, the distinction between life on and off camera collapsed. This entailed the blurring of social boundaries previously taken as concrete, such as those between actor and character, those between spectator and participant, and those between temporalities (the 1970s and 1990s). Even those lines normatively separating living and dead bodies were temporarily dissolved, which thus challenged the spatiotemporal distinctions between the realities depicted in the film and the realities lived by the actors and professionals who were filming it. The often incredulous responses of onlookers and participants alike—which ultimately lived on in the memory of the people involved and justified the filming of a documentary *about* the making of *Man on the Moon* nearly two decades after the original film was released—were the result of this complete blending of spatiotemporal and cognitive frames.

We ask readers to compare this description to the common manifestation of spirit possession events in such contexts where they are considered credible. Typically, as a long tradition of cross-cultural ethnographic literature has suggested, spirits often possess their mediums unexpectedly, and, like the experience depicted in *Jim & Andy*, they tend to possess them both "on" and "off" the stage of formalized ritual contexts. The difference between the social context in which Andy could be said to possess Jim—a secular, artistic environment in the United States—and the contexts wherein spirit possession is an institutionalized social action, lies in the extent to which the singular possession event is understood to change the lives of the people who are exposed to it. Initiation into an established spiritual context that demands the ongoing manifestation of possession creates new social connections with kin and kindred, both humans and other-than-humans, while at times destroying older ones. It ultimately necessitates the restructuring of mundane life in ways that enable the occasional intrusion of spirits, who normally exist somewhere else, and who then become an integral aspect of the world of the living. In the case of *Jim & Andy*, the extent to which such restructuring was allowed was inevitably limited to the space-time of the filming itself.

And yet, even then, the dynamical interactions revolving around the blurring of boundaries between Jim and Andy enabled an "intrusion" of sort. For instance, during his acting career, Kaufman sometimes performed as Tony Clifton, a fowl-mouthed cowboy who would go on stage and cause scandals. At times he would perform on stage next to Clifton, with Kaufman's close friend and performance associate Bob Zmuda playing Clifton. A scene depicted in the 2017 film *Jim & Andy* showed how Clifton was resurrected in the afterhours of the filming of *Man on the Moon* in 1999 to quite literally intrude into a real-life party that the billionaire Hugh Hefner had organized for Jim Carrey. It shows Clifton dancing provocatively, making jokes, and generally creating havoc. Hefner, like everybody around him, thought that it was Jim acting as Clifton and so he danced with him cheerfully. Some minutes later the real Jim, appearing as himself, wearing shorts and a robe, nonetheless showed up, behaving as if he did not know of anything suspicious. It was then apparent that it was Bob Zmuda, an uninvited guest, who was playing Clifton all along. Subsequently, Zmuda was thrown out by security.

The resemblance of this event to that which often happens in possession rituals, indeed sometimes even in the mundane lives of people engaged in a possession-based religious lifestyle, is quite striking, albeit unintentional. The initial blurring of identities between Kaufman and Carrey, and later between Kaufman and Clifton, and then between Zmuda and Kaufman and Clifton and Carrey, have all accumulated to create a real-life intrusion, an unexpected resurgence of imaginary figures from immortality into mundane life, which ultimately also caused embarrassment. We can talk analytically about *"possession"* in this case because it manifested in ways that resembled the manifestation of *possession* in such contexts where this is a heuristic, generic term. In both "possession" and possession there is an implicit "theatrics" that cannot be reduced to the "theatrical" as such, understood as somehow previously engineered or scripted in minds. Think, for example, of Bruce Kapferer's use of the term "phantasmagoria" in his description of how Singhalese healers create dynamic spaces with their own logics, which thereby engender worlds that are regenerated anew for the victims of sorcery (1997). This engendering of worlds through possession, both in the case of Jim & Andy and in contexts where possession is underscored by deeper cosmological settings, is essentially about potentiation (Don Handelman, personal communication July 2021), about understanding a particular moment in becoming something new, an activity that can be understood as dynamical in its "own right" (Handelman 2004) because it suspends everything else around it, whether that includes psychological dissociation or not.

Indeed, our analytical intention here goes beyond this structural analogy between "real" and "fake" episodes of possession. We seek to justify a wider understating of possession that goes beyond those cases wherein it is anchored in cosmological convictions and ritual traditions. We decided to use the case of *Jim & Andy* as our opening example because it demonstrates our point beautifully, that is, that the temporality of both possession and "possession" events can be analyzed under the analytical guise of *play*.

In essence, play is a social action "in which you create a context marked by brackets {} and then say {'everything I say in these brackets is false'}" (Nachmanovitch 2009, 5, parenthesis in origin; cf. Bateson 2000 [1972]). This happened during the filming of *Man on the Moon* in 1999 because multiple, mutually exclusive identities, personalities, and subjectivities enmeshed together *off camera* as much as they did in front of it. People's reactions flowed from amazement to amusement to anger precisely because they did not expect the play to go on after the acting was finished. What is striking here is that even without a cosmological theory that justifies co-presence of humans and entities in some fantastic or extra-human way, those present on the film set still attached spiritual meanings to the simultaneity of identities they witnessed. Evidently, Andy Kaufman's daughter spoke with her father *through* Jim Carrey, treating him as a sort of medium. And Jim Carrey himself chose not to take part in the shooting of the clip for the theme song of the movie because he felt that Andy was no longer there and that consequently he could not artificially act him out. The continuation of the play frame thus conditioned the emergence of different sets of relationships, ideas, and experiences in the everyday lives of those involved.

Play theory ultimately makes it possible to think critically on possession events because both play and possession are premised on the simultaneous manifestation of previously separated entities and temporalities. The simultaneity of play, in other words, allows us to integrate the notion of paradox into the critical reading of possession events. After all, the mutuality of actions and the simultaneity of identities during the filming of *Man on the Moon* communicated for actors, the film industry professionals, spectators, and even Andy Kaufman's own family members, a series of confused messages. In order to make sense of these messages, they quite literally had to overcome their own mundane habits, which generally dictate that one person cannot all of a sudden be another (cf. Handelman 1998, 68). The simultaneity of identities here becomes paradoxical because it allows for two distinct things to coexist in a single frame of reference (Neuman 2003). It is the presence of paradox that made possible actions usually taken in this social context to be preposterous, such as talking to the dead.

The case of Jim & Andy is so illuminating because it demonstrates that even in a social context where spirit possession is *not* a credible possibility, or is at the very least an esoteric one, the simultaneous co-presence of previously distinct identities, temporalities, and subject positions *can* inspire the cultivation of new relationships, the initiation of new kinds of movements, and the opening of new links made explicit as they are transmuted from the fantastic realm of the virtual into the materiality of the actual. And if paradox can be seen as the hallmark of dynamism—rather than as a state of stasis or a kind of stuckness—it can open exciting analytical perspectives in the cross-cultural study of spirit possession. At a wider scope, as we explicate further below, we hope that such perspectives will help scholars rethink the limits of anthropological representation. We argue that a new form of anthropological description is needed to account for forms of emergence (the idea that a structure or social phenomena can develop in ways that are irreducible to the sum of its parts), one that will shift the focus away from the areas in which dynamic social forms such as possession find rest (e.g., their social function or utility in the context where they take place) to the self-organization that characterizes them *qua* dynamic phenomena (Handelman 2021, 179; cf. Shapiro 2021).

In this edited volume, we collectively seek to theorize the movements that are created both during and as a result of heuristic spirit possession events in different social contexts across the globe. We use terms such as simultaneity, play, and paradox for this task because we believe that anthropology is in need of finding new conceptual languages that do not determine a priori a figure-ground distinction between persons and spirits, and which carefully consider the invention, as well as the appropriation, of new vocabularies that transcend the logical dualisms implicit in much of the ethnographic descriptions of possession to date. Such a new vocabulary, we believe, would promote the quality of the "absence of gravity" (Handelman 1998, 68) that characterizes the experience of simultaneity, an experience which is so central to possession events cross-culturally. In this reading, "absence of gravity" means that there is nothing really predictable even in the most predictable of events, ritualized possession included, as well as the now quite common assumption in anthropology that the concrete meanings of the unfolding of social events such as possession are not predefined by those involved in them (Kapferer 2005, 1997). Precisely because possession is a moment in which alterity is suspended, a moment in which paradox and simultaneity take hold of people quite literally, we wish to challenge the utility of figure-ground terms for the understanding of possession. How can we redefine the analytical terms, as well as the relationships between the social figure and the ground that shape the context of possession events, in such a way as to allow for the rethinking of the phenomenality of possession through these notions of paradox, play, and simultaneity?

Play: Simultaneity and Paradox as Enablers of Change

In a famous text originally published in the 1950s, Gregory Bateson describes a trip to the zoo where he observed monkeys playing. The interesting thing about play, Bateson claims in this foundational text, is that it is not easily distinguished from not-play. The monkeys he observed were mocking a fight, but it appeared as if they also clearly realized this was *not* a fight. They were playing by acting *as if* they were fighting, maintaining a fine line between real aggression or animosity and its mimesis. Bateson thus reasons that playing can only occur when participants exchange some kind of meta-communication (2000, 180), that is, a higher level of communication that comments about the values, meanings, and rhetorical acts taken within the perceived framework of communication at hand. The meta-message conveyed during playful action, he argues, is "This is play" (ibid., 179). As with monkeys, this exchange of *messages about messages* between people, which conditions playful actions, is often nonverbal. "Expanded," argues Bateson, "the statement 'This is play' looks something like this: 'These actions in which we now engage do not denote what those actions *for which they stand* would denote'" (ibid., 180).

In play, then, things always have a double meaning (Huizinga 1970 [1939]). They denote one thing, but in the context of play they denote something else. Only by knowing and understanding both these contexts simultaneously—that which is denoted during action and that which "would have been denoted" if it was *not* play—will we in fact know ourselves to be playing (Handelman 1992). Bateson develops this line of argumentation later in the same article by claiming that "the messages or signals exchanged in play are in a certain sense untrue or not meant," because "that which is denoted by these signals is nonexistent" (ibid., 183). Bateson's hypothesis is that the meta-message "This is play" consequently establishes a paradoxical frame comparable to Epimenedes' Liar paradox of self-reference (ibid., 184). Epimenedes, who was Cretan, said that all Cretans were liars. Being Cretan, he knew the truth and spoke it out. Yet, if that was the case, and he was to be believed on the basis of his intimate knowledge of Crete, then we must assume he was also a liar. If Epimenedes was telling the truth, then he was naturally lying, and if he was lying, he was still telling the truth. For Bateson the logic of play is *inherently* paradoxical; just like the Liar's Paradox, it simultaneously includes things that are contradictory—friendship and animosity, for example, to remain with the example of a mock-fight—within a single framework. Building on this background, Don Handelman (1998) has taken Bateson's assumption one step further in the direction we would also like to develop here, by claiming that the meta-message "This is Play" also communicates uncertainty. Using another of Bateson's examples, concerning the resemblance between nips and bites during the mock-fight, Handelman argues:

> A phenomenon is one thing (a bite) and another (a nip) simultaneously. Therefore, at one and the same time it is both, and so it may be neither. Uncertainty permeates this meta-message of play. And this, of course, is the lesson of true paradox: so long as one holds to its internal logic of operation, one cannot solve or escape its ongoing self-contradictions and self-negations that continually resurrect their

antitheses. True to itself, the paradox is in perpetual motion, in a sort of fluidity and flux that knows no resolution or stability except that of movement. (1998, 69)

Play, Handelman argues, promises neither this nor that, neither truth nor untruth; it can be both, and it can be neither. Think of the broom that becomes a horse, the fingers that mimic the shape of a pistol, and the doll that is treated "like" a baby (Anchor 1978). In all these instances of children's play that are widespread across the globe, we cannot distinguish between the binaries. The distinction between an object and its symbol, or even ego and alter, is distorted as they become one. Crucially, this suspension of normative distinctions, the seemingly smooth "movement" or immersive flow often experienced in play (Csikszentmihalyi 1990), influences relationships and dynamics happening beyond the play frame itself. The impact can be instrumental, as with the acquisition of new skills or mental structures (Winnicott (2005 [1971]), but it can also be purely contemplative, as with individual feelings of joy, inspiration, or awe (vis. Caillois 2001 [1961]). The "unseriousness" of play, in other words, must not be confused with irrelevance. Its "relevance to human existence is this very quality of absence of gravity, of the flux and fluff of ongoing change, of the everpresent (sic) sense of the possible" (Handelman 1998, 68). The ability of play and fantasy to create this "absence of gravity" through the implementation of paradox makes part of that which enables people to experience change. While this experience includes a measure of uncertainty—we can lose ourselves in the whirlpool spinning of self-referential paradoxes in play—the temporary manifestation of simultaneities is also a force that moves things in the world.

As it may have become clear by now, we believe that similar points about paradox and play can be made of spirit possession. The idea that a person can be "oneself" and "another" is only paradoxical in light of the assumption that in regular sociality one can be identified only *as a single person who is always available to him or herself as such*. However, simultaneity—two events, or entities, or personalities, or dispositions, contradictory or not—happening at the same time in the same frame of reference (or body), *which is often gleaned as paradoxical*, is in fact absolutely essential to spirit possession. What if we think of simultaneity as something that both reflects and reconstitutes cosmological assumptions in new ways, rather than as a spatiotemporal "breaking" of dialectical or otherwise binary classifications? What if we think of possession as a cross-cultural manifestation of play, not in the sense of play-acting or theatre but in the sense of enabling the manifestation of paradox in people's lives? And, consequently, what if that which is at the center of spirit possession is not *radical alterity*, the binary "other," but rather a phenomenal play with uncertainty, which thus allows for several contradictions to happen simultaneously? We now turn to explore this possibility further.

From "mind" to "Mind": Rethinking Alterity through Paradox

Informed readers will no doubt find in these lines an analytical reference to another one of Gregory Bateson's contributions to anthropological theory, his famous "ecological" or interactional-cybernetic approach to the study of life forms (2000 [1972]). The main principle that guides Bateson is that "the mental world—the mind—the world of information processing—is not limited by the skin" (2000, 460). Consequently, claims Bateson, any study of sociality must move away from an analysis of single, pre-defined, enclosed, self-contained units in the observed structure—such as "entity" and a "person" who "receives" or "contains" it, in the case of possession—to the analysis of the mutuality of interactions that sum up together a holistic, dynamic conceptual-perceptual ecosystem wherein individuals and systems reciprocate messages (and transform each other continuously as a consequence) on a continuous basis.

Bateson uses the term "Mind," as distinguished from "mind," to describe this grand dynamical mutuality, an overall holistic system of constantly interacting dynamic forces, which work simultaneously "inside" and "outside" bodies. For example, Mind includes both the "metabolic energy" (2000, 459) that animates the senses from within the neuronal body—which Bateson understands as information that runs through the senses—as well as external phenomena that interacts with the senses, such as traveling waves of light and sound. In fact, only the combination of these forces is effective in an ontological sense. Every perception is impressed and impressing—facilitating while also simultaneously being shaped—the multiple interactions existing between all these external and internal forces together. "The individual mind is immanent," Bateson argues (2000, 467), "but not only in the body. It is immanent also in pathways and messages outside the body; and there is a larger Mind of which the individual mind is only a subsystem." While the Freudian tradition has tended to insulate minds as internal structures of communication, Bateson's analysis expands the mind beyond the boundaries of bodies, widely defined, and transforms them in this way into an interconnected chain of subsystems, whose overall mutual coexistence ultimately constitutes an immense, infinite complexity of Mind.

Let us take Mind as a springboard to explore paradox further. Rather than a disposition, an individual mind in this theoretical framework is imagined as a system of cooperating and mutually relational effects located both "inside" and "outside" the human body (or brain, for that matter).[2] This system is constantly created, recreated, and also at times degenerated as the rolling effect of a multiplicity of dynamical forces in action. Here, interaction of any kind is always about the transfer, reception, interpretation, and processing of information. Minds, with an "m," thus operate both internally and externally of their body-matter, within the vastness of Mind. And Mind, in its immensity, is also intrinsic to mind, mainly because Mind has no perceived boundaries at all, be that at the ecological and planetary or cosmic levels (Bateson 2000, 469).

Setting the boundaries of the subsystem of the individual mind at hand, which is the object of our observation, thus requires understanding how boundaries are generated in the course of the processual unfolding and enfolding of any dynamical occurrence in the world. This is opposed to the predisposed idea that there is a given separation between individual elements, or the notion of an "inside" mentality totally distinguishable from the "outside" world. Bateson brings the following example (2000, 464–5) to elucidate this point:

> Consider a tree and a man and an axe. We observe that the axe flies through the air and makes certain sorts of gashes in a pre-existing cut in the side of the tree. If now

we want to explain this set of phenomena, we shall be concerned with differences in the cut face of the tree, differences in the retina of the man, differences in the central nervous system, differences in his efferent neural messages, differences in the behavior of his muscles, differences in how the axe flies, to the differences which the axe then makes on the face of the tree. Our explanation ... will go round and round in that circuit. In principle, if you want to explain or understand anything in human behavior, you are always dealing with total circuits, completed circuits. This is the elementary cybernetic thought ... the unit which shows the characteristic of trial and error will be legitimately called a mental system.

Bateson, in short, explains the world in terms of minute transformations—numerous acts of boundary making—which create distinctions (or "differences" as he puts that) between objects of perception *as they interact*. These transformations, for Bateson, also include the invisible, or unknown, or even the undone, such as an unwritten letter, a word not uttered, a void just being there in mind or indeed in Mind, which are integral to all other causes and effects, intrinsic to the forces that are intra-connected holistically (Handelman 2008) and infinitely always communicating with each other. This is the reason why paradoxes in Mind do not necessarily disturb routine dynamics, nor are they an ultimate form of inertia, but rather, the enablers of creative movement away from the common meanings of everyday life and back into them.

Mobius: The Structure of Mind Systems

Since Mind facilitates movements and transgressions across different surfaces—if we are allowed to think of bodies and ecosystems as surfaces of sort—it acquires the shape of a Mobius Strip, "a surface with just one side, in the sense that a bug can traverse the entire surface without crossing an edge" (Neuman 2003, 142). This image of a Mobius Strip stands at the heart of our own attempt to study possession events as a manifestation of paradox in Mind. The cognitive scientist Yair Neuman (2003, 143) explains the internal logic of movement on a Mobius Strip:

Our common sense suggests that if we want to move from the outside of a form into its inside, we must cross a boundary through a material region of discontinuity. A sphere has an inside and an outside, and the only way that a bug traveling on the sphere can get inside the sphere is by passing *through* the sphere, through a hole. However, moving from the outside of the Mobius strip to the inside of the strip and vice versa is done without crossing a boundary! In this sense, the Mobius strip shows us that it is possible to move from the inside of a form to its outside (i.e., from one value of a binary system to its other value) without crossing material boundary. There is no hole in the Mobius strip — just a catastrophic point (a point at which the value of the bug cannot be determined) that moves us from the inside to the outside. The Mobius case shows us that it is possible to think of a boundary not necessarily as an entity, a set of points, or a point of material discontinuity, but as an *event*, a certain dynamic, that moves us from the inside of a system to its outside, and by so doing delimits the boundaries of a form. This point is specifically important because the dynamic that creates a binary world of self versus non-self, true versus false, sign versus signified, and other binaries, is the dynamic of boundary construction that underlies many phenomena. In this sense, the dynamic underlying the Mobius example may be used to teach us a general lesson concerning the dynamics characteristic of many other systems and how they constitute their self vis-à-vis the environment, that is, how they constitute their own boundary. The next step is to conceptualize these dynamics.

As he develops his argument, Neuman goes on to suggest that the Mobius can also teach us something about the general nature of paradox. Striving to think beyond the accepted definition of paradox as "a seemingly sound piece of reasoning based on seemingly true assumptions that leads to a contradiction (or other obviously false conclusions)" (*Cambridge Dictionary of Philosophy*, 1995, quoted in Neuman 2003, 145), Neuman claims that paradox is in fact a form entering into itself. The Mobius is a good example—it is a distinguished object, which nonetheless becomes as such only by re-entering its constituent parts. Think also about Bateson's example of nips and bites—it is the recurrence of bites as nips, and of nips as bites, within the course of the activity at hand, which constitutes the paradox of play. In Neuman's terms, a "war" is here entering into itself, in distinguishable ways, alas acquiring a different intensity or density as it is performed, to produce play, which is a mock-war (cf. Handelman 2021, 289, Nachmanovitch 2009).

Neuman's explanation allows us to begin thinking about possession as an eventful enactment of a certain paradoxical dynamic that takes place in Mind. Like play, it is paradoxical because during possession people appear to those who look at them from the outside as both themselves and other—or, more accurately, their regular selves are both here and not here, simultaneously "inside" and "outside" social reality—and it is dynamic because both the identities of the possessed person and the possessing entity do not precede each other at any given point in time, as they are both continuously redefined by the multiple, additive reciprocal actions that make their mutuality meaningful across time. The open-ended unfolding of relationships between possessed and possessing entities, and between them and both their earthly and otherworldly kin, is at the center of the event, rather than a focused, rigid, or static formal exchange of gifts for favors between "self" and "alter." This is a "dynamic" because there is no binary fixation in time and space, only co-working, or mutual engagement of minds, in and through a wider Mind system that includes the relational trajectories and spaces of contact between entities and humans alike.

And it is here, in this paradox of possession, that the negotiation of alterity becomes apparent as a dynamic event—not a simple situation of transformation through transgression, which is later dissolved or is undone through reintegration and separation between possessed and possessing agents. Rather, possession is here revealed as a focused reiteration of certain ongoing reciprocal relationships in the "critical point" of passage between an "inside" and an "outside" of a system of communication (viz. Neuman 2003), whose different parts or elements (e.g., "this world" and the "the world of the spirits") continuously interconnect. If we think of the

Mobius again, we could think of possession as being the point of passage in the strip, linking inner to outer edges. The paradox of possession can thus be defined in this light as a spatiotemporal "critical point" within the system, a warped or twisted region that allows passage without requiring the crossing of a threshold, an event which enables participants to negotiate alterity and harness it, productively or not, into the everyday dynamic of relationships.

The Dynamic Cosmos

This notion of paradox as an *enabler* of movement is well inscribed in myths across the world. Think, for example, of the image of the trickster, a much-recognized figure in mythology, which is always depicted as a paradoxical entity because it unites oppositions in the ongoing creation of society's "tolerated margins of mess" (Babcock-Abrahams 1975). Tricksters often evade clear-cut classification because they are both A and not-A; as Lewis Hyde argues, the trickster is "at once culture hero and fool, clever predator and stupid prey" (1998, 19). Most aptly, a trickster is often an innovator (Handelman 2021, 36) who suggests new directions for established cultural forms. Tricksters can operate in this way precisely because they are capable of assuming diametrically opposite roles in their own life story—they contradict their own existence as a very condition of their existence (Wagner 1981). Circus clowns are an archetypical example: they embody within themselves sense and nonsense in ways that annul the boundaries between these two forms of human meaning making (Carmeli 2001). Clowns are figures that offer mutually exclusive moral narratives, which are nonetheless contained in a single aesthetic unity, and this is the reason they are allowed, in most cases, to challenge every commonsensical societal convention (Handelman 1998, 246ff). Lewis Hyde (1998, 72) demonstrates this point brilliantly with his treatment of the trickster obfuscation of binaries, especially as related to established notions of truth and false:

> Our ideas about property and theft depend on a set of assumptions about how the world is divided up. Tricksters' lies and theft challenge those premises and in so doing reveal their artifice and suggest alternatives. One of the West African tricksters, Legba, has been well described in this regard as "a mediator" who works "by means of a lie that is really a truth, a deception that is in fact a revelation." That's how Krishna works, too. When he is the thief of hearts, for example, he disturbs all those who have been foolish enough to think that their hearts are their own property, not the property of god. As the thief of butter, Krishna upsets the categories that his mother has established to separate him from that food or foods. It is in this sense that his lie subverts what seemed so clear a truth just a moment ago. Suddenly the old verities are up for grab.

Mythological play with verities is embedded also in the liminality of spirit possession, which condenses and articulates boundaries in ways that at least temporarily cancel that which is located at each of their sides (Handelman 2021, 177–9). Paradox thus creates a kind of experiential cleavage in the irreversible passage of time. When people are engaged in a paradoxical activity—and, as Bateson and Handelman suggest, when people exchange paradoxical messages about something that is at the same time something else—the experience of reality changes from something generally detracted with more-or-less clear boundaries (e.g., virgins can't get pregnant), to something that is free-flowing, open, and (potentially) possible (when the divine operates, virgins *do* get pregnant). This also happens in fantasy: the opening at the back of the closet that seamlessly integrates Narnia with London of the 1940s, the rabbit hole linking Wonderland with Alice's world. It is this quality that creates a powerful sense of enchantment. In each case, and we think that possession fits well into this scenario, in the kinds of passages, trajectories, intensities, movements, and flows that the paradox enables—indeed, movements that are empirically presented, represented, and enacted in front of spectators when possession happens publicly—normative truths can be questioned, verified, contested, or reapproved, depending on the case.

Possession, which nearly everywhere includes the simultaneous manifestation of distinct "things" made manifest in and through body vehicles (Boddy 1988; Danforth 1989; Lambek 1980, 1996; Stoller 1989), here emerges as a temporality that enables practitioners to negotiate questions of social alterity. Such questions often focus on the differences between self and other, or between "us" and "them," but they also concern the relationship with wider cosmological notions, such as luck, fate, and the role of extra human entities in the determination of one's happiness, misery, success, or failure in life. These questions differ of course across different social and cultural traditions. Yet the trope of paradox, along with the simultaneity imbued in it, is a gateway to exploring these questions about alterity. A careful look at paradox is key to understanding how threshold moments such as possession are ones where categories are suspended, where alterity is held at bay, and where movement is instigated across that which in everyday life is often seen as an unbridgeable barrier or an unattainable void.

This approach to possession is novel because it considers the relational play between dynamics and continuities, on the one hand, and dialectics and disjunctions, on the other. The simultaneous inclusion of both finitudes and flows in our analytical framework differs from the bulk of possession literature, which tends to focus only on one of these aspects. As an example, take the anthropology of African witchcraft, where religious cosmology at large and spirit possession more specifically are taken to be *about* something else: gender inequality, political or economic strife, colonization and domination, the dark side of a postcolonial order (Comaroff & Comaroff 1993; Geschiere 1997, 2013; Sanders & Moore 2001). At large, the tendency in the literature is to either focus on possession as an event primarily defined by its radical alterity to mundane events, identities, gestures, language, etc., an approach wherein spirits diametrically mirror the earthly, finite, existence of the possessed, before, during, and after the possession event—*or* to focus on the intrinsic everydayness of possession. This latter position assumes that spirits in fact extend worldly political, economic, psychological, and emotional or affective realities that predefine the context, mark the actions enacted within the possession event, and ultimately are integrated back into that very same context after the possession ends. The first approach offers that we look at possession always through the prism of otherness and alterity; the second offers that we look at possession always through the prism of sameness, mimesis, and perpetuity. In both cases, the result is a linear, straightforward relationship between possession and other localized social action. Evidently, on the one hand, if there are always strict boundaries, possession is an external comment on reality, a vehicle by which people around the world "tell themselves a story about themselves," to use a famous Geertzian perspective. And if, on the other hand, there are no boundaries at all, possession is merely another socioeconomic and political tool to live through these realities, give meaning to difficulties, and improve the human condition in the process.

Recent scholars in the anthropology of religion have begun to shift this tendency, to resist this figure-ground reversal, which they take as limiting, often employing languages from outside the discipline to unpack their respective ethnographies, for instance, from philosophy or even physics. The field of Afro-Latin religious studies is especially fertile for this abstract kind of theorization, because in these contexts possession events expose continuously shifting ontological assumptions about the nature of matter and spirit (see, for instance, Beliso-de-Jesús 2015; Goldman 1985, 2005, 2007; Holbraad 2012; Ochoa 2010; Otero 2020; Wafer 1991). For example, Ochoa seeks in Hegel a language for understanding his interlocutors' "turns" of the dead, like ebbs and flows of the sea, in their bodies (2010); Beliso-De Jesús reconsiders transnational religious flows in the light of Karen Barad's notions of "entanglement" and "diffraction"; and Holbraad understands deities as relations, which must be set in motion through the diviners' board markings (2012). Immanence is the theme in all these ethnographic contexts.

In this light, it may not be far-fetched to claim that paradox is embedded in the ontological structure of such Afro-Latin socio-political-religious geographies. For instance, in his book on spirit possession in Brazilian Candomblé, Jim Wafer makes distinctions between Catholicism and Candomblé, only to dissolve them. He says, "In practice the two models do not necessarily exclude each other. It is rather a question of which aspects of which model are emphasized in which contexts by people for which purposes" (1991, 15). Another example is the Trickster. In the universe of Candomblé practitioners, *Exu* is one of the primary entities. Often associated with the devil in Christian cosmology, this association is nevertheless deceptive. Wafer says that *exus* are not identified with absolute evil; like people, they are capable of both good and bad, and humans may enlist their services, persuading them to do one thing or another, by making offerings (ibid., 14–15). Indeed, *exus* are the tricksters of this cosmos; they open and close paths, and their complicity must be sought at the beginning of any ritual. But to understand how *exus* can embody opposites, one only has to look at the architecture of Candomblé's, and indeed Cuban Santería's cosmology, at the heart of which is the Brazilian notion of *axé*, or *aché* in Cuba. This is how Wafer describes it.

> It means something like "the quintessence of the ethos of Candomblé." In this usage things "have" *axé*, though not indefinitely. The term "presence" would express something of its intangible quality, but not its dynamism. *Axé* moves around. A thing that "has" *axé* at one moment may lose it in the next. From this perspective *axé* has a lot in common with fashion. Like the *exus* and the stock market, it is not entirely predictable. (ibid., 19)

While we wholeheartedly respect and admire these ethnographies, with which we have often crossed paths, here we propose something different, perhaps even heretical to some of these authors, that is, theoretical heuristics that at least as a thought process imposes itself temporarily on the diverse ethnographic theories of our respective fields. In a strong sense, we believe that it is an *experimental* heuristics and that is how we wish to be read. As mentioned before, we claim that it is essential to understand spirit possession beyond linearity. This approach focuses on the spatiotemporal suspension of binaries that possession produces because it views possession as a frame of reference heavily dependent on a certain affective and maybe also cognitive *experience* of paradox. But possession does not merely *represent* or *mirror* normative social values, narratives, symbols, or structures. In its inherently dynamical flow, it becomes a nonlinear ontological force in Mind. In line with localized notions of power and dynamics where possession is taken to be credible, which often attach cosmic and mythical meanings to the manifestation of nonlinearity in possession, we thus think of the dynamics of paradox as facilitators of movement in *cosmos* (Abramson and Holbraad 2014). Within this framework, we assume that paradox may not be an operational concept at all in people's minds, but a form of *practice,* an action, whenever certain contradictory conditions of being enable certain types of becoming; spirit possession being one of these. The issue is not whether paradox is present in all cases of spirit possession; it is whether an understanding of the paradoxical *movements* that possession processes make-do with might be good to think with.

With this in mind, we must briefly elucidate here what we *are not* trying to do in this book. There is a long history to the term "possession" as something that implies a "dramatic displacement of everyday consciousness" (Johnson 2014, 3). In his edited volume *Spirited Things,* Paul Johnson traces an intellectual genealogy of the term, as well as its infiltration into religious practices (especially, the Afro-Atlantic kind). Definitions of persons and things become primary here, namely because, in plantation societies, where the term evolved, "human bodies *were* very often things and property, or possessions" (ibid., 5). Spirit possession, in contrast to shamanism, which was regarded as more masterful and controlled, "indexed the absence of control, the body without will," and thus, the figure of the slave, who was not, by most laws, understood as a *person* (ibid.). But while this may appear archaic, the "substitution of self or consciousness" hypothesis, read through dissociation and its conceptual corollaries, still prevails as a primary theoretical modality in contemporary spirit possession studies. Possession is conceived through a figure-ground model in which a certain social and political context is seen to precede the form and content of this dissociation episode, and thus to define or impregnate it with predisposed meanings.

Inspired by the writings of Don Handelman (2004, 2021), Bruce Kapferer (1997), and Gregory Bateson (2000), we propose to circumvent this prevalent methodological assumption—by focusing on the interior formation of paradox as a dynamical phenomenon in and of itself. We propose that the scholarly discussion of possession will gain enormously if we analyze the micro-scripts and minutiae of the enactment of a possession episode as it happens, in a particular sociocultural context. This is so because such a focus might help us see how some social formations inherent to possession relate *dynamically* (and thus also change, impact, or indeed transform) to the social surround in which the possession episode takes place. This method, we suggest, will allow us to grasp analytically how the dynamic movement of emotions, feeling, and bodies in possession quite literally moves into and changes wider societal contexts in complex and ultimately unpredictable ways.

The Chapters of the Book

We asked the different contributors to think through their ethnographic material with a language of dynamism, paradox, simultaneity, and play. We did not ask them to *explain* possession via one or another preexisting anthropological, psychological, or historical modality (cognitivist, structural-functionalist, phenomenological, interpretive, etc.). Rather, our intention was to encourage the different contributors to conceptualize possession in terms that do not alienate its opposites, that is, to analyze their material using words and concepts that do not exclude any such predisposed analytical or heuristic explanations, including and especially those of the possessed themselves. We did so by positing paradox as an insight into the dynamics of spirit possession—a means to renegotiate its basic assumptions as anthropologists of the phenomenon. Together, all of the case studies at hand demonstrate that it is impossible, in fact, to see and analyze possession in a single dimension. As much as we the editors claim the experience as a paradox of no-alterity for the event itself, with transformational properties, this experience can and must be refracted through its many edges and processes, some of which do not directly refer to paradox itself. The point of theoretical experimentation was to see where this could lead us, as a collective. The order of the chapters was chosen not to exemplify a journey, or a story, about spirit possession, but to make salient each of the contributions in relation to the broader theme of no-alterity.

In the first chapter, Diego Maria Malara considers how "movement" can become a major analytic tool in the unraveling of multiple relationships between mediums, spirits, and their kin-persons in the context of contemporary Ethiopian Orthodox notions of the sacred. Emphasizing such notions of flux, velocity, and "deadlocks," Malara traces how people's spiritual "journeys" in sacred sites where angels and saints materialize both reveal and reconstruct the "entangled predicaments" his research interlocutors continuously construct as they measure their mutual relationality, both in the context of the "sacred" and beyond, in the mundane world of everyday interests. Of particular interest is a holy water shrine, associated with Saint Michael, where, upon contact with the water, "demons become mediators of the messages of an angel that no one can see"; messages, like water, that flow through kinship ties and expand and "thicken" them. In a sense, it is the demonic that flows effortlessly through family ties, reinvigorating and creating all forms of articulacy between its members. The demonic is thus a dynamic contained within a holier frame—the Shinkuro Mikael. Malara elaborates these notions using innovative concepts, such as "telos" and "curvature," first made explicit by Don Handelman (2004) and later elaborated by such authors as Jens Kreinath (2012), Matan Shapiro (2016), and Diana Espírito Santo (2016). Kinship and possession here become mutually defining; two sides of the same Mobius surface.

In the second chapter, Anastasios Panagiotopoulos explores the causal immediacy between representational and ontological domains as these manifest in possession events. Indeed, these terms are not unrelated opposites, he argues. He problematizes this distinction (representation, ontology) in an account of the manifestation of racialized spirits in the context of Afro-Cuban worship practice. He claims that possession in this context can be understood as an ontological racialization of blackness – a process of "blackening" in the terminology of Fanon – that nonetheless simultaneously recedes "back" into performative representation. Movement here is central. The category of "race" gains meaning as it shifts from representation-cum-ontology into the opposite direction, ontology-cum-representation. This is done through "sweat-soaked" possession performances, but also through the use of dolls, that is, objects that mimic and exaggerate a local representation of "blackness" and its potent qualities. The analysis unfolds how this process happens as a form of simultaneity, in which what is "represented" becomes that which represents, and vice versa, thus making any essentialization impossible. More importantly here, there is an ontological "conversation" that affects how the spirit both sees and represents *itself*. Panagiotopoulos thus emphasizes co-constitutive forms of mutuality on multiple levels, forms which depend on the movement of forces, whose realization as particular modes of living takes place through structures of language, body, and materiality.

The third chapter examines notions of power, spiritual force, and their management in possession phenomena in Trinidad. Brent Crosson goes back to the roots of the notion of "possession" in our intellectual history—sensu Paul Johnson (2014)—to show that "catching power" in Trinidad, the term used for spirit manifestation, is more complex and paradoxical than the notion of a relinquishing of control, so typical to possession scholarship. Trinidadian Spiritual Baptists, or Kali Mai pujaris, understand possession as a constant "journey," in which selves do not become instruments of "external forces" but create something novel in co-constitution and co-habitation. The idea of "power" as a field of force here becomes imperative, and Crosson describes how practitioners "work" and "contain" power in their mastery of the coexistence that defines and brings both worlds together in a single time frame. In essence, Trinidadians *matter* power, enacting agential "cuts" by virtue of their growing expertise with spirits, of the craft of learning how to "let go" while still being in control, thereby creating all kinds of objects and subjects in the process. This does not mean, at once, that conflict and affliction are not constitutive aspects of this process. Rather, it means that "mediums act within and are imbued with field (sic) of spiritual and material power," that the "work" that goes into assuming such a position goes through an ability to see play as the transformation of the real.

Miho Ishii's fourth chapter asks how spirits are "actualized" in relation to their witnesses. This chapter focuses not just on the experience from the point of view of the possessed, but from the standpoint of an emergence that occurs between different elements of a life-form. Ishii argues that it is "not self-evident that people take 'spirits' as given existences" or as "thing-concepts," as ontological anthropology would posit. Rather, when comparing possession events in Ghana and South India it is necessary to shift gears and understand how an event (possession) occurs "of its own accord." After surveying functionalist and ontological approaches to possession—the former celebrating sociological utilitarianism and the latter the radical alterity between different forms of possession—Ishii moves on to claim that human subjectivity is in fact uncertain, or contingent, and on this basis it is possible to think about possession not in ontic terms (as some form of tangible idiosyncratic experience that is defined entirely by its otherness to other such experiences) but as *pathisch*, a concept she uses following the theoretical physicist and philosopher Victor von Weizsäcker; who looks at organisms not as acting agents that assume life but rather as receiving life in myriad, continuous forms. In anthropological terms, *pathisch* is about existing as a result of the other's actions, rather than your own. Developing another concept— "the middle voice"—Ishii then moves on to demonstrate how we can conceive of possession as something that is not exactly done "inside" the mind, or inside anything else in particular, but rather, in between, a processual coming into being of shared consciousness between the medium, the spirit, and the mediator. The witness here is crucial to actualizing the possession event as a social process.

In the fifth chapter, Diana Espírito Santo focuses on Cuban creole forms of spirit mediumship to ask how spirits "come into view." Following Jensen, Ishii and Swift (2016), Espírito Santo argues that the predominant factor is the generation of *movement* during ritual. Cuban espiritismo has the "muerto" (or spirit of the dead) as an internal feature of a human self; it needs to be exteriorized in order to come to fruition and to attain presence. Differentiations between interior and exterior versions of the self here become moot in processes of development, when we consider that certain spirits (*muertos*) are virtual aspects of a self-in-motion. Espírito Santo consequently uses Handelman's "Ritual in its own right" to analyze how espiritista rites "curve" into themselves, and subsequently to their exteriors, with corresponding effects. Ritual activities not just foment the appearance and actualization of these *muertos,* but open up perceptual faculties, giving rise to a particular space-time, to mundane information, and knowledge of one's self. Notions of flexibility and modularity, or plasticity, are fundamental elements of this cosmos: as Malabou says, "[plasticity] renders possible the appearance or formation of alterity where the other is absent. Plasticity is the form of alterity without transcendence" (2010, 66). The "self/ spirit" in this ethnography is in constant paradoxical self-formation, Espírito Santo suggests, precisely because they are impelled (or sometimes not) by the movement (and the concrete curves) of ritual.

In the sixth chapter, Bruno Reinhardt delves into notions of embodiment and asks exactly what we mean by them. He argues that there is a "dialectics of embodiment and transcendent excess" among Pentecostal believers in Ghana who cultivate the Holy Spirit, which limits embodiment-centered approaches in his ethnography. Learning, through imitation among other means, is simply not a cognitive process, but one which implies a "yielding" of oneself in order to attune to a disembodied other. Reinhardt suggests that being "acted upon" by the Holy Spirit requires a competency that is hard-sought and worked—what he calls (en)spirited pedagogy. Whereas anthropologically they are seen as different processes of converting, or coming to God, "submission" and "attunement" are paradoxically present in any form of Pentecostal enskilment in Ghana. Indeed, to be "acted upon" is to "flow in the spirit": "Performance and charismatic flows coincide in the experience of exceeding embodied skills," which

Reinhardt calls "navigational dexterity." Navigation—a skilled kind of improvisation of the part of the pastor in conjunction with its surround, be it human or not—contrasts here, to orchestration. Possession requires an "atmospheric sensibility to spiritual presence," which is both diffuse and condensed, embodied and disembodied, simultaneously.

In the seventh chapter, Matan Shapiro analyzes how charismatic neo-Pentecostal pastors exorcise demons in contemporary Brazil. Possession by demons in this context is discovered accidentally after the demons were "inside" people's bodies for long periods of time. Shapiro analyzes the intense rites of exorcism used to extract the demons out of the body as the untying of a paradox, which consists in the unity or continuity between humans and demons. He argues that the ritual separates between surfaces, much like the cutting of a Mobius Strip in the middle, so that it becomes possible to segregate between cosmic spheres preserved for evil demons and cosmic spheres preserved for those who follow the good Word of God. If possession by demons destroys the order of God and replaces it with chaos and destruction, expelling of demons is a correcting mechanism by which the cosmic domains can be rearranged and re-owned by moral human beings. As opposed to straightforward functionalist conclusions however, Shapiro develops the ethnographic focus on paradox and its provisional resolution in this context to offer a wider anthropological discussion on theories of passage between cosmic domains, which he argues that at least in the Brazilian context become the main aspect of the expulsion rituals. Building his argument in dialogue with Tanya Luhrmann's (2012) Theory of Mind, Shapiro thus concludes with a call for colleagues to consider the analytical value of local theories of passage to cross-cultural comparisons of rituals and play scenarios.

Katherine Swancutt develops an interesting debate on the ins and outs of possession from a different perspective, in the eighth chapter. Exploring different conceptualizations of "thresholds" among Nuosu, a Tibeto-Burman people of highland Southwest China, Swancutt examines how the crossing of boundaries of different kinds in this context can shed light on our own anthropological understanding of a social boundary, and threshold. She examines how heuristic concepts can be seen analytically to pertain to two main types of thresholds. These are priestly thresholds, which are progressive in the sense that they are meant to be crossed in the pursuit of ritual knowledge and wisdom; and shamanic thresholds, which Swancutt associates with a void, a black hole of sort, that attracts the ghosts into a perceived oblivion. While priests have expanding thresholds and powers, shamans have shrinking ones, because the "wild-qualities" of the spirit-helpers that descend on the shaman are both an asset and a liability. Wildness diminishes, and thus potency, as the shaman becomes familiarized with these spirits. Swancutt ultimately develops an inspiring argument about Nuosu cosmology that builds on individuals' imagination of the type of threshold they need to encounter and cross as they deal with the traffic of spirits, ghosts, and lost souls. She argues that to understand spirit possession the anthropologist needs to ask herself what kinds of thresholds are operative in it, and to acknowledge that the crossing of thresholds leads to the renewal of everyday life. Indeed, thresholds outline movement in the Nuosu cosmos.

Jon Bialecki's ninth chapter traces the changing history of communication with the dead in the Mormon Church of Jesus Christ of Latter Day Saints. Beginning with the practice of "indexing" the dead—a form of channeling of spirits into this world, which both proves the truthfulness of church cosmology and gives guidance to individual members as to how to avoid sin in their everyday life—Bialecki goes on to think about the utility of the term "possession" when this is not heuristically defined by research interlocutors as a relevant category. In line with the argument we presented above, Bialecki also thinks that we as analysts can allow "possession" to do "far more than it does in more standard uses of the term." The result is a historical journey into the depth of Mormon play with their dead, and even with other Christian and Jewish "souls," which includes postmortem baptism of far relatives and the future potentiality of the incarnation of the dead through cutting-edge modern genealogical charts composed of DNA tests and other technologies. What Bialecki ultimately does is point to the redundancy of a pre-given understanding of "possession" itself for anthropology. Rather, concepts need to be dilated and reinvented to suit their ethnographies. Bialecki's chapter does not refer to "classic" forms of possession, and thus it links back to our initial example of the film Jim and Andy, where the "opening" of dynamic, cosmological worlds, is still apparent yet harder to define in the absence of heuristic categories.

In the final chapter, Marcio Goldman goes back to the Candomblé practices in the northeast of Brazil that he has been studying for over thirty years. He argues that in a satisfactory anthropological analysis, one needs to place *more* things in relation to each other than the natives themselves intend to. Indeed, the only way to "symmetrize" an anthropological rendition of spirit possession is to take relations, not substances, or actions, as the operating concept. According to Goldman, conceptions *breed* existence. Anthropology, too, is a type of performance, or even art. But he also says that what we *do not know* is also critical to anthropology. This is an ultimate paradox, which is also an ethical quandary. In the tradition of "symmetrical anthropology"—the idea that the production of anthropological knowledge in the field through unmediated encounters with research interlocutors should be used to undermine and even transform value judgments prevalent in the anthropological discourse itself, along with other elite groups—Goldman thus deconstructs the process of reasoning and analysis in anthropology as something that essentially belongs to the realms of the ethical and the political. A reanalysis of several cases of possession in the *terreiro*—the Afro-Brazilian cult house—which is beautifully woven with Evans-Pritchard's famous discussions of witchcraft among the Zande, serves for Goldman as a fruitful ground to question how spirits can change our own notion of politics, ethics, and power. In the true spirit of symmetrical anthropology, Goldman ultimately turns the question of spirit possession on its head for anthropology; by positing an anthropology through a type of transcendental we simply *don't know*, he emphasizes its inherent cosmopolitical dimension and ultimate analytical utility.

In his afterword, spirit possession expert Michael Lambek comments on each of the chapters and adds his own take on the utility of such concepts as paradox, play, simultaneity, and movement in the exploration of dynamic possession events. Complementing this introduction, Lambek surveys the history of the study of possession in anthropology and comments on the analytical force and weakness of the different terms suggested throughout the volume, as well as on the potentially transformative power of a framework that takes simultaneity and paradox seriously.

In proposing a paradoxical approach to the continuous generation and destruction of alterity in possession events, the chapters of the book collectively seek to shift the attention from the spherical image of possession events—the idea that entities and humans are initially bounded in different realms of thought and perception, and that they must "cut" a cognitive boundary in order to meet (Cohen 2007)—toward a Mobius-like image (cf. Handelman 2021, 177–9). In this framework, social relations emerge through the alterity retractions that are enacted in the "critical point" of passage along the "inside" and the "outside" axes of a local cosmos. Social relations are no longer conceived here as something that precedes the possession event or indeed as its "base" or "ground." Possession, in turn, is not seen as something out of this world, but rather, as something integral to the lives of the people who are entangled with it, even when they are not literally possessed. This idea, as the ethnographies collected in this volume testify, could inspire creative new ways for the study of what possession does cross-culturally, as well as for how it does that, in different ways.

Conclusion

In this edited volume we perceive of theoretical anthropological "oppositions"— such as concept/cognitive-based and phenomenology/experience-based theories of possession—as frameworks that are empirically double-edged. By this we mean that any theoretical scheme can be self-perpetuating and holistic, on the one hand, from "within" its own guiding logic, but also, and simultaneously, undone and made illegitimate by their counter-explanations from "without." When the two opposing perspectives meet, both with their inherent logic, they create a paradoxical continuity, which just as in theory also takes place throughout the instantiation of possession and possession-like events in different sociocultural contexts. In this continuous scale, the term "spirit" can then be doubly seen both as a subjective and objective "thing" (mental construct and physical being), something which simultaneously preexists people but which is in constant need of creation or performance and invention *by* people. Spirits are understood in this volume both as taking a form that is culturally staked and one that exists *outside* of culture, both as self and not-self, both as subjected to sociohistorical configurations, moments, and events, as well as totally immune to them, eternal in their unique existence. Spirits, in short, always require representation *and* immediacy for effect. And in that sense, we contend, the act and experience of spirit possession is an *archetypical experience* of paradox: it contains within itself all of its opposites at once (Bateson 1972, 172ff; Handelman 1992).

This volume collects analyses and ethnographies of possession from across the globe. However, the volume represents Afro-Latin contexts more than others, and it does not include references to the rich Islamic tradition of spirit possession. We therefore call our colleagues who work in other contexts to scrutinize the theoretical propositions we the editors have made in this Introduction—as well as the arguments presented by the different contributors—in the contexts of their own ethnographic fields. Based on the collective work presented here, we suggest three main directions for future research, which can guide this critical engagement, all of which focus on boundary-making in the constitution of possession events. The first direction is the holding together of possession as a tension or dynamic of boundary making, which is focused on persons, personhood, and the integrity of "selves." Here the creation of difference is done within oneself, at the psychological level, with the ultimate goal of maintaining the tension of the self in flux vis-à-vis the threats and obstacles of everyday life that may encroach on it. The second direction is the holding together of the phenomenon of possession as a social structure. Here, the boundary is located in the ecosystem that identifies possession as such, for whatever reason, thus urging the intensity of the "critical point" at the moment of possession, after it had happens, or even before its manifestation. And the third direction concerns the boundary between cosmic and earthly spaces, especially with regard to *how* they are integrated (or interacting and interfacing). Here, analysis can focus on the ways by which imaginaries and theories about the universe, which inform local cosmologies, become *real* as they are actualized in everyday realities. All these directions are general potentialities for boundary making and unmaking that might well be relevant to the analysis of possession cross-culturally, and we hope that they will be useful to think with.

The phenomenological and conceptual impression of paradox, impossibility or negation, ultimately allows considering these multiple interactions and mutual effects as ontological transformations of and within the cosmos, wherever and however it is articulated locally. Paradox, we argue, is a crucial element in each of these analytical directions because its performative utterance and continuation are that which ultimately maintains the dynamic that holds different sides of the boundaries here described in a constant dialogue. And it is this dialogue, a form of linguistic as well as corporeal movement, that should be at the heart of the analysis. Rather than an attempt to infuse the world with stability and permanence, or restore some kind of lost harmony, the dynamic communicational event of possession, whether it is fleeting or a routine practice, continuously *reforms* social boundaries through creative instantiations of paradox.

Angels and Demons: Notes on Kinship and Exorcism at an Ethiopian Orthodox Shrine

Diego Maria Malara

Angels, Demons, and Families

A skinny man, frail and dark of complexion, Abebe was initially too shy to look me in the eye. He sat, nervous, sunken into a cheap armchair in the Taytu Hotel lobby. "Don't worry, he acts like this in his shop when a customer comes in too," said a mutual acquaintance who had accompanied him. Abebe smiled timidly, and nodded silently in confirmation.

When we spoke about religious topics, Abebe's shyness gave way to a certain severity. He talked with the soft but decisive tone of one who takes the subject seriously, and feels that his direct experience confers the authority to produce a truthful narrative—a narrative validated by a suffering that others could not understand or explain. It was in this tone that he recounted his story in full for the first time since we had met a month earlier at Shinkuro Mikael, an Ethiopian Orthodox shrine near Addis Ababa.

Abebe's problems had started when he was working in a carpentry shop. A generalized sense of "stress" (*cinqet*) made him unable to focus: "Even if I worked, I was never satisfied with what I did. I even started to spoil other people's work." He began experiencing severe pain in his joints and chest—"as if they were pierced by a spear"— which made working even harder. His poor performance and growing irritability led to countless fights with his employer, who eventually fired him. The stress soon turned into anger. "I lost patience easily. I was constantly angry and I started talking back to my elders ... I, who used to be such a shy and respectful son," he said. Abebe perceived the quarrels he had with his father as being particularly at odds with the Ethiopian

I would like to thank Tom Boylston, Janet Carsten, Magnus Course, Koreen Reece, Maya Mayblin, Mellatra Tamrat, and Bruno Reinhardt for their insightful suggestions and criticism on different versions of this chapter during its long gestation. Diana Espírito Santo and Matan Shapiro provided invaluable feedback and support during a difficult phase of human history. A previous version of this chapter was presented at "The persona and cult of the Archangel Michael" workshop, University of Bergen; I am grateful to the participants for their comments. The research and writing of this article have received generous support from the University of Edinburgh (School of Political and Social Science), the Tweedie Exploration Fellowship, the Royal Anthropological Institute (Sutasoma Award), and the Institute of Advanced Studies in the Humanities (IASH).

etiquette of deference—"it is outside our culture," he explained—and a "behavior which is not Christian." According to his mother, the chief reason for the quarrels was Abebe's inability to keep the job secured for him by his father through personal ties with the owner of the carpentry shop. At that time, Abebe's actions were considered shameful signs of ingratitude, jeopardizing his father's reputation.

Unemployed and hopeless, Abebe developed an addiction to *khat*.[1] The family tried to cover it up for some time, but it soon became public, piling further shame onto the household. He succeeded in convincing his mother to give him money on several occasions, but the money was soon spent on feeding his addiction. Too ashamed to admit his failures to anybody but his mother, Abebe begged her to intercede with his father and ask that he lend Abebe a sum to start a small business. However, any attempt at mediation was met by his father's unconditional refusal. New quarrels erupted, and Abebe's father stopped talking to him, but not before threatening to banish him from the house. Abebe decided to leave.

He left the house in a state of confusion, which he described as "not knowing myself." Resolute on leaving Ethiopia in order "to change life," Abebe embarked on a journey east. He explained: "I remembered that when I was little I overheard that this is the passage to Djibouti that people take when they want to leave the country." But, by the time he reached Metehara, a town in central Ethiopia, he found himself short of money. One night, he was sitting on the shore of nearby lake Basaka when he felt an uncanny desire to enter the water even though he could not swim. He recounted: "It was like being in a movie: I could see this happening but I could not control it. [...] My body was moving, and I was desperate because of the life I had ... Then, when I was almost in the water I said: 'My Lady [Mary], come to me' (*Immebeté derrashiliñ*)." After this desperate appeal, he experienced a sudden sense of relief: "I felt that the spirit that was on my back was leaving." This was the first time Abebe realized that he was under the influence of an alien force. Confused and frightened, he returned to his family, but kept what had happened by the lake to himself.

Abebe heard from a close friend about Shinkuro Mikael, a famous *s'ebel* (holy water) shrine located in the mountains around Addis Ababa. With no particular expectations, he decided to visit the site. There he met a "kind stranger," a man who advised him to bathe in one of the many *s'ebel* pools. As he immersed himself in the water, something unexpected happened. "I lost consciousness (*rasen satku*; literally, I lost myself)," he told me in an agitated fashion. He struggled to leave the pool, his limbs moved frantically in the water, he asked for help to get out, he cursed the stranger who took him there. But something was holding him down. Then, the spirit inside him finally spoke.

Abebe said gravely: "I have to thank God that there was a woman sitting there [near the pool] ... She and the man who took me there listened to what the demon said." As he regained consciousness, the two reported to him what had happened. "They told me that I said: 'I will return with my mother and my sister on Saint Michael's day.' But it wasn't me speaking. It was the spirit ... I went home and I told my mother what happened. She loves Saint Michael very much so she said: 'It's an invitation from Michael, I won't miss it for any reason.'"

On the appointed day, Abebe went to Shinkuro Mikael with his mother, sister, and older brother. As he touched the holy water, the spirit spoke again: "I screamed a lot, I struggled a lot ... The spirit said that it was a *zar*,[2] a kind of spirit that affects different people within the same family, and had been in the family for a long time. My mother was frightened. She had never seen anything like that. She cried a lot. I didn't know all this [he was in a trance] but the spirit told my mother: 'Don't worry, Saint Michael has seized me.'"

Abebe and his mother stayed at the shrine for several months. His brother and sister also spent protracted periods there. They all regularly underwent ritual ablutions, and eventually, something even more extraordinary happened: the same spirit manifested itself through Abebe's mother and revealed itself to be at the root of many family conflicts. As time passed, these revelations led the kin to reconfigure their mutual relationships and care for each other in ways that allowed divine powers to free the family from its spiritual affliction.

Abebe was freed from his spirit after two months, his mother after six. Throughout their stay, mother and son woke up at dawn, attended the pre-mass service (*kidan*), took regular early-morning baths in the s'ebel pools, and drank holy water in the nearby eucalyptus forest before eating anything. They underwent confession regularly and sought the advice of local priests. Abebe said that this experience radically changed his life: "Now I know the importance of prayer. I pray every morning and every night. Now I know the power of s'ebel. I saw that God is above everything." Both Abebe and his mother maintained that the family quarrels had disappeared, enabling various family members—including Abebe's father—to agree to start a modest business where Abebe is currently employed. It has proven to be quite successful.

* * *

Drawing on this and similar stories, this essay traces the intersecting relationships between humans and non-human persons at the Shinkuro Mikael shrine. It shows that although the declared telos of exorcism remains the restoration of individual agency through the excision of a demonic other, in cases like Abebe's, exorcism is concerned less with individual demoniacs than it is with the intricate relationships and histories of suffering in which they are entangled. I chart the ecologies of communication through which a demon's presence is detected and through which demons, in turn, reveal critical truths about the relationships that bind kin together. And I illustrate how such relationships are shown both to cause possession and to be fundamental to the success of exorcism—a paradoxical simultaneity that, to echo the introduction to this volume, instead of constituting a deadlock begets creative possibilities for social action and healing. Demons, here, are not external to relatedness, but inherent to kinship networks.[3]

The study of deliverance from demons in African Christianities has focused mostly on Pentecostal ritual frameworks in which, according to prominent interpretations, a marked rapture with an idolatrous pre-Christian past and its far-reaching demonic influence is also achieved by breaking ties with kin who are still involved in non-Christian practices (Meyer 1998, 324–9; but see Lindhardt 2017; Quiroz 2013). In Abebe's case, instead of these familiar tropes of breakage, we see a concerted recalibration of extant, but fraught, kin relationships to displace a common demonic enemy. And, rather than assertions of discontinuity, we are confronted with a sort of recuperative change, whereby the same kinship ties that were implicated in the onset of possession are at once subtly modified and graphically reinstated. I foreground a cosmology in which kinship and possession are not just intimately linked, but mutually constitutive—one which contrasts with assessments of similar Ethiopian shrines that portray healing as instigating disconnections from mundane relations and spaces in order to authorize access to a new, therapeutic community of fellow sufferers (see Hermann 2010). In so doing, I suggest that the boundaries between the domains of kinship and spirits should not be approached as readily given but as necessitating the intense, coordinated socio-ritual labor of priests, kin, and divine beings in order to be demarcated and reasserted, all the while remaining dangerously fuzzy and permeable.

Presence and Voice

Situated a few kilometers outside Addis Ababa, the Shinkuro Mikael shrine is a vast open field, dotted with pools of holy water and dominated by a church consecrated to the archangel Michael. The pools' names evoke the imagery of biblical geography: Meskel Bet (the house of the cross), Yordanos (Jordan River), and so forth. In Shinkuro Mikael, everything is saturated with divine potency: the water is s'ebel, which burns demons and cures every sickness; the soil is *imnent* (literally, faith), which heals wounds and skin diseases. This pervasive holiness is a consequence of the fact that the site is Saint Michael's property, imbued with the charisma and force of his sacred persona. Saint Michael is referred to as the "owner" (*balebetu*) of the site and everything within it falls under his scrupulous control. This ownership, as we shall see, is not that of a bureaucrat, but rather of a jealous lord who exerts his violent power without restraint.

The flux of people, bodily substances, objects, and activities at the shrine is regulated by strategies of separation, aimed at preventing the cross-contamination of the "spiritual" (*menfesawi*) and "worldly" (*alemawi*) spheres. Before entering the site, visitors have to pass over a bridge, described as a "customs control" (*kela*), where they might be asked if they had sex the night before, or, in the case of women, if they are subject to any postpartum taboos—conditions deemed incompatible with access to the many sacred spaces. Those who have open wounds and women who are menstruating are not allowed to enter the pools. People are forbidden to step on holy ground wearing shoes, just as in Ethiopian Orthodox church buildings. Smoking and chewing khat are strictly prohibited.

People speak of their visits to the site as a pilgrimage from the most polluted and worldly of all places—the capital city—into a place not-of-this-world. These movements across the heterogenous moral geography of the city and its surroundings resonate with Brown's description of saints' shrines in late antiquity:

> By localizing the holy in this manner [in holy sites] [...] Christianity could feed
> on the facts of distance and the joys of proximity. [...] The pilgrim committed

himself or herself to the "therapy of distance" by recognizing that what he or she wished was not to be had in the immediate environment [...] Pilgrimage remains essentially an act of leaving. But distance is there to be overcome; the experience of pilgrimage activates a yearning for intimate closeness. (1981, 86–8)

Spending a period of time at Shinkuro Mikael is described as *subahé*: an ascetic retreat from the anxieties and desires of worldly existence, which is often rendered as a time of "temporary monkhood." However, as I will argue, this ascetic idiom does not always neatly map onto the actual experiences and practices of people like Abebe who move to the site with their families, or others who are frequently visited by family members. Indeed, the persistence and relevance of mundane mutual relationships throughout the ritual process complicate the possibility of tidily disentangling the sphere of the spiritual from that of this-worldly affairs.

The proximity that people seek in Shinkuro Mikael is to a sacred power embedded in various materials—the water or the soil—available to sensory experience. But, people also visit this site to meet a powerful person and patron: Saint Michael himself. Shinkuro Mikael is thus "not just the site of holiness and power, but rather the site of an encounter" (Josipovici 1996, 61). At the same time, people often come here to confront the demon lurking within their bodies. Shinkuro Mikael is, thus, a site of ominous revelations, where Michael's raw power coerces demons into visibility, creating a space in which to address malevolent spirits under his tutelage.

At the shrine, elusive entities become audible and responsive, entering relationships with humans that concretize and amplify their impalpable presence. The presence of the angel is dramatically evinced through his interactions with demons that suffer under his force, confess their misdeeds, scream, and beg him to stop inflicting pain on them. To echo Brown again, "nothing [gives] more palpable face to the unseen *presentia* of the saint than the heavy cries of the possessed" (1981, 108). As Abebe explained, "Michael obliges demons to talk [...] You can't expect anything good from an evil spirit, but because they are afraid [of Michael] they say what Michael asks them to say." He further added, "The demons talk always about Michael. They say: 'descendant of Adam, Michael rose for you.'" Demons declare their vicious hate toward the human race, but also bitterly admit to their vulnerability: "he is burning me, Michael is burning me! The water is fire and his sword is like a flame on my head. Enough!" These messages are both frightening and comforting, revealing the unruly power of the demonic, but also testifying to the benevolence of divine power, and to its ultimate superiority. Demons become de facto mediators of the messages of an angel that humans cannot hear or see. And, as in the case of Abebe—whose demon reported Michael's request that the entire family should come to the shrine—it is often the demons' own messages that make the possessed person's kin aware of his or her situation, and which mobilize their support.

What distinguishes Shinkuro Mikael from most shrines is that, here, priests and monks are forbidden from performing exorcisms. The angel takes full charge of curing all kinds of diseases, and hostile spirits are cast away by his wrath. Michael is not just the owner of this vast field, but also the only officiating "exorcist" (*atmaqi*; literally, baptizer). Stories suggest that, in the past, priests tried to exorcise demons on this site, but were either thrown violently on the ground by an invisible force or became sick and temporarily paralyzed. As Tesfay, a formerly possessed man, narrated:

> There was a priest called Abba Tadesse who tried to baptize [exorcise] people here many years ago. But when he raised his cross, it was taken from his hand by an invisible person and stuck into the trunk of a tree. The priest was shocked and scared, and bowed down to ask for forgiveness. I have seen this cross and I can tell you that there is no nail or glue holding it on that tree.

One of the outcomes of the absence of priestly mediation is that the quotidian ritual routines of those who seek a cure in this shrine are less strictly regulated than at other similar sites. Priests only provide advice to visitors through sermons and personal counseling, but the degree of adherence to the suggested ritual protocols varies significantly. Lay assistants, often formerly possessed people themselves, help ensure orderly access to holy water, facilitate the search for accommodation, and provide encouragement by sharing the stories of healing they have witnessed or experienced. Visitors are advised to drink s'ebel or bathe in it early in the morning. Oral intake of s'ebel brings clean, divine power directly into the body, and causes the evacuation, through vomiting and defecation, of various materials—eggs, stones, and worms—taken to be signs of demonic intrusion. Bathing in a s'ebel pool makes demons "shout and talk" so that, in cases like Abebe's, they reveal a picture of flawed relatedness which might contain the clue to its own cure.

During their stay at Shinkuro Mikael, visitors live in one of the small huts scattered around the site. Besides bathing in and drinking holy water, daily routines might include fasting, church attendance, and confession. The possessed persons, and often their kin, eat together, pray together, read religious texts to each other, and assist each other during ritual ablutions. Their presence at the healing site often leads kin to focus on the inevitability of their relationships to one another—the fact that they are stuck with each other, as it were, bound by demons, a shared familial history, and divine forces.

Before I turn to unpacking the intersections of the demonic, the divine, and the domestic, I wish to shift the analytical focus away from the shrine as a site of revelation and heightened communication, and concentrate instead on a different social arena where order is achieved and sustained through silence, pretense, and concealment: the household.

Hierarchy and the Order of Silence

There is a broad academic consensus that hierarchy and deference are crucial fibers of the Ethiopian Orthodox social fabric. Levine notes that "reverence for one's father is perhaps the key legitimating principle in the structure of [...] morality" (1965, 83). Ideally, as my friend Seyoum put it, "When your father asks you to do something, 'yes' is the best answer ... Or you can just remain silent and do what he asks, even if you don't want to do it. But you do it because he is your father." In many households, especially in the absence of a father figure, mothers are granted similar deference. Seyoum insisted that "respecting one's elders is the first commandment of home life." Mothers are perceived as somewhat more accessible, and interaction with them, though also regulated by hierarchical codes, is often more informal. Deference toward authority is conveyed through various bodily and verbal idioms. Avoiding eye contact with one's father when receiving a severe command and bowing silently is, for example, a graphic demonstration of obedience. In conservative households, fathers can be addressed with epithets such as "my shield" (*gashe*) that ratify hierarchical distance and acknowledge protective authority. Although comportment and degrees of intimacy vary greatly, the ideological basis of submissiveness was largely upheld by most of my interlocutors. However, they stressed that these principles can be hard to live by, especially in contemporary Ethiopian society, which is characterized by increasing aspirations to economic emancipation among young people, but also stronger dependence on one's parents due to widespread destitution.

Abebe's story illustrates how filial respect can often imply suppressing one's own desires when they are not approved by elders. After losing his job, and squandering his family's money, he was refused credit by his father. Rather than questioning his authority more than he had already done, Abebe preferred to leave the house. In the words of Fanta, a formerly possessed woman, "The price of *kibur* (respect or honor) is often suffering." Many narratives collected within and outside the shrine suggest that the domestic sphere is a social field where individuals occupying lower hierarchical positions are often condemned to silence, and that silence is a chief means to order relations. Abebe's father's refusal to speak to his son was described as a *korfia*, a term that can be roughly translated to mean a silent feud. Silenced tensions, as I will show, find loud articulation in Shinkuro Mikael, while also becoming transfigured into something altogether different.

Of course, young family members are not straightforwardly deprived of persuasive agency vis-à-vis their elders. Yet, often, for their desires to be made known, the intercession of mediators is indispensable. Recall that Abebe's request was not presented directly to his father, but was mediated by his mother—mothers being perceived as "closer" to the father, and willing to intercede endlessly for their children due to their intrinsic love for them (Malara & Boylston 2016). Failures at maternal mediation are particularly tragic from the point of view of children, as in the absence of an effective advocate, their grievances may be more easily dismissed as transient signs of immaturity or plainly ignored.

For many interlocutors, domestic forms of self-discipline and the unanswerable nature of patriarchal authority contribute to the onset of "stress" or cinqet. In Abebe's story, cinqet figures as a generalized and diffused malaise that is hard to pin down to a single etiology or manifestation. On a few occasions, Abebe seemed to imply that this condition was due to the internalization of silenced conflicts. As Abebe and his father stopped talking to each other, cinqet was revealed as a body engulfed by words that Abebe had not said and could not say: "I had many words inside but I felt scared to speak."

The injunction *lik mawek*, that is, "know your place" but also "know your limits," informs various aspects of domestic ethics. It suggests the necessity of respecting authority, of speaking properly, or refraining from speaking when appropriate, and, more broadly, of accurately assessing and acknowledging the constraints of one's agentive possibilities. If a child speaks against elders inappropriately, I was told, s/he might be reprimanded with admonitions such as: "you don't know your place/limit" (*lik atawekim*), "are you not ashamed?" (*atafrim*), or "you have been seized by a demon" (*saytan yazeh*). The lattermost expression is commonly taken to mean "you've gone mad" but, as the story of Abebe shows, it can have a more starkly literal meaning.

While certainly veering on the normative, the picture I have sketched gives a sense of the impasses that disciplines of silence—both imposed from without and self-imposed—can beget. In the domestic space, I suggest, we see a turning inward (Handelman 2004) of the experience of spirit possession: prior to diagnosis, Abebe's wants, tensions, and spirits were painfully contained within his person, as the image of the bodily engulfment of stress conveys. As I show next, this "inward curvature" (ibid.) is the prelude to a folding outward of possession dependent on the movement of kin, and their spirits with them, to a qualitatively different space where demons reclaim their voices and reveal salient aspects of fraught kin relationships.

Revelation and Witnessing

In mundane spaces, possession can easily go unnoticed or misdiagnosed. Its typical signs range from gastritis to temporary paralysis, from apathy to stress. The polysemy of such signs makes detecting demons a complicated business. The only incontrovertible diagnosis of possession comes from the painful cries of the demons themselves. Often, these loud and violent manifestations take place in sacred sites like churches or shrines—and are contrasted by my interlocutors with the interpretative angst ensuing from demons' enigmatic silence in the home, where families like Abebe's are left to wonder helplessly about the causes of their kin's problems. As Brown aptly put it, "the horror of the demonic [is] its very facelessness" (1981, 110).

The catalyst for these demonic revelations is the holy water, whose silent flow instigates the raucous flow of spirits outward into sacred arenas and across individuals, rendering tangible flawed sociality and voice (cf. Espírito Santo 2013). It is in the water that demons take movement and force, conveying messages that allow for social entrenchments to be dissolved and recalibrated. And yet, as I show below, this revelatory process would be incomplete and ineffective without the performances of human audiences—other demoniacs at the shrine but also, crucially, one's kin—acting as witnesses.

At Shinkuro Mikael, demons manifest in all their vehemence. The people who witness the ghastly scene of trance feel morally compelled to listen carefully to what is said. Remember that two strangers reported to Abebe what his demon declared, of which he himself had no recollection. This reporting, in turn, allowed Abebe to convey the invitation of the angel—mediated by the demon—to his mother, instigating the family's movement to the sacred site, where the deep entanglements between kinship and the demonic were unraveled over months. The demon eventually also manifested through Abebe's mother and, as the demon spoke through mother and son at different moments, they acted as witnesses to each other's trance. This web of mediated communications allowed for a cumulative process of elaborating and consolidating a shared interpretation in which murky passages in the family's history were illuminated. Family members came to learn about themselves and the intricate tapestry of their mutual relationships through a common, vexing demonic other. At the same time, they were exhorted to relinquish agency to the sacred potency surging in the place they visited, and to the angelic protector who acted both on their bodies and their relations.

In contrast to the "inward turn" of possession (Handelman 2004) experienced at home—where the demon hid in plain sight, silently contained within Abebe's body—the folding outward of possession at the shrine produced all manners of connections and effects in its social surroundings. These effects were enabled by human acts of testimony and mediation which, I suggest, have important implications for the selfhood of the possessed. With reference to spirit possession in Mayotte, Lambek notes that the insertion of an intermediary in communications between spirit and human host is essential to maintaining their separation: "Were host and spirit to regularly communicate directly between each other, their distinctiveness would be broken down" (1988, 322). Indeed, before Abebe was able to undergo a trance and recruit external parties as witnesses, he wondered restlessly: "Is this my own thought? Or does it come from a demon? What is the voice I hear in my head saying 'I should … ?' The demon doesn't say 'you should kill yourself' but 'I shall kill myself.'" In brief, the ecology of communication at Shinkuro Mikael helps diagnose subtle malignant forces which refuse to speak in their own voices and facilitates the recovery of a threatened notion of self-identity.

As human witnesses helped demarcate between spirit and host, they also contributed to shaping, propagating, and validating a public narrative about possession. Those who witness trance events are predisposed to listen with compassion in its literal, etymological sense of "suffering with." Witnesses convey their emotional state through expressions of dismay such as "in the name of the father" (*besimihab*), statements of pity such as "poor thing" (*miskin*), or exclamations like "*wayne*," which suggests amazement, worry, and pain. The unentranced audience appeals to a multitude of celestial beings as advocates of the Christian body usurped by unclean spirits. The audience's responses punctuate the demonic tale, conferring upon it its characteristic rhythm. Similarly to what Seremetakis (1990) notes for Greek funerary laments, this acoustic interplay ratifies the intersubjective truthfulness of demonic speech and, most importantly, confirms its vital capacity to reach others. Indeed, through these processes, Abebe's demon effectively gained a sympathetic audience for his host's case when he had lacked one. Without the successful dissemination of demonic messages the social efficacy of trance performances would be entirely lost. To reiterate, what allowed the family to overcome the initial deadlock was the indeclinable invitation of an angel, conveyed by an unlikely demonic emissary and reported to Abebe and, later, by him to his mother.

The mechanics of revelation and witnessing are not simply predicated upon a collective, dispassionate reporting, but rely on the visceral dimensions of seeing and hearing (see Pandolfo 2018). The expressions of the audience members are solemn, marking the gravity of the occasion. Listeners bring their hands to their faces, dig their nails into the skin of their cheeks, plant their fingers into dark soil moistened by holy water, and cover their mouths in scandalized astonishment. They beat their chests with open palms in a rhythm reminiscent of mourning, and tears often accompany the acts of seeing, listening, and responding. The embodied reflexes of witnessing, and the verbal responses of the audience, amount to "ontological acts" (see Introduction) whereby the reality of possession and spirits is brought into being through human performances and stylized iconographies of veridiction (see Seremetakis 1990).

Lambek notes that religion establishes its truths "by means of performativity, such as that [...] the facts are expected to conform to the performative utterance rather than the reverse" (Lambek 2013, 253), and that this conformity is also established retrospectively. By entering sensorially dense circuits of witnessing, the messages conveyed by the demon produced the very thing they purported to describe: a haunted family history and kinship. And yet, as I illustrate in the remainder of this chapter, demons do not just transform kin relationships in specific ways but, much as interactions between kin are key to revealing the workings of the demonic, the excision of demons is contingent upon specific realignments of kin relations.

Thickenings and Reconfigurations

Saint Michael coerced the zar spirit not only into revealing how it had sabotaged the well-being of Abebe's family, but also into disclosing how, in the absence of its mischievous interference, the family would have prospered due to the profound love that its members bear for one another. Despite its patent animosity, the spirit served as a potent "sign of the unity, distinctiveness and continuity of the family," speaking "with the voice of someone who has an enduring association" with it (Lambek 2003, 47). While the spirit's revelations certainly consolidated a sense of cohesion among family members, Abebe thought that this outcome also obtained from his and his mother's visceral realization that they were vessels invaded by the same evil. Being possessed by the same spirit is, as Boddy suggests, "a means of relating," not just "through words or overt acts of allegiance" but also "through embodied experience" (1993, 33). Here, kin relations are not just relationships *between* people but relations that are painfully lived *within* their body. Possession rendered dramatically clears the fact that kin share a history, and this is the reason why they were possessed in the first place (ibid., 32). Simultaneously, the stay at Shinkuro Mikael revealed that the key to deliverance lay in this same tumultuous family history and the reconfiguration of kin relations. In short, kinship emerged as both the cause of, and solution to, a problem.

Shinkuro Mikael provided mother and son a safe space to confront the unruly forces of the demonic under the supervision of an angelic patron. It was also a space that encouraged, oriented, and rewarded specific gestures of compromise, understanding, and affection patterned on the normative registers of Orthodox ethics and piety. The priests who advised the family admonished them that, for God to show his mercy, kin must be merciful to each other. In enacting this analogical incitation, kin mediated each other's relationships with the divine, thereby displacing the demon. Significantly, the time Abebe spent at the shrine didn't engender an entirely new set of social relationships, nor did it compensate for the loss of kinship attachments (cf. Hermann 2010, 237–0). Rather, it "thickened" existing relationships (Boddy 1993), adding renewed urgency to the mending of familial ties and new layers of affective and spiritual relevance to reciprocal care among kin—as well as encouraging new ways of inhabiting relatedness.

In retrospect, Abebe's mother commented that her experience at the shrine taught her that "without the love of one's family life is like exile," adding that the conflicts troubling the intrinsically nurturing bond between mother and son widened her distance from God. Abebe came to a similar conclusion when seeing his mother's body overtaken by an alien evil—a terrifying sight that also made him intensely aware of his own vulnerability by confronting him directly with a vision of the nefarious entity lurking within himself. He compared this insight to "a spiritual X-ray." Mother and son began to see pedestrian acts of care, such as cooking and feeding, as imbued with the highest spiritual significance. By praying together and for each other, as well as jointly attending church services, family members partook in the holiness of the surrounding space. Their stay at the shrine enabled them to "improve their relationships in a way that pleases God," as Abebe put it, activating the channels through which the salvific intervention of Saint Michael could heal the family.

Differently from assessments of similar Ethiopian Orthodox shrines that portray healing as predicated on an ascetic pilgrimage that leaves behind enmeshment in worldly affairs to reinsert the sufferer into the therapeutic *communitas* of fellow pilgrims (e.g., Hermann 2010), Abebe didn't seek alternatives to his troubled kin relations in new social collectives. Nor did he consider severing ties with his kin or asserting discontinuity with family history—operations that are central to some ideologies of deliverance described in studies of African Pentecostalism—as necessary, beneficial, or even possible (cf. Meyer 1998). Rather, the power of exorcism was obtained from its capacity to move part of the family into a qualitatively different, sacred setting, where existing kin relations could be simultaneously sustained and modified.

The relative restoration of harmony depended also on a recalibration of the relationship between Abebe's mother and father. Unwilling to forgive and further support his son despite the repeated pleas of his wife, Abebe's father never visited the shrine. So far, I have described the autopoietic dynamics of exorcism in the self-contained space of Shinkuro Mikael, and the ways in which ritual elements are held together from within, as it were (see Handelman 2004). However, the efficacy of exorcism is heavily reliant on continual communication across boundaries, from the shrine to Abebe's house, and back. What is integral to ritual efficacy is the capacity of the sacred potency of the shrine to spill out from its ritual confines and reach Abebe's father through human messengers, drawing him away from his stagnant position. Social context and ritual, home and shrine, are tightly intertwined from the onset of exorcism, complicating the possibility of disentangling these domains, even temporarily and for purely analytical purposes (cf. Handelman 2004).

Abebe's father eventually reconsidered his uncompromising stance after his wife and Abebe's siblings reported what had happened at Shinkuro Mikael. Discussing zar possession in Sudan, Boddy notes that spirits possessing various female family members provide "threads of coherence" in complex kin relations, foregrounding matrilineal continuity as an "embodied counterpoint" to patriarchal authority (1993, 33). In the case of Abebe, the process of exorcism created an affective and embodied cohesion between those kin who underwent or witnessed each other's trance, providing evidence of the depth of their essential connection and uniting them against a common spiritual enemy and under the guidance of Abebe's mother. Drawing on the support of her offspring, the mother communicated with her husband—either directly during her short visits or, less frequently, through her children going back and forth from the shrine—with renewed persuasive force. And this persuasiveness partly derived its momentum from the fact she did not just speak for the rest of the family, but mediated the will of a higher angelic power that was willing to heal fraught kinship relations, provided its demands of family reconciliation were met.

The therapeutics of exorcism has as its declared end the restoration of individual agency; but, in Abebe's case as in others, it appeared less concretely preoccupied with the individual than with an intricate tapestry of relations. Crucially, the outcomes of exorcism did not subvert the ideological scaffolding of kinship hierarchy and dependency, but subtly recalibrated domestic relations. Indeed, in facilitating compromise with Abebe's father, who eventually agreed to support his son emotionally and economically, Abebe's mother enabled the very asymmetrical divisions that had been at the root of the original impasse (see Malara & Boylston 2016). Indeed, by facing her husband, speaking for and on behalf of Abebe, she both lent her son a voice and confiscated it, shaping the narrative of possession according to her own views and agenda, and actively impeding direct and nonhierarchic communication between father and son (see Pandolfo 2018, 48). In conclusion, while these "acts of kinship" (Lambek 2013) undoubtedly brought about incisive changes, they did so in ways that tended to reproduce socially and religiously sanctioned relational arrangements and the roles assigned to family members within them—at least for a time.

Exorcism offered Abebe's father, a pious man, the occasion to submit to divine power and its designs, in a context where rebellion against God can invite serious repercussions (Levine 1965; Malara 2020). Meanwhile, upon re-entering the home, Abebe also submitted to his father's authority, begging for his protection. He considered this display of deference as reinforcing his own submission to God and thus tantamount to eliciting divine mercy (*mihret*) and blessing (*bereket*). Exorcism made the vulnerability of intimate relations visible—unveiling the painful truth that one is more vulnerable to one's protectors—but also made palpable the caring potential of hierarchy and patronage. Indeed, after his stay at the shrine, Abebe did not seek an escape from asymmetrical relations of dependence, but new, sustainable, and productive ways to inhabit them.

These dynamics, as I have shown, are at odds with views that unilaterally emphasize discontinuity with mundane relationality as a distinctive feature of healing. To be sure, I do not suggest that there aren't a number of people who travel to and stay at Shinkuro Mikael alone, or who see severing relations with a kin who has, for instance, bewitched them, as necessary. Indeed, while exorcism at Shinkuro Mikael encourages adherence to a normative model of relatedness, there is nothing deterministic about its outcomes. My point, as I elaborate below, is simply that despite the ascetic idiom and aesthetic of otherworldly escapades that suffuse descriptions of pilgrimage to shrines, in the Ethiopian Orthodox context we can't overstate the extent to which spiritual relationships are made *through* kinship relationships, not *apart from* them (see McKinnon & Cannell 2013, 10; cf. Reece 2019).

Coda: loops

Kinship emerged, simultaneously and paradoxically, as the fertile ground for demonization and the indispensable instrument to overcome it. In contrast to functionalist and representationalist readings, this conception cannot grant analytical priority to troubled human relationships as the real, material ground of which possession is essentially a refraction (see Introduction). But, equally, it doesn't allow for an interpretation of possession as causally independent from the social context from which it arises and which it affects. Rather, our case presents us with a loop of sorts, where kinship and possession are not just mutually related, but are, in many ways, mutually constitutive. This loop is somewhat reminiscent of the paradoxical geometry of the Mobius Strip evoked in the introduction to this volume, as kinship and spirits can be seen as recursively entwined in a single-sided spiral. As Vilaseca put it, "[w]hat distinguishes the 'Moebius strip' is its subversion of the usual (Euclidean) way of representing space: the strip appears to have two sides when in fact it has only one: hence the impossibility of distinguishing its 'back' from its 'front'" (1999, 427; see also Tsintjilonis 2019). Although the domains of kinship and spirits have, at some level, demarcated boundaries—their separation is, after all, the aim of exorcism—these boundaries are often tenuous at best, especially during people's presence at the shrine. Crucially, boundaries between the domains of kinship and the demonic are not a given; they require instead the active ritual and affective work of penitents, priests, and angels to assert specific distinctions, and even so, a profound interdependence remains (see McKinnon & Cannel 2013, 11).

In Abebe's and his mother's hermeneutics of affliction, such looping effects confound and conflate notions of cause and effect (see Hacking 1999). At times, family members seemed to imply that Abebe's repentance of his chronic insubordination was key to the success of the exorcism: as his mother said, "Abebe's bad behaviors opened the gate to a demon, which was fed by the fights in the family." But, most of the time, Abebe's kin maintained that the situation wasn't his fault, and that his behavior was due to an inherited spiritual agent, which was also operating through his mother. Hence, the ritual process did not straightforwardly produce order or certainty out of messy lived experience; it also engendered its own indeterminacy through the paradoxical simultanety evoked by Espírito Santo and Shapiro in the introduction to this volume (see Malara 2019), which allowed for individual accountability to be mitigated, redistributed, or obscured (cf. Lambek 2003). Abebe was thus able to act as both penitent and victim, or could shift between the roles in different contexts. Meanwhile, the absence of definitive judgment about his responsibilities made it easier for the family to forgive his transgressions or to simply not to discuss them as intentional: to forget them and move on, or to pretend to forget them. This indeterminacy also facilitated the exorcism of the shame Abebe brought on his father and family: while giving in to the request of a disrespectful son would have generated further ignominy under normal circumstances, in this case it became an index of the piety and decency of the family. Here ambiguity verging on paradox doesn't constitute a deadlock, but is generative of possibilities, as "people [...] deliberately use the simultaneity that the paradox entails in order to put emotions, words, feelings [...] in motion" (Introduction). Forgiving, forgetting, and pretending are inconspicuous, understated, and perhaps anthropologically under-explored means through which kinship is reproduced and households are rendered habitable.

So far, I have foregrounded the interdependence between kinship and the demonic. I want to conclude by suggesting that a different type of circular relation ties together Saint Michael and Abebe's family. While relationships between demons and kin are markedly predatory, those between kin and saints are predicated on intense reciprocity. People visit Shinkuro Mikael because of its holiness and because the angel's power is known to be intensely manifest at this shrine. Yet it is only through the witnessing of visitors that the power of the shrine and its owner is renewed and amplified. It is commonly understood that in exchange for their miraculous assistance in daily affairs, saints ask nothing back but "worship" (*mesgana*) from devotees; but, in practice, worshippers also witness and broadcast saintly efficacy through their lives and devotion in their social surroundings. Worship effectively gives saints perpetual remembrance, a social life in the world of humans, and potentially expands their circle of influence to new devotees who learn about the wonders of their powers. Saint Michael became an essential part of Abebe's family's history, and all family members now offer a feast on Saint Michael's day to publicly acknowledge their debt. These devout acts of witnessing and passionate recounting can be seen as a reciprocation—perhaps the only one possible—to an angelic patron. Moreover, the story of the family also became part of the miraculous history of the shrine and contributed to its fame, as it is now told and retold to others there. Much like the story of Abba Tadesse, which I recounted earlier, Abebe's story became tangible proof of Saint Michael's efficacy. Significantly, this story also traveled outside the shrine, along the trails of pilgrims returning home. In fact, before meeting Abebe, I had heard his story from a friend, who heard about it from a relative who knew Abebe's mother. My own ethnographic account, perhaps, functions as a continuation of this chain of testimony, widening the reach of narratives of Michael's efficacy across farthest borders, and attesting to exorcism's capacity to ensnare one as witness to the grand spectacle of submission of all things human and nonhuman to the divine.

Spirit Possessions, Racial Dispossessions: The Second Diaspora of Race in Afro-Cuban Religious Experience

Anastasios Panagiotopoulos

Fanon through Cuba, Cuba through Fanon

One of Frantz Fanon's most powerful and often quoted textual moments refers to something he once experienced on a train. A white child, seeing him, exclaims to its mother: "Look! A Negro; I'm scared!" (2008, 91). Fanon vividly describes how blackness intrudes on him from the outside, taking place inside his skin: a visceral rather than merely mental or verbal assault: "I am a slave not to the 'idea' others have of me, but to my appearance" (2008 [1952], 95). The aggression condensed in such a short phrase, expressed by such a short human being, no matter how innocently, affects Fanon profoundly:

> As a result, the body schema, attacked in several places, collapsed, giving way to an epidermal racial schema ... I was no longer enjoying myself. I was unable to discover the feverish coordinates of the world ... Nausea. I was responsible not only for my body but also for my race and my ancestors. I cast an objective gaze over myself, discovered my blackness, my ethnic features; deafened by cannibalism, backwardness, fetishism, racial stigmas, slave traders ... Disoriented, incapable of confronting the Other, the white man, who had no scruples about imprisoning me, I transported myself on that particular day far, very far, from my self, and gave myself up as an object. What did this mean to me? Peeling, stripping my skin, causing a hemorrhage that left congealed black blood all over my body. Yet this reconsideration of myself, this thematization, was not my idea. I wanted quite simply to be a man among men. (ibid., 92)

Powerful words! A host of them would not be out of place if they were to describe instances of spirit possession: "the body schema, attacked in several places, collapsed," "feverish," "nausea," "ancestors," "fetishism," "slave traders," "disoriented," "transported," "object." From a broader perspective, spirit possession is meant to be a process of interiorization, of something coming from the outside and intruding on oneself: the Other becoming the Self (and vice versa), a process of incorporation (Boddy 1994; Johnson 2011; Lambek 1998; Stoller 1995) or, as the editors' Introduction of this present volume commences, a "twilight zone" wherein identities blend. In this broad sense, spirit possession is very reminiscent of Fanon's account of how "blackness" is a violent intrusion from without, a process and experience of "blackening," as he calls it. The exterior becomes interior, abruptly yet repetitively, each time with the same negative and violating "freshness," and, simultaneously, as if it has to do with something constitutive of oneself. This is temporally translated into *eternity*: both looking back (past) and forward (future), perpetually (present). Both "blackness" and spirit possession seem to be imbued with an almost unfathomable but intense ambiguity between the given (nature?) and the made (culture?), the interior and the exterior, the Self and the Other, reality and fiction or *Jim & Andy* (see Introduction to this volume), ontology and representation, more significantly in this chapter. The way something or someone (Fanon or the possessed, in these cases) is perceived from the outside, from the Other(s), is constitutive of being ("ontological"), although not necessarily in a closed and fully encompassing manner. The "point of view" *is* (or *becomes*) part of the very concreteness of being, whether this latter can be further negotiated or not, resisted or accommodated. Such an affinity between the experience of "blackening" and spirit possession could make us venture to treat them together through the ethnography of possessions by spirits of blacks or Africans, something often evinced in the field of Afro-Cuban religiosity.

An initial ethnographic observation is that Afro-Cuban religiosity is not solely concerned with contact with the spirits of blacks or Africans, and that participants in Afro-Cuban religiosity are not limited to Afro-Cubans, as this is understood in the broader Cuban society. Neither the spirits nor the living humans that constitute the Afro-Cuban religious milieu are strictly "black," although the milieu is unequivocally recognized as a legacy of Cuba's African heritage, however transformed (improved or degenerated) this might simultaneously be perceived to be. Yet this observation, with both its cosmological (the society of the spirits) and sociological (the society of the living humans) dimensions, is only a prelude to the much stronger point this paper seeks to unpack. This is that "blackness," through spirit possession by the black spirits themselves, is an indigenous critical theory and praxis wherein race is exposed as a historical process comprising its transformation from "representation" into "ontology" (Fanon's "blackening"). Spirit possession, rather than faithfully reflecting (on) the process, simultaneously reverses it, race being returned to its strange and twisted homeland: from "ontology" to "representation;" twisting the twist, as it were, diving into the waters of "paradox," to employ this volume's central concept. But, then, the dive occurs into even deeper waters.

One of the two main pillars of my meta-ethnographic argument is that the passage *from representation to ontology* (following section) and then *from ontology to representation* (third section) is not digitally linear. The destabilization of the one by means of the other is constant, at least as a potentiality. Race is de-ontologized *at the same time* as the spirits of Africans and their buried magical skills and oracular sensibilities are excavated and ontologically constituted as such (i.e., as spirits of wizards and diviners), in the midst of possessing the living (black, white, and everything-in-between) humans and through subsequent "representations" such as dolls. Through spirit possession and other "paradoxical" acts and objects, race is dispossessed, undergoing what I call a "second diaspora," in the sense of *dispersal*, the very dispersal to which black-African "subjects," from Africa to Cuba, were subjected in the first place by means of slavery. But the second diaspora, and here lie the foundations of the second main meta-ethnographic pillar (fourth, and last, section), is not just a symbolic and symmetrical reversal of the first diaspora. It is not a typical *rite of passage*. Rather, the second diaspora is the "space" wherein the conditions for radical, and not linear, dispersals are created. Radical dispersals, or second diasporas, unlike the first ones, do not follow a single path, the reverse of the first (a kind of *eternal return*). They follow many paths, as these cross each other, and at the same time, not necessarily excluding the reverse path, but not just that. For this to occur, the very structures that tried to cement a first diaspora and its perpetual hauntings should be blown. Spirit possession plays the role of the dynamite, although, in its multiplicity and simultaneity, is also partial and it never succeeds to *fix things*, not even in their fluidity. Under such scope, "paradox" is worth the inverted commas, because its paradoxical character lies in the fact that within it a more "rational" linearity can be included. If it was paradox, plain and simple, this inclusion would be incompatibly paradoxical.

The present account *is not* an attempt to give academic voice to living black subjects, at least not directly and inclusively. It is also not about representing them nor doing so unwittingly by claiming that it is about their ontological (non-representational) constitution. Rather, this paper *is* about black practices that have managed to escape their distinctive racial color, but not through their becoming "color-blind" or losing their "cultural" color or flavor. The way out of, the escape from, racial color is instantiated not as an act of accommodation but, as said before, through the dispersal that the second diaspora effects. It is an escape from single and linear paths (as that of race), partial but powerful. On a more theoretical level and as hinted before, I adopt a critical but engaged stance toward the so-called "ontological turn" (see Holbraad & Pedersen 2017), by examining instances where "ontology" can be a negative thing or effect, and where "ontology" and "representation" are not necessarily unrelated opposites; rather, they are a pair in which one may transform into the other or even coexist critically. This is of import, I argue, because there lurks in the "ontological turn" a tendency to obfuscate and essentialize the capacity of the ethnographic Others to act ontologically and not representationally. To be sure, this is a reaction to the contrary tendency, well held within traditional anthropological theory, of the exact opposite; that is, that only the "West" is capable of ontology (science) while the rest only of representations. What guides this present chapter is the understanding that we are all equally capable of both ontology (relative solidification) and representation (relative de-stabilization). What differs is that we *create* different *kinds* of them. I thus employ an ontological proposal to call for the need for even more contingent nuances.

Spirit Possessions: from "Representation" to "Ontology"

Spirit possession and "blackness" or "Africanity" in Cuba are very much linked in the following sense. In a highly complex, diverse, idiosyncratic, open, inclusive, and ever-transforming field of Afro-Cuban religious experience, there are certain practices that lean more distinctively toward the "Afro" part of what is an otherwise multiplicitously "inspired" (echoing Ochoa 2010) ritual reservoir. The most fertile and commonly desired conditions that lead to spirit possession are ceremonial instances of oracular consultations in front and with the aid of consecrated objects, of consecrated percussion producing African(-inspired) rhythms; of people (not necessarily black and not necessarily initiated) being physically and affectively moved by these rhythms, of a kind of collective effervescence that animates and is animated by an "electric" (echoing Beliso-de Jesús 2015) environment that—without any intention to produce essentialisms, whether stigmatizing or exoticizing—still evokes a visceral sense of "Africanness" (a collective Afro-efferv-essence?), which, in my opinion, is hard to dispute. It is also hard to dispute because it is an "essence" that has to do more with affective and performative intensity, rather than with a clearly demarcated and abundant content of intractably frozen principles or values, rigidly attached only to certain bodies. In other words, it is not a performed DNA of sorts.

Beyond this hard-to-substantiate-but-easy-to-sense "African" *habitus*, what can be ethnographically asserted is that the identities of the spirits who possess Cubans are more often than not identified as black, whether they are spirits of the dead or deities, such as the *orichas* of Santería and the *mpungos* of Palo Monte. In contrast, the more saintly (Catholic) dimensions of divinities or spirits of whites tend not to possess people, but appear in the senses and perceptive sensibilities in more solemn ways. Sobriety is their common mode of manifestation. The fair question arises, then, as to whether spirits of blacks may truly suffer from some kind of violent repression that keeps on resurfacing through possession, a deeply repressed and possessive collective trauma that goes beyond the actual bodies of living black Cubans and is surreptitiously ingrained in and diffused through the whole of the society through a ritual/performative idiom. The common scholarly answer to this has been in the affirmative so far, but what I assert and substantiate here is that it may well be more complicated. The same goes for how Fanon and his notion of "blackening" are commonly understood: as an ontological constitution that seems impossible to overcome. Let us first examine exactly how this ontological constitution is *constituted*, how it comes to manifest itself as ontological in the "*blackening*," Fanonian sense. The following section deals with how this "blackening" is being *deconstituted* or *dispossessed* by simultaneously constituting "race" as a historical and representationalist construct and asserting that "blackness" is a non-biologically predetermined, yet still ontological, category of magical and oracular sensibility and perceptibility.

"Too black … almost blue"

"The spirit that possesses me is black; too black!" These words were exclaimed by Celia, a self-proclaimed black woman. Revealing a wide range of "blackness" on Cuban (epidermic) soil, Celia's spirit, called Tomás (see also Panagiotopoulos 2011, 100–2), is described by Celia as more black than herself. This is not only in terms of skin color, as the spirit has been visually perceived by mediums as deeply black, "so black that he is almost blue," as Celia, in a typically Cuban figurative fashion, puts it.

While Tomás possesses Celia, her body emits a very powerful and unpleasant odor, framed by Celia in both quantitative and qualitative terms: "He sweats like a pig." She explains that, firstly, both the quantity of sweat and its degree of unpleasantness are higher than is analogous to the degree of movement he exhibits while in possession. Even though Tomás often possesses Celia in the midst of drumming and dancing, and once having possessed her, is constantly on the move, the quantity of sweat is not justified by this (or at least, "always justified", according to Celia). Secondly, Celia's sweat never smells this way in non-possession instances. Even if she happens to sweat a lot (which does not happen frequently), the odor is distinct, less intense, and unpleasant. Then Celia goes on to describe other characteristics of Tomás. He is a "brute," "bossy," and a "witchcraft" (*brujería*) expert. Are all these, along with the outpouring of bodily substance, concomitant with being "too black?"

I have witnessed Celia being possessed by Tomás several times and, although I have not managed to assess the odor, s/he indeed sweats a lot, becomes abrupt, even rude at times, and the accent is hard to understand, as it has an "African" sound and vocabulary. What would normally be interpreted as an arrogant and aggressive attitude is welcomed or, at least, diplomatically tolerated by those present in the possessions (c.f. Lambek 1993) as the taken-for-granted accompaniment to the presence of Tomás, who is there to speak the truth, give advice, incite action both practical and magical, and ask for offerings, among other activities. Speaking of her Congo, runaway slave, possessing spirit, one of Beliso-De Jesús' interlocutors, Zoraida, says: "He is tolerated because of his good sight" (2015, 115). One could argue that the sweat, the bodily gait, and all the other manifestations are necessary ingredients so that *oracular articulacy* (see Panagiotopoulos 2018) is ignited and enabled. As Beliso-De Jesús aptly puts it: "Various copresences demand an attunement to odors as communicative potential" (2015, 174). Tomás's possessing Celia is the whole affective, perceptive, and material "package," so to speak, which puts into motion this kind of *articulacy*, something not easily divided into a cause-and-effect classification (What comes first? What gives rise to what?), but is a simultaneous flow of words, images, sensations, movements, and smells. To put it more graphically, while Celia is emitting an altered kind of sweat, she is also able to emit oracular utterances, otherwise thought impossible to be retrieved. The emission of this flow is vested with a phenomenology and ontology of suffering, unpleasantness, abruptness, and rudeness. These, in their turn, are linked with the somatization of "blackness" brought about by spirit possession brings. Sweat pours out and "blackness" pours in! "Africa becomes a form of blackened humanity within Santería and other diasporic assemblages, operating with geographical, metaphysical, and ontological assertions," Beliso-De Jesús asserts (2015, 95). She goes on:

> [H]arnessing the powers of blackness ... counterdialogics ... experiences of being-strange-in-the-world ... in an unnamed ontology ... these spirits conjure produce a distinct feeling of *being different* ... a racialized queerness that makes their ontology feel decidedly unique from Cuban (global) society [an] ontology of the strange. (ibid., 117; emphasis in the original)

Ontology here, unlike conventional renderings of it (see Holbraad & Pedersen 2017), is seen as stemming from without (through possession) and not as a necessarily positively valued manifestation. The sweat of Tomás is an odorful condensation of his biography as a captured Congo man forced into labor in slavery-driven, colonial Cuba. Its excess is a somatic effect of a historical phenomenon, slavery, and all the repression and violence it unleashed on its subjects. Celia tells me that the sweat is a product of harsh labor as a slave: "Can you imagine working for hours non-stop, in the hot and humid Cuban climate, and doing something you do not want?" I would like to believe that I can indeed imagine it; what I could not imagine until then is this being translated into the *presence* of possession; the presence of Tomás. It seems that, in the Afro-Cuban religious idiom of spirit possession, "blackness" is *more* of itself (more than Celia's blackness, for instance) when it is linked to this affective genealogy of slavery, a historical experience made (forced) to become an apparent ontology of "blackness" in the New World: slavery-suffering-enforcement-blackness-sweat becomes one complex whole; history is embodied, it becomes ontology, it "blackens:" "I am a slave not to the 'idea' others have of me, but to my appearance," to recall Fanon's words at the beginning of the paper. An idea finds (creates) its sign in appearance, and then intrudes it violently; "representation" becomes "ontology," and an utterly negative one; it *enslaves*. This is the historiographical experience of "blackness" in the New World, expressed both by Tomás and Fanon. It is perhaps a kind of "blackness" that it is so black that it becomes blue, as Celia said (see also Gilroy 2010), *blues* that have been sung and danced to across the New World.

Racial Dispossessions: from "Ontology" to "Representation"

If one were to follow a "pure" phenomenology of spirit possession in Cuba, it would be very probable and tempting to conclude that all there is to it is precisely a phenomenology of "blackness." Possession in itself seems to allude to an expressive manifestation of violence, while all the "Africanisms" displayed, be they stylistic, bodily, or discursive, complement such a picture. Is this really all there is to it? Is the theme of racial exhaustion exhausted in this kind of phenomenological *epidermics of spirit possession*? Is the sweat that runs through such *epidermis* an end in itself? Is Tomás just a much-too-black sweating spirit?

In the course of Tomás's possessive interactions with Celia, as is the case with most possessions by other spirits in Cuba, the need to "represent" him has emerged. In the Afro-Cuban religious idiom, to "represent" (*representar*) signifies a material manifestation of sorts, often also called "materialization" (*materialización*). The spirit is "represented" in a way that a visual resemblance is materialized in the form of objects, which in the case of possessing spirits is most often a doll (see also Panagiotopoulos 2017). In the more particular case of possessing spirits of blacks, their "blackness" is "represented" and "materialized" through the color of the doll, which is dark. As dolls are most commonly made of plastic or cloth, the darkness is achieved by either painting over white dolls or by using a black or brown material. Semi-nakedness, headscarves, rustic clothes of bright colors usually adorn surround the dark bodies of the dolls. A cigar or a shot of rum may accompany them, when the specific spirits, while possessing their living counterparts, make them smoke or drink. Female "representations" are often adorned with jewelry.

"Representations," such as dolls, are deemed important for two interrelated reasons. Firstly, they are said to attract the spirit they betoken. This creates a more solid and interactive kind of ceremonial center, as the spirit is somewhat more present, playing a more integral part in the abode (houses constitute the most central and stable physical space of Afro-Cuban ritual expression). For instance, they become the most frequent receivers of offerings and sacrifice. Secondly, "representations" effect vital transformations, both in the spirits they "materialize" and, in consequence, the life-courses of their living counterparts. Being confronted with an indigenous term, what are we to make of "representations"? Do they *represent* the spirits or *are* they them? Representation or ontology, in other words? My quick answer is both. The ontology of "blackness" is turned into a representation, while at the same time "magic" is ontologically constituted. The remainder of the section elaborates on this.

Tomás's biography has been exposed during his possessions as that of a Congo slave, oozing "blackened," arduous, forced labor. The phenomenology of a sweat-soaked possession seems to be highlighting precisely this. Yet, another biographical element crops up, with less phenomenological obviousness but, perhaps, more powerful grip. Celia describes Tomás as a "witchcraft" expert. The Cuban equivalent term, that of *brujería*, is a tricky one, exactly like other terms which refer to Afro-Cuban religiosity (see Palmié 2013). Its precise meaning may range from a largely descriptive denomination to a more value-laden one, tinted with amoral (even immoral), "animist" superstition (see Ortiz 2001 [1906]). The full implications of this range would require a whole study of its own. From the point of view of Celia and for all those Cubans who are active participants in Afro-Cuban religiosity, "witchcraft" is principally taken as expertise with a definitive "Africaness" to it, the Congo inspiration (translating into the religious tradition of Palo Monte) capturing and condensing one of its most archetypal solidification. Indeed, one of Tomás's biographical revelations has been that he was a Congo man brought to Cuba as a slave. His "witchcraft" expertise is biographical baggage which precedes that of his enslaved transition to Cuba, and it does not only precede it *historically* but it also superimposes itself as the dominant element, transcending the past and infusing the present with its much-valued attributes. Celia says:

> Tomás was a great "knower" [*conocedor*] of "the religion" [*la religión*] and a great "witch" [*brujo*]. He was the holder of many secrets and knowledge that have now been lost, as is the case with many of these old Africans. At important times, though, he has revealed some of his secrets to me so that I, combining them with my own knowledge and experience, can provide solutions to urgent situations and help people who come to me. When he "mounts" me [the verb *montar* is an alternative to possess] he is able to see things no one else can and offer solutions to the most urgent of cases.

Celia, through an allusion to a never-conclusive excavatory and ever-creative archeology of magical and oracular knowledge, foregrounds the "witchcraft" element, as this links Tomás's biography with hers and the people she ritually attends. The arduousness of forced labor is displaced by the arduousness of a "secret" knowledge not readily shared, but with occasional and extremely rewarding revelations. The dialogic possibilities opened up, pursued, and further cultivated in the proliferation of possession instances, along with the complementary "materializations" of the spirit through "representation," harness two simultaneous paths: its biography-cum-representation and its "necrography-"cum-ontology (see Panagiotopoulos 2017).

The most obvious part of the spirit's biography is manifested as a seemingly necessary condition of the spirit's presence. Yet spirit possession is not a stable and faithful repetition of itself, exactly as the possessing spirit is not an unchanging entity, as it is normally presented in the cross-cultural literature, to the contrary. The first instances of possession are often manifested as raw, violent, and ambiguously insinuating situations. One basic ethnographic explanation that I have gathered from various interlocutors is that the person being possessed is either not used to the experience of possession in general or possession by the specific spirit (or both). The violence of possession, here, has more to do with an initial and provisional incompatibility of incorporation which needs time to become smooth, rather than just the resurfacing of a specific violent biographical event of the spirit's past life, an otherwise recurrent element in possessing spirits of the dead. This is the passage from an inarticulate to an articulate state. The absolute inarticulacy of the spirit before its first possession is relativized precisely through the latter. The first possessions are a breakthrough of silence into voice, but the voice is still conditioned by its previous inarticulacy. Here, what is voiced is not so much a wide range of clear utterances but the previous inability to express them, and an insinuating and overarching call for this impediment to be overcome.

At this stage, the biography of the spirit comes more to the fore, materializing in a mixture of intense verbal, affective, and physical expressions. For instance, the first possessions of Tomás were "pure" biographical expositions, simultaneously intense and shallow, so to speak. Precisely because of his inarticulate state, Tomás did not recount his biography as a life lived in the past, nor in its unraveling depth, but performed it as if it were *still a present, a still present, a present still*. Tomás sweated excessively and uttered an unfathomable bundle of words, a loud syncretic mixture of African and Spanish, only a few of them captured by those present. Celia describes a progressive smoothening of such crudeness in subsequent possessions, considering the step of "representation" a critical (turning) point.

Initially stemming from a few hints revealed in the first possessions, those described as the most violent ones in terms of movement, the people present started to put the pieces together. The words that stood out from this otherwise inarticulate storm were the name "Tomás," the Spanish words "slave" and "Congo," as well as "*bilongo*," "*lukansa*," and "*munafinda*." Celia tells me that these last three words are of Bantú origin and mean "witch" (*brujo*), "diviner" (*adivino*), and "jungle" (*selva*), respectively. Subsequent possessions initiated a kind of dialogue between Tomás and the ritual specialists present wherein the latter, employing these words, tried to gain a more detailed biographical profile. For instance, they learned that Tomás had been a slave around the metropolitan area of Matanzas and that both back in Central Africa and in his enslaved and eventually freed life in Cuba he was widely known and extremely respected and feared for his knowledge of the "jungle," and for being a great "witch" and "diviner."

Celia, here, places great emphasis on the transformative effects of the whole interaction with the spirit of Tomás. Running parallel with a progressive transformation of relative inarticulacy into relative articulacy, the possessions themselves have lost their initial extreme violence and wild movement. Even the sweat, according to Celia, has become less intense, although it has never lost its distinctiveness (when compared to Celia's "normal" perspiration). Tomás has lost his pressing urgency to communicate his condition as a "slave" or "Congo," although these have not vanished completely. What I find extremely interesting here is that these biographical elements have undergone a kind of transformation that, while not eliminating them, has converted them into aspects of the past, it has *historicized* them, that is, made them biographical in the full sense. It is precisely here that "representation," through "materialization" becomes a vital catalyst for this transformation. In the effort of attaining more dialogical terms with the spirit of Tomás, of trying to fathom his speaking and posing questions and eliciting answers, "materializations" such as dolls facilitate all this transformative effort (from inarticulacy to articulacy).

What the spirit of Tomás has *learned* (spirits learn too, not only living humans [c.f. Halloy & Naumescu 2012]) is to recognize himself as the spirit of a dead person (*muerto*), something of which he was initially unaware. The first possessions were themselves possessed by his barren and problematic state of not being fully aware of being dead. This is the reason for their inarticulacy and for the unreflexive resurfacing of biographical elements as if they were unraveling in a living state. Engaging dialogically with Tomás and presenting him with a three-dimensional mirror of himself in the form of a doll all came together as a critical step toward making him realize that his "Congo-ness," his enslavement, his precarious freed life in Cuba, even his racialized blackness were elements of his past. As such these were "represented" in the doll, made black, half-naked, with torn rustic trousers. These elements are important in their dual and extremely dynamic (precarious too, at times) quality of attracting the spirit of Tomás to the doll and simultaneously reminding him of being dead. Celia pinpoints that this effect is neither stable nor guaranteed. The lurking danger always exists that Tomás will act *as if* he were alive. That would render his "witchcraft" expertise uncontrollable, a wild and untamed beast of the jungle or a furious vindictive slave, "an angry black man," as Celia says, very likely to harm the people near him: Celia in the first place, her family and all those who frequent her house, in the second. Tomás' ritual expertise is what is activated, rescued, and made to live in the present, as a "necrography" (i.e., the unfolding present of the spirit of a dead person) in a parallel effort to render other biographical aspects as things and memories (no matter how vivid) of the past. The former is controlled and made beneficial for one's own ends through the "representation" of the latter.

Looking at the doll, what one *sees*—exactly as the spirit of Tomás himself does—is a typical image of "blackness" in Cuba. But the doll is ritually "charged" (*cargada*), that is, consecrated, including the hidden materials inside it which activate the "magic" of the doll: the "magic" which has emanated from Tomás. "Blackness" or "Africanity" is made relevant for the historical and cultural reasons of their having created a *living* tradition of ritual expertise and *not* for their biological and immutable laws that have constituted (through cunning acts of representation) race as an "ontology." While race and ethnicity are de-ontologized and "represented," what is constituted with more solid ontological foundations is "witchcraft" knowledge and praxis. This finds its most de-racialized manifestation in the sociological fact that spirits of *brujos* now possess a wide range of racial, ethnic, and cultural backgrounds in Cuba and beyond, from less black bodies (like Celia's), to mulattoes, whites, and other local categories, as well as non-Cubans. What comes to the fore is Tomás-the-*brujo* not Tomás-the-black or Tomás-the-slave; or better said, these latter come to the fore as long as they activate (in both their archeological and creative dimensions; c.f. Espírito Santo and Panagiotopoulos 2015) the former. They have to perform this double role of reminding (us) how representations can turn into ontologies (and, more so, into negative ontologies) and, at the same time, reverse this direction but without guaranteed results.

Spirit possession is constituted as an ontology, not so much through the strict reproduction of the biography of the spirit, but as a "technique" for the ignition of oracular articulacy and the acquisition of magico-practical knowledge. Various deities, identified as of African origin, may possess living humans in Cuba apart from the spirits of blacks: the *orichas* of the Lucumí (Yoruba)-inspired traditions or Congo-inspired *mpungos*. As noted earlier, spirits of non-blacks tend not to possess, nor do deities identified as non-black (Catholic saints, for instance, although the issue can be more complicated given that there is a historical equivalence among African deities and Catholic saints). If the spirits of blacks are praised for their magical ritual expertise and if this is, importantly, motivated through a *habitus* of possession, this is not out of an ontological "blackness" or a "blackened" ontology. The motivation, no matter how corporeal, is historical and cultural, not genetic and not even "ethnic." Armando, a white Santería initiate and a scholar, argues:

> Spirits of blacks possess us, the living, not because they were black, but because, while they were alive, they too would get possessed by their *orichas* and their own spirits, who, for the known historical reasons were Africans. Maybe, in the future, we will get to see spirits of whites who, because they too used to be initiates of Afro-Cuban religions and would get possessed while in life, will in their turn "mount" their "horses" [*caballos*; those who get possessed].

Armando includes himself among potential possessing-spirit candidates because of his already "developed" capacity to get possessed. Possessing spirits of the dead are those that, while in life, used to get possessed by their own spirits and deities. This "paradoxical" multiplication (or, at least, doubling) of possession as a means of achieving ritual expertise is ontologically constituted in parallel with the deconstitution of the category of "race" as a representation forced to be lived as an ontology. Spirits possess, while race is dispossessed. Possession becomes a vital "path" (*camino*) of the retrieval and manifestation of magical and oracular knowledge, which in its turn finds a way out of stagnated and deviated life-courses (some of which were and are indeed "blackened"), not of a barren biographical exposition nor of a genetic disposition.

The Second Diaspora of Race

If Afro-Cuban religiosity is treated as a strictly "diasporic" religion, then what is automatically implied is an overdetermination of a specific historical point that comes to encompass all its previous (past), actual (present), and potential (future) unraveling. This overdetermination ironically transforms a historical point into an archetypal and, thus, linear and immutable point of reference and influence; it ultimately becomes *ahistorical*. If this is linked to the category of "race," Afro-Cuban religiosity is in danger of becoming fixed as a mere reflection, even if critical, of the linear transformation of "blackening," from a representation to ontology. That would be the first diaspora of race: possession by spirits of blacks and African deities *performing* race in a spectacular manner *par excellence*. This might be true, because Afro-Cuban religiosity has indeed incorporated the historical experience of this kind of diaspora, but it is *only partially* true; if this is not clearly stated and further elaborated, it becomes analytically perilous in its overdetermining approach. To the rescue, however, comes the "second diaspora" of race.

The Greek root of the word "diaspora" signifies *dispersal*. In other words, the root of diaspora is plunged into its uprootedness. The "second diaspora" that spirit possession and Afro-Cuban religiosity in general instantiate is a much more powerful kind of diaspora in the sense that it potentializes the possibility for the warping of diaspora itself: the dispersal of dispersal. This involves a powerful, even violent, inversion. The category of race is forced from a representation-cum-ontology into the opposite direction—ontology-cum-representation—through sweat-soaked possessions and half-naked black dolls. The inversion of direction along the same (diasporic-colonial-racial) line—although a possibly empowering positionality with all its famous "mimetic" qualities (see Kramer 1993; Taussig 1993)—nevertheless preserves the line itself. It also preserves the analytical argument of a return to a proud all-too-black Africa, an *eternal return* (to echo Eliade 1974 [1949]). Yet if it is indeed a return to Africa, it is not in its racially genetic dimensions, but in its mythopractical, magical, and oracular sensibilities: back to Africa as "culture" not "nature," and not a kind of encompassing but singular Africa (leaving also room for alternative "Africas"). This kind of "return" *cannot* be just linear, because "culture" is a highly inventive and transformative entity (see Wagner 1981 [1975]). In that sense, we cannot strictly homologize nature with ontology and culture with representation (or body-matter and spirit-mind, respectively), as "culture" contains and entertains, not to say invents, both ontology and representation ("nature" would perhaps be indifferent to both, but let's leave this aside for the present purposes; c.f. Descola 2013; Viveiros de Castro 1998). Thus, if we would like to analytically make sense of ontology and representation and their relation, a more suitable homology is needed. Perhaps a homology with solidification and destabilization is more apt.

Both ontology and representation are relative processes; they are hardly ever total and immaculate achievements and states. This is so because they are antithetical tendencies of which their direction is endangered and destabilized, actually or potentially, by the other tendency and opposite direction. Conditions of ontology are relative to acts of representation (de-ontologization), just as the solidification and stability of "things" are relative to their exposure of the creativity and to the inventiveness that inhere in them or, better said, that make them up, institute, and instantiate them. Theories of *being* and theories of *becoming* are sides of the same coin and, additionally, go hand in hand with their undoing, that is, *nonbeing* and *unbecoming*. Of course, this is so often a story to be told after the event, if an event can ever be said to be terminated.

Colonial racism is an event that has, literally speaking, terminated in the sense that colonialism has done so. Nevertheless, this cannot be said to apply for racism itself (nor of other colonial remnants after and despite the official end of colonialism), an event that has been unfolding before and after colonialism, up to the present and, very likely it seems, to the distant future. Spirit possession, as an effervescent event of Afro-Cuban religious *habitus*, is an act of radical destabilization of the category of race. A certain analytical frame could draw a historiographical path (from representation to ontology and then from ontology to representation), extremely revealing in itself; but the most faithful ethnographic depiction is that these two processes, in spirit possession, unfold simultaneously. This simultaneity creates a "paradoxical" space and moment, wherein fixity-cum-ontology and exposure-cum-representation coexist. Such coexistence also includes a contingent instance where the two opposing tendencies mutually neutralize each other, and different possibilities make their appearance. The same colonial context that instituted Afro-Atlantic slavery and race to such a stabilizing effect that it (almost) became an ontology, it also strived to expose Afro-Cuban magic and divination as a backward fiction, that is, as a primitive and fetishized representation (see Matory 2018; Palmié 2013; Ortiz 2001). To that effect and because, as has been the case with the category of race, this was an imposed perception, spirit possession, dolls, and Afro-Cuban religiosity in general, institute magic and divination, in their myriad and everyday acts of solidification, as (almost) an ontology.

While an inverted linearity is being entertained through the acts of representation and materialization of the blackness of the spirits, at the same time an opening-up is facilitated. The magical and oracular potentialities unleashed in possessions bring the biographies of spirits and living humans together into an explosive crossroads of "paths" (*caminos*). Previous biographical elements of both parts, which had led to stagnant or deviated ("blackened") life-courses, are manifested as representations; as *caminos* they find a way out of their ontological dead-ends. While race is de-ontologized, magic and divination are ontologically constituted, that is, entangled in the entanglement of the lives (biographies) of the living and the afterlives (necrographies) of the spirits or the mythographies of the deities.

Is this a "color-blind" attitude toward the category and experience of race? Not in the least; rather, it is a quite singular and unexplored position which obviates the polarity between "color-blind" and angry black politics (see Bonilla-Silva 2003; Essed & Goldberg 2002). A color-blind attitude rejects the notion that there is *a problem* with race or claims that racial differences should undergo an assimilationist process wherein everyone adopts the dominant "culture" (the white, in this case). Conversely, an angry or loud kind of racial assertion, parting from the claim that race is an all-important factor of inequality, inverts the roles in terms of signification and asserts a proud and even aggressive role of racial difference.

This polarization between aggressive and mute politics has had various manifestations. It has been present in the most direct politics of race, variably translated—especially in North America—as the opposition between "race-based" politics and that which is "postracial" or "transracial" (see Fraser 2009; Hill 2009, see also Steinberg 2014). "Postracial" politics, for instance—materialized through Martin Luther King and more currently with Barack Obama—tends to seek citizenship, reconciliation, assimilation, and a universal, all-embracing definition of society or culture, considerably downplaying race as a mark of difference. An academic version of this is the Chicago School of the 1950s (see Park 1950; see also Marable 1996). "Race-based" politics (e.g., Malcom X or the Black Panthers Party), on the other hand, incorporates a strong, even aggressive, affirmation of difference, cultural pluralism, hierarchy, even opposition. In academia, such a stance became particularly popular in the 1960s in North America, precisely as a critical reaction to the assimilationist tendencies of the early Chicago School (see Gans 1999; Glazer & Moynihan 1970). These polarities can also be gleaned in anthropological approaches to these issues (see Piot & Allison 2013) and, more particularly for the purposes of the present chapter, to Afro-Latin and Caribbean culture, including religiosity (see Bastide 2007 [1978]; Capone 2010; Frazier 1957; Herskovits 1941; Johnson 2011; Mintz & Price 1992 [1976]; Palmié 2013; Yelvington 2001).

As noted at the start of the chapter, the present ethnography does not offer a representative and direct voice to black living subjects. Whether religious or not they would most probably have a different story to tell from this one (see de la Fuente 2001) but not, I hope, one in stark opposition to it. This is because this story has not *replaced* in the strict sense the two aforementioned conventional paths of racial politics. Rather, it has *displaced* them or *dispersed* them, in the sense that it appears and breathes in parallel to them. As it belongs neither to institutional nor to anti-institutional forms of racial politics, but stands ethnographically in parallel and analytically beyond them, I thought the story, in its originality, was worth telling.

The "ontology" *and* the "representations" of spirits are constituted as a way out of essentialist or stagnant linear paths of "blackened" diasporas. Spirit possession by spirits of blacks and African deities affirms alterity but not on an essentialist or genetic basis. The basis is ontological, corporeal, perceptual, and affective but not "natural" in the racial-racist sense. This is precisely the *spirit* in possession, something that is often neglected in favor of its possessive phenomenology. Maybe here a warping ontology of Tomás's sweat is being circulated. While never forgetting its "blackened" (colonial) conditions of production, it simultaneously goes beyond them to unleash (or free) a potentiality of magical and oracular efficacy that can reach (and indeed reaches) all kinds of peoples, races, and cultures. Sweat, then, is not just a powerful odor, but a catalyst ingredient of motion and transformation, of both possessions and dispossessions, and of the intricate interrelationship between "ontology" and "representation." Returning to Fanon, maybe this is what he alluded to when, while describing the negative representation-cum-ontology of "blackening," he finally exclaimed: "Yet this reconsideration of myself, this thematization, was not my idea. I wanted quite simply to be a man among men" (2008 [1952], 92). Not a white man, nor a "blackened" one, just a man, a black man.

Between Possessor and Possessed: Warping Spacetime and Agency through Co-Presence

J. Brent Crosson

Introduction

In an annual review of a discipline that has come to dissociate itself from the fiction of exotic others, it was strange to read of a phenomenon still regarded as "dramatically and intransigently exotic" (Boddy 1994, 407). Perhaps it is no coincidence that such a characterization references spirit possession, one of those quintessentially anthropological objects of inquiry. As Janice Boddy notes in her review, discourse on spirit possession has been "thematic for the discipline [of anthropology] as a whole in its confrontation with the Other" (Boddy 1994, 408). For Boddy, and a long line of anthropologists, spirit possession has embodied all that is the radical other of a rational, materialist West. It is a phenomenon that supposedly rests on assumptions about the boundaries between self and other that are very different from the materialist thrust of capitalism and Western modernity.[1]

If we accept that anthropology as a discipline has been founded upon a "confrontation with the Other," then spirit possession, rather than denoting an "intransigently exotic" practice for the discipline, would seem to share its fundamental concern with the representation of alterity. What has united a variety of scholarships on possession is the recognition that it is a practice whereby otherness, whether defined in terms of culture, race, gender, or class, is represented by the possessed medium (Albers 2008, Boddy 1989, Gibson 2001, Stoller 1995, Taussig 1993). The anthropologist, as medium between an Other culture and her own cultural system of representation (Western academic), performs a magic of representation analogous to a Zar medium embodying a European spirit (Boddy 1989), a Hauka medium representing a colonial official (Stoller 1995), or, in my own field work, an Afro-Trinidadian Spiritual Baptist claiming a South Asian "spiritual" identification (Crosson 2020a).

Such a view of "possession," rather than making it intransigently other, places it firmly within a Western genealogy of colonialism and representation. This colonial construction of "possession" has been exhaustively detailed by Paul C. Johnson (2011a, 2014b). He shows how European Enlightenment ideas about spirit possession in sub-Saharan Africa were central to the justifications for slavery in the age of the so-called Rights of Man. These Rights were supposedly borne by a self-possessed subject that was defined through his opposition to (Western ideas of) the self possessed. Spirit possession thus defined post-Enlightenment conceptions of agency through what Johnson (2011a, 2014b) calls a vast "labor of the negative." Contrary to anthropological characterizations of spirit possession as a property of the non-Western other, Johnson argues that the province of spirit possession is the West (Johnson 2019). The relationship of radical alterity between self-possessed Man and the self possessed signals a relationship of co-construction rather than some kind of unbridgeable cultural divide. This genealogy reinforces the idea of spirit possession's "intransigent" otherness in exactly the terms described above—as the radical limit of Western ideas of personhood. However, in this reckoning, such alterity was itself the shadow that Western fantasies of self-possession cast.

In the first section of this essay, I rehash Johnson's argument. Admittedly, this section is based on a paper I wrote as a graduate student before Johnson's detailed genealogy of spirit possession had come out in *Comparative Studies in Society and History.* Happily, Johnson performed a much more exhaustive and nuanced version of this genealogy than I had done in my bumbling grad student attempt. His masterful essay on the Western genealogy of "possession" left me wondering what else there was to say about this story of the constitutive play between ideas of the self-possessed property owner and the self possessed. I thought there was certainly no point in writing more about a Western genealogy of self-possession and selves possessed. Yet, after doing more field work, what I realized was that my interlocutors in Trinidad conceived of spirit manifestation in terms that differed from this Western genealogy of agency and its "possessed," intransigent others. Rather than speaking about "possession" (with its constitutive opposition between possessor and possessed), they talked about "catching power." More than a mere difference in English word choice, this latter phrase signaled a divergent and paradoxical notion of agency. "Catching," after all, is both active (catching a fish) and passive (catching a cold). Another sense of personhood and spirit manifestation, I will argue, lies in this space between agent and object or possessor and possessed.

As Paul C. Johnson's genealogy of possession articulately suggests, to be in possession of one's self entails rational self-control, but it also assumes the ability to possess others through representation and property relations (others as possessions). Catching power in Trinidad, however, suggests that less dichotomous relations of agency, involving conflict, cultivation, and dialogic negotiations among persons and spiritual powers, form important parts of possession practice. To address these questions of agency in spirit manifestation, it will be necessary to examine how common conceptions of control are embedded within constructions of power as sovereign, which still haunt liberal, ostensibly post-sovereign societies (e.g., Foucault 1991). It will also prove necessary to complicate questions of authenticity in possession practice, as arbitrated by the medium's loss of self-consciousness and the non-willed nature of their performance.[2] As Morris (2001) shows, this desired authenticity expresses a fantasy of transparency, which has pervaded not only scientific representation, but late capitalist discourses of proper market relations and neoliberal ideals of accountability. In contrast, this essay asks what a less-than-transparent practice of mediumship might look like. For grassroots mediums in Trinidad, the initial moments of catching power must be unwilled, often to the point that they are experienced as unwanted afflictions. Catching power, however, often begins a lifelong process of living with and cultivating spiritual powers. By looking at broader practices of living with spiritual power, rather than fetishizing the moment of unwilled possession, I will focus on the negotiated coexistence, cohabitation, and co-constitution of persons and spiritual powers in Trinidad.

As a departure point for this look at "catching power," I will first trace a brief genealogy of "possession," intended to be more provocative than definitive, which asks what resonances material and spiritual possessions may share. Rather than maintaining this analogy between spiritual power (possessing spirit) and material power (possessive ownership), I will then ask how "catching power" might unsettle the relation between possessor and possessed that has structured scholarly and popular ideas of "spirit possession." My interlocutors thus tell a story of spirit manifestation that is different from both the eclipse of the self-possessed subject (i.e., the story of possession as the Western subject's radical other) or the recapitulation of a Western genealogy of possession (i.e., Paul C. Johnson's story of possession as a performance of the dynamics of slavery [see Johnson 2014a, 2019]). As suggested in the Introduction, I will thus weave a story of spirit manifestation based in neither radical alterity nor colonial mimesis. "Catching power," I argue, warps space-time through a seemingly paradoxical (yet mundane) experience of intimate alterity, in which two distinct kinds of being occupy the same position in space and time. I show how my interlocutors' foregrounding of sound rather than vision to describe spirit manifestation affords a means by which to conceive of this warping. While a Western visual logic of Cartesian space assumes two entities cannot occupy the exact same point in space and time, sound (with its inherently wavelike properties) allows for the simultaneous "copresence" (Beliso-De Jesús 2015) that the editors of this volume call "paradox." Such copresence is harmonious and dissonant, active and passive, defying neat oppositions between possessor and possessed.

Self-Possession/Self Possessed: Preliminary Definitions

In this section, I will follow Johnson's (2011, 2014b, 2019) foundational interventions, working to unsettle the "intransigent otherness" of spirit possession by showing how the representation of possessing spirits constituted and was constituted by ideologies and practices assumed to be Western and modern. I would like to conduct what Sydney Mintz, in the midst of anthropology's postcolonial crisis of representation, called an "anthropology of ourselves" (see Carnegie 2006). From the exotic other, anthropologists were beginning to turn that gaze on themselves. Years later, anthropologists have experienced the pitfalls of this self-consumed reflexivity, recognizing the value of turning their gaze outward. In the spirit of Mintz, however, an anthropology of ourselves is one that seeks to bare the otherness at the very heart of the domestic, defying the developmental distinctions between colony and metropole. In *Sweetness and Power*, Mintz (1985) anchors the story of the industrial revolution in the Caribbean, showing how the tastes and labor disciplines of the English proletariat were dependent on colonial others.

In a similar way, I would like to tell the story of private property from the vantage point of a phenomenon that apparently reverses the relations of ownership between the subject and its possessions in the colonies. The first use of possession, circa 1500, to refer to private property coincides historically with the first recorded use of possession in the "demonic sense" (*Oxford English Dictionary*, "possession"). Previous to this sixteenth-century transformation of meanings, possession was tied to land tenureship and residence. Indeed, the Latin etymology of "possess" literally translates as "to be able to sit" (ibid.).

Thus, possession, in the sixteenth century begins to take on the contemporary senses of "property ownership" as well as the sense of "being dominated by something (as an extraneous personality, demon, passion, idea, or purpose)" (*Webster's New International Dictionary*, 3rd ed., "possession"). Inherent in the word possession itself, therefore, is the question of external power, domination, or control. While this sense of ownership means the ability to dispose of objects or control human labor, to become possessed means to be controlled or dominated from without. Even though these two definitions appear to be polar opposites, they in fact rest on the same relationship of possessor to possessed. In one the human possesses an object or labor resource, in the other the human is possessed by a spirit, idea, or emotion. Both relations are ones of control and domination by possessors.

The genesis of the concept of "spirit possession" in English, therefore, is inextricable from changing relations of property tied to the beginnings of mercantile capitalism and European colonialism in the sixteenth century. Property under a landed aristocracy, understood in terms of land tenureship, was coming to include a notion of property as capital. Far from being a phenomenon "intransigently exotic" to Western modernity, the category of spirit possession emerges at the very genesis of modern relations of property. This may help explain why, as scholars have recently shown (Boddy 1989, Morris 2000, Palmié 2002), modernity has been accompanied by a profusion of possession modalities.

Departing from this admittedly Euro- and Anglo-centric etymology of "possession," the social conditions of the multiethnic savannahs surrounding the Bight of Benin during this same time period must play a central role in any analysis of "Black Atlantic" possession modalities (Gilroy 1993, Matory 2005). This cradle of what would later be called "Yoruba" religion was forged through the imperial conquest of the region by the Oyo-Yoruba people beginning in the seventeenth century (Matory 2009, 233). Their orisa deities were fundamentally intertwined with the exercise of political power, as priests acted as provincial viceroys and kings ritually embodied a deity named Sango (Matory 2009, 242). Sango himself was a deceased Oyo king, representing an ancestral lineage of political power as well as the force of thunder.

Most important for the purposes of this document, Yoruba religious practices involved "spirit possession," and, during the time of their imperial spread, the slave trade was becoming a very lucrative business in the region. Matory (2009, 243) has speculated that it is no coincidence that "elaborate spirit possession religions" proliferated "at the slavery-ridden borderlands between Africa and the Islamic worlds [i.e. the bight of Benin]." The implication of his argument is that control over people rather than control over land had become the "cultural priority and the limiting factor in African political power" (ibid. 243, Thornton 1992). While the etymological roots of the Oyo words for spirit possession do not directly imply property ownership as they do in English,[3] the conditions by which human labor was becoming the most lucrative good in the Bight of Benin must be addressed in a study of black Atlantic possession practices. Slavery and plantation labor discipline, of course, served as the setting for the development of possession-based practices on the other side of the Atlantic. While it would be simplistic to draw a simple, cause-effect relationship between human-as-property and human-as-possessed, this essay will ask how the practice of possession reflected creative responses to the possession of humans as labor, while also disrupting the tendency of scholarship to figure African diasporic possession as a recapitulation of slavery (e.g., Hayes 2011; Johnson 2011, 2014a; Matory 2005; Palmié 2002, cf. Lambek 2014, Ochoa 2010).

By paying attention to ethnographic detail within southern and eastern Caribbean styles of "possession," we can begin to turn the troped power relation of self-control to self controlled on its head. My argument will aim to disrupt the dichotomy between rational, instrumental selves and selves who become the instruments of external forces. This reworking of possession mediumship aims to conceive of subjects as not separate from, or subject to, power. Rather (to re-voice Foucault in a quite different context) mediums act within and are imbued with fields of (spiritual and material) power, rather than simply being the subjects of a possessing sovereign.

"Catching Power"

The story of possession's etymology, at least, helps to explain the category's development in the English language. This story is necessarily grounded in Western European (and West African) transformations of state and society. The implications of this story are still with us, as the twenty-first-century dictionary definitions of spirit possession as domination show. However, as the ethnographic details I will examine illustrate, the notion of possession as domination from without reflects a limited understanding of this phenomenon. Practices termed "spirit possession" do relate to the experience of external force or power, yet they are not simply a relation of domination. In fact, modalities of "possession" in the southern Caribbean (and elsewhere) aim for individual manipulation of these possessing powers. This manipulation is not exactly control, because that would reproduce the dominant logic of ownership inherent in the English-language etymology of possession. Rather it is a relationship of channeling, containing, or "working" the possessing spirit.

In southern Caribbean parlance, it is not "possession," but "catching power" which we must examine.[4] Indeed, Trinidadian congregants referred to the possessing deotas of the Kali Mai temples I visited as "powers" rather than spirits. As Vertovec (1998) has shown, "catching power" is the phrase denoting "spirit possession" that is common to Spiritual Baptist, Shango (or, to use a more contemporary term, Orisha), and Kali Mai practices in Trinidad. As the colloquial phrase implies, we must here rethink the relations of power between force and medium in the realm anthropology has typically called "spirit possession." If possession is not the experience of being owned or dominated by a spirit force, but rather the "catching" and embodying of a power, we must reconsider the relations of control that adhere in the anthropological conception of possessed bodies.

As Foucault (1977, 1991) insisted, though we may have beheaded the monarch, the notion of sovereignty still permeates our theorizations of power. My examination of the English-language genealogy of "possession" seems to underscore this insistence. Whether we are talking about property ownership (to possess), domination by spirits (to be possessed), territorial sovereignty ("colonial possessions"), or "control over oneself" (self-possession), the notion of power as sovereignty repeats itself. Foucault, however, repeatedly called for a re-theorization of power not defined by an above (a sovereign or God) and a below (a subject). Rethinking sovereignty and power, therefore, also means rethinking Western conceptions of immanence and transcendence. As Bhrigupati Singh (2012) has argued, conceptions of sovereignty in Western political theory have remained premised on Christian (or, perhaps, "Abrahamic") theologies of a transcendent God, and other religious worlds of power might revise these ideas and reveal less monolithic conceptions of sovereignty.

Before Foucault redefined discourses on power in the academy, southern Caribbean notions of possession as "catching power" acted out force as a permeating field. Rather than possessing or being possessed, mediums that catch power embody, in socially positioned ways, this assumed field. This field of power is called shakti (divine energy or force, gendered feminine) in Kali Mai temples or Holy Spirit in Spiritual Baptist congregations. In both instances, the divine is not a single sovereign persona, but a field of force. The medium who catches this power is neither dominated nor purely dominates such force. Rather, they learn to manipulate powers which also remain beyond their full control. For these reasons, the medium is more like the "conducting" subject Foucault invoked than the subject of a possessing sovereign. In the next section, I will use ethnographic detail to show how the medium in southern Caribbean practices, rather than simply being possessed or dominated by power, catches and works it.

Spirit Manifestation and Bodily Discipline

In southern Caribbean parlance, spirit possession, in addition to being referred to as "catching power," is also called "manifestation" (McNeal n.d., 2). The distinction, between malevolent possession and cultivated "manifestation" of spirits, calls the relationship of controlling spirits and controlled selves into question. If one "manifests" a spirit rather than becoming possessed by it, the locus of control (at least linguistically) is not external to the medium. In fact, the partial control of spirits by a medium is one of the chief goals of southern Caribbean possession-based religious practices. Spiritual Baptists or Kali Mai pujaris in Trinidad express this process as one of "hosting" the spirit force. Far from a romanticized loss of control, assumed in much of the Western writings on possession, the manifestation of spirits is incumbent upon learned technique and the performance of mastery, itself denoting leadership roles within congregations. This mastery manifests as a measure of bodily control—expressed by practitioners as a hierarchical distinction between modes of manifestation.

In his study of Vincentian Spiritual Baptists, Wallace Zane reports this distinction as one between "shaking" and "'doption:"

> In most of the churches I frequented, the shaking person was supposed to gain control of the shaking and transfer the spiritual power into 'doption. Those shaking are told to 'Work it out.' 'Working the Spirit,' 'working penitent,' or 'jump Spirit' is an ordered sort of Holy Spirit possession. (Zane 1999, 100–1)

Gaining control of possessing forces, therefore, is central to the performance of progress within Spiritual Baptist (also known on St. Vincent as Converted) teleologies of growing in the spirit. As Zane notes, the "uncontrolled jerking and spasms" that occur when the Holy Spirit "seizes" a congregant is a less tutored form of manifestation (Zane 1999, 100). "Prolonged shaking is frowned on in most churches," Zane observes. Rather this "uncontrolled" shaking should be channeled into "ordered" or recognizable forms of bodily movement (ibid.). These recognizable forms are the patterns of bodily movement recognized as "'doptions." These 'doptions may take the form of bending at the waist while stamping on one foot (Zane 1999, 101) or rhythmic sighing (Ward and Beaubrun 483). These patterned bodily disciplines distinguish "uncontrolled jerking" from choreographed travel through the "spiritual lands." Each 'doption denotes travel through a different "spiritual city," and these itineraries of bodily movement to distinct song repertoires are the focus of Converted spiritual progress.

In a different, yet analogous context, manifestation in Trinidad and Guyana's Kali Mai Puja is classified by a control of bodily movement that can denote one's station within temple hierarchies. In the Kali Mai Pujas I witnessed in central Trinidad, there is a distinction between generalized shakti (divine force) "play" and the manifestation of specific deotas (Hindu divinities).[5] The play of shakti is generalized throughout the congregation and may involve more uncontrolled bodily movements, while the manifestation of oracular deotas is confined to ritual specialists and manifests as a more stationary shaking.

On repeated occasions, I witnessed the officiating priestess[6] of the temple controlling or containing the bodily movements of shakti play when they became particularly intense in devotees. This was done by holding the head of the shakti player to her chest, typically resulting in a lessening of bodily agitation. Manifesting mediums would often tap the tops of their heads, thus containing the force of shakti in their bodies. This reproduces the orgasmic analogy of body as phallus prevalent in strands of Hindu practice. In this bodily cartography, divine energy rises through the spine and ejaculates through the top of the head. By containing the ejaculation through the application of pressure to the crown, one can symbolically contain shakti.

The realization of bodily control distinguished the manifestation of official mediums during the later stages of the Puja from the earlier shakti play, generalized throughout the congregation. Congregants stood in line to consult these official oracles regarding everyday dilemmas. The bodily style of possession for these mediums was characterized by a more stationary shaking or swaying. Thus, the ability to control or contain shakti was associated with oracular mediumship, confined to certain ritual specialists.

These ethnographic details convince me that, far from playing the other to a rational, materialist self seeking to control external forces, these possessed selves aim for a certain performance of control. As Erika Bourguignon notes in a Brazilian context:

> Umbanda centers make an organized effort to teach novices how to enter trance states, and "how to be possessed by, and control the behavior of four spirit types." Such learning is not unique to Umbanda but inherent in possession trance ritual in general, in the many societies in which such beliefs and practices are to be found. (1989, 376)

Thus, learning to perform and channel possessing spirits, rather than simply succumbing to them, seems to be a cross-cultural theme (see also Halloy and Naumescu 2012).

From Possession to Paradox

The idea that "spirit possession" might involve the coexistence of different agents rather than the displacement of one personality by another relies on a notion of personhood that is more sonic than visual. The visual notion of Cartesian space, in which two different material bodies cannot occupy the exact same point in space and time, differs from a conception of entities as sound (or waves more generally). Such a notion of place and person as sound is evident in Spiritual Baptist notions of spiritual travel and manifestation. When Zane asked his Converted interlocutors to draw a map of the Spiritual Lands to which they travel, they were at first puzzled and then replied, "The sounds are the route" (Zane 1999, 82). As Zane observes, "The tunes (also called songs, although they are usually without words) are what carries one to specific spiritual lands" (Zane 1999, 81–2). A person as sound is different from a person as a visual body with defined contours, and a place as sound is different from the visual off-earth perspective afforded by a map. It is often assumed that possession bridges a vast distance between immanent body and transcendent divinity, thus recapitulating what Beliso-De Jesús (2015) has critiqued as an "Abrahamic" logic of transubstantiation. Spiritual Baptist practices of "sounding," however, suggest something different. The sounds that a congregation makes carry a church to different spiritual locations, and congregants often liken a church to a ship (with some churches even possessing ship's wheels attached to their center poles, which leaders sometimes steer [Duncan 2008]). These sounds, however, also reflect back the qualities of those spiritual places, making them viscerally present in the church as a kind of sonic architecture. This is the paradox of movement in a Spiritual Baptist church, which remains fixed in space while being a moving ship.

This paradox of movement also characterizes the Spiritual Baptists' central ritual of "mourning." In mourning, a practitioner is blindfolded and secluded in a special room for at least three days (with longer periods undertaken by more experienced mourners). Physical immobility and sensory deprivation (the series of blindfolds, decorated with esoteric signs, covers both eyes and ears) are supposed to provoke spiritual travel, in which a mourner learns about Africa, India, China, and other spiritual realms. The breadth of places to which a congregant has traveled in 'doption or mourning and the spiritual-ethnic "true natures" they acquire there confer status in church hierarchies. As Zane notes amongst Vincentian Spiritual Baptists, "Usually more-experienced mourners go to places like Africa, India, or to the bottom of the sea. Less-experienced mourners tend to have spiritual experiences that reflect their day-to-day life" (Zane 1999, 20).

This mourning travel for Spiritual Baptists is also figured as auditory. "From each city you visit on a spiritual journey," Vincentian church leader Mother Haynes asserts, "you must bring back its sound. Africa has a sound. China has a sound. Every place has its own sound" (Keeney 2002, 99). Such a practice of auditory travel recalls the centrality of sound and music in the literature on trance induction (Becker 2004, Rouget 1985), or the importance of acoustic spaces and "sound systems" in the practice of diaspora (Henriques 2008, Veal 2007). In a very real way, the spiritual territories cannot be mapped as territories or ethnic groups usually are—visually and/or from above, as in what Feinberg (2003) calls a "linear" style of specialist identification of cultures or religions. The place is the sound, and sound, of course, is harder to see from a distance or to circumscribe in a visual form. Instead of studying a map, the mourner must go there to hear (and spiritually become) India, Africa, or China.

All of these examples show how practices of spirit manifestation are not necessarily defined by the relationship between foreign power and possessed self. Fixed oppositions between selves and others are characteristic of the "linear" style of representing difference. The "constant journeys," soundings, and transformations that characterize encounters with alterity in spirit manifestation suggest a modality of action that is perhaps more akin to what some scholars have called "play" (e.g., Bateson 1972, 1988; Handelman 1992; McNeal 2011). A cosmos based (at least in an ideal form) on opposition and dichotomy stands in productive tension with a cosmology of play. Play tends to subvert dichotomies through movement and transformation. Such movement can result in irony or mockery, such as when lower-class Black women dressed up as higher class women in a common Trindiadian carnival masquerade (the *Dame Lorraine*). This is perhaps the more common association of playing a particular character that the word "play" evokes, and there are some partial resonances between this kind of play and spirit manifestation, as scholars have noted (see Adelugba 1976, Gibbal 1982, McNeal 2011, Stoller 1995).[7]

Play rests on a tension between a frame of "as if" and a surrounding frame of "reality," but play is not only humorous or unreal. Play is often a transformation of the real. Kali Mai devotees often talk about "Shakti play" or about specific devotees "playing" a particular power in episodes of spirit manifestation (see McNeal 2011). Yet, Shakti or spiritual power does *not* exist in a realm opposed to the real for Kali Mai pujaris. As Aisha Beliso-De Jesús (2015) has shown for practitioners of Afro-Cuban Santería, the spiritual power that devotees manifest is coexistent with practitioners' bodies, in that specific Orishas are inserted into their heads (*orí*). Once again, such a conception refutes the notion of "possession" as the descent of foreign power and its displacement of human personality. In contrast, "manifestation" suggests the appearance or foregrounding of something latent.

As Wirtz (2014) has noted, however, the compound being of human bodies and spiritual powers in Afro-Cuban practice does not diminish the distinctions between spirit and matter that practitioners constantly make. Spiritual Baptists also constantly avow that spiritual power is different from what practitioners call the "carnal" world of physical bodies, in that spiritual power saturates or imbues material bodies without being reducible to a particular body or to an ontology of matter (in which bodies occupy singular locations in space-time—the assumption known is physics as locality [Barad 2007]). This is why practices that scholars have called "spirit possession" are not reducible to material possession (and the attendant theory of possessive individualism that Paul C. Johnson traces). Such possessive subjectivity rests on an assumed difference between animated, agential selves and passive objects rather than a *paradoxical*, compound relation of agency-passivity, self-other, or movement-stasis (see also Introduction). Instead of a relation of ownership between a self and its material possessions, spirit manifestation entails a capacity for transformation between what might appear to be the self and others (but what is actually a compound or non-local assemblage-being).[8] This notion of personhood depends less on a monolithic sovereign entity than on the self-contradiction of "paradox," without the attendant notions of impossibility or irrationality that this word usually entails.

Paul C. Johnson (2011a, 2014b) treats theories of possessive individualism and spirit possession as inverted analogues in order to describe Western constructions of the Enlightenment man and the African slave. This is precisely why the analogue between spiritual possession and possessive individualism may be less useful for describing actual practices of spirit manifestation. Nevertheless, this analogy has seeped into scholarly and popular accounts that make practices of spirit manifestation a reenactment of precisely the relationship of property that Johnson places at the center of his genealogy: chattel slavery. The next section concludes this article by foregrounding the limitations of this description and the paradigmatic relationship between possessing self and self possessed that underlies it.

Conclusion

Chattel slavery has often functioned as a root metaphor in scholarly descriptions of Afro-American practices of spirit possession, implicitly referencing the Enlightenment genealogy of possession that Paul Christopher Johnson traces so carefully. As noted above, this is perhaps why the language of "possession" rather than "shamanism" or "travel" has been the overriding frame for these practices in the Americas. Indeed, as Johnson (2011, 2014b) notes, the "possessed" African, in this figure's European inception, was a constitutive other for the sovereign political subject of Enlightenment liberal economic and social contract theory, an inversion of the modern, self-possessed political subject.

This racialized "labor of the negative" joined representations of "spirit possession" to forms of juridical displacement and dispossession, in which individual agency was supposedly lost. As scholars have noted, a model of "displacement"—defined by "the complete displacement of the host's agency by another agent's agency" (Barrett & Cohen 2008, 247)—has characterized the overwhelming majority of anthropological representations of "spirit possession" (see, e.g., Bourguignon 1968, 1976; Frazer 1958 [1890]; Hayes 2011; Stoller 1989, 1995; Behrend & Luig 1999; Lum 2000; Lewis 2003 [1971]; cf. Espírito Santo 2017 or Lambek 2014). The prevalence of this displacement model, as Paul C. Johnson (2014a, 4–5) notes, continues to conflate renderings of spirit possession as "the absence of control" or "the body without will" with the juridical dispossession of "the figure of the slave."

Possession has long been construed as pathology, and the reading of possession as a recapitulation of (a reductive idea of) slavery as loss of self risks echoing the loss of self-possession that has often defined psychological pathology in the West. This trope of possession-as-slavery does not simply have ramifications on the level of the self. For contemporary observers of the Caribbean, an anxiety over national borders and the sovereignty of state entities has often been conflated with the improper sovereignty of possessed bodies in African religions. In his magisterial work on African Caribbean culture, *Afro-Creole* (1997), Richard Burton thus makes it his scholarly task to "link the phenomenon of [spirit] possession to the experience of slavery, colonialism, and the politics of the postcolonial Caribbean" (223, qtd. in McNeal 2011). This project begins by invoking the dynamic of self and exogenous power implied by the very choice of the word "possession" to encapsulate a number of disparate phenomena from across the Caribbean. In this dynamic, the divinity or spirit that "possesses" the devotee reproduces a relation of possessing sovereign to dispossessed subject:

> For whether it is the power of the slave master, the colonial apparatus, or the charismatic political leader, power, as we have seen, always *descends*, like the spirits, onto the powerless below. It may empower them–for a time–but it does so only by dispossessing them of themselves and filling them with a power that, since it is other and originates elsewhere, can be taken away as quickly and as easily as it was bestowed. (ibid.)

While Burton's account is somewhat more sensitive than popular (and, sometimes, scholarly) attributions of Haiti's contemporary lack of proper political sovereignty to "voodoo" (Brooks 2010, Harrison and Huntington 2000, Harrison 2010), the link between failed political sovereignty, legacies of slavery, and African-inspired religions of spirit possession remains quite clear in all of these accounts. The notion that spirit possession is the dispossessed other of proper political sovereignty and personal self-possession is even stated (in strikingly exoticized terms) by the great French Caribbean theorist of postcolonial national liberation, Franz Fanon (2004 [1961], 19–20).

In contrast to such polarized representations, agency and patiency for mediums in Trinidad were more uneven and negotiated. Rather than the notion of one agent totally displacing another or two agents fusing into one, a more appropriate metaphor might be that of rider and horse. This metaphor is used extensively by actual practitioners of Haitian Vodou to describe the relationality of "spirit possession" (see Dayan 1995). A rider and a horse are a coherent entity that, at the same time, does not form a single organic, biological being. In other words, rather than conforming to the organic assumption of "one body, one mind," the horse and rider are a relational assemblage. Certainly this relation is one of hierarchical, unequal power, but as anyone who has ridden a horse knows, the relation involves a frictional, contested molding of potentially agonistic agencies. That a horse must be "broken" in order to be ridden resonates with the common narrative in the Caribbean of a human having to be afflicted by an other-than-human power to become an assemblage-being with that power.

While the history of slavery has greatly impacted religious practice in Trinidad and the Caribbean, to conceive of the relation between humans and spirits as one of slavery risks misrepresenting (and even insulting) practitioners. The very word "possession" contains this assumption, suggesting a property relation of agential possessor and objectified possession or a juridical fusion of owner and property. This is partly why "possession" is a negative term in Trinidad (see McNeal 2011); it is a relation that makes the human into the object of another agent's desires. Nor is it possible to simply say that an ambivalence regarding the representation of African-identified religious practitioners as "slaves of the spirits" (Hayes 2011) is peculiar to Trinidad.[9] As the Haitian oungan and painter André Pierre told Colin Dayan when describing his experiences of spirit manifestation: "I do not mean domination ... the spirit is dancing in the head of his horse" (Dayan 1995, 74). Speaking back against scholarly characterizations, another of Dayan's interlocutors asserted emphatically that spirit manifestation and devotion to the *lwa* (deities, powers) is "*not* another form of slavery" (ibid., 72, emphasis in original).

This does not rule out slavery as a possible way of conceiving of spirit-human relations—particularly negatively valued "possessions"—but it does significantly decenter (a certain idea of) slavery as the encompassing root metaphor for thinking about Africans as simply possessed bodies in their cultivated practices of living with other-than-human power. Perhaps more importantly, the scholarly insistence on the relation between devotee and deity as one of "possession-as-slavery" recapitulates the sometimes violent condemnations of Pentecostal-charismatic spiritual warriors in the region, who see African religionists as enthralled to demonic powers—a kind of enslavement that can only be broken by the liberation of being "born again" as (the right kind of) Christians.

As Halloy and Naumescu (2012) suggest, it is important to focus on spirit manifestation as a learned and cultivated phenomenon. Yet, such a focus should not make spirit mediumship into a willed or chosen practice. Within the worlds of African religion in Trinidad, the experience of affliction and hardship is often a sign of being chosen as a medium by a spiritual power. No one wants to be severely afflicted, and manifestation was often referred to as an uncomfortable, frightening, and tiring experience by my interlocutors in Trinidad (see Crosson 2020a, 2020b). Nevertheless, such manifestations were empowering experiences of becoming other and integrating an exogenous presence into one's daily life. Perhaps, rather than slavery, the more fitting metaphor might be kinship, with all the feuds, frustrations, and intimacies that cohabiting with family implies. This means that spirit is not transcendent in the way that God is typically conceived of in the West, but neither is spirit simply human. Somewhere in between immanence and transcendence, or possessor and possessed, sits the experience of manifesting spirit. Perhaps that is why it remains such an intransigent object of study for anthropology.

4

Waiting for Deities:
Spirit Possession in the Middle Voice

Miho Ishii

I am hot liquor. I am hot liquor. I'm drinking hot liquor and the liquor is myself. If you cook *kwakwa* to make a soup and put palm kernels into it, you are putting yourself into it. [...] So, I'm sitting here and drinking myself. (Nana Yakubu, October 15, 1999)

Introduction

In this chapter, I will investigate the relationship between spirit, medium, and mediator or "witness," focusing on cases of spirit possession in Southern Ghana and South India. I will first examine the functionalistic analyses that explicate spirit possession as representation of people's response to modern sociopolitical circumstances, as well as more recent studies that presume the existence of spirits in the ontological world for people in the field. Although these previous studies have presented important approaches to understanding spirit possession, it is insufficient to regard the phenomena merely as either the symbolic representation of people's sentiments against modernity or as indication of the radical alterity of a particular ontological world. Then, how can we understand the phenomenon called spirit possession without either reducing or substantializing it?

To answer this question, I will present in this chapter an alternative perspective that sees spirit possession not as "possession" of the subject by an external subject-agent, but as the actualizing process of an event occurring at the site—a phenomenon that should be understood in terms of the *middle voice*. Based on the work of Victor von Weizsäcker (1997 [1950]), who investigated the *pathisch* way of being of an organism in its *umwelt*, as well as a study by Takeshi Matsushima (2014)—examining performers' bodily movements in an experimental drama in Italy—I will consider the spirit-medium's body as the site where the manifestation of spirit occurs of its own accord. I will also examine how spirit is actualized as a transient becoming or sojourner in relation to the witness, who stays beside and receives the occurrence.

Through these investigations, I will present a fresh perspective that sees spirit possession neither as the representation of people's response to modernity nor as a radically unique phenomenon that is incompatible with Western ontology, but rather as a phenomenon that has something in common with our ordinary experiences. By shifting our focus from the *ontisch* to the pathisch aspect of the phenomenon, and from the opposition between the active voice and passive voice to that between the active voice and the middle voice, we realize that spirit possession has some essential traits that form the basis of our experience of *life itself*, which may be acutely sensed in terms of affect, passion, and care.

From Functionalism to Ontology

Since the early modern period, magical-religious practices such as spirit possession and witchcraft in non-Western societies have been represented as the opposite of the ideal image of person and society in the West. As Johnson (2011) argues, for instance, the possessed person has been regarded as the reversal of the rational, autonomous individual who should possess and control himself or herself. Meanwhile, in a strand of anthropology that has grown since the twentieth century, magical-religious phenomena in non-Western societies have been a key subject. Among various explanations developed to understand these phenomena, the analyses that elucidate people's magical-religious practices in terms of their social and psychological functions have flourished (e.g., Beattie 1969; Lewis 1966).

In line with this perspective, since the 1980s, studies that focus on the relation between modernity and the occult in non-Western societies have been especially prevalent.[1] Most of these studies share the idea that magical-religious practices in non-Western societies are incompatible with modern rationality, and yet/therefore function as criticism of ideologies and systems originating in the modern West. Magical-religious practices have thus been linked with ongoing global issues, such as penetration of capitalism, globalization, and the intensification of neoliberalism. Here, these practices are analyzed both as symbolic protests against modernity and as inventive mimicry of its power. At the same time, they are also imagined as escaping the control and scrutiny of modern rational systems and discourses.

Since the end of the 1990s, a new trend has grown in anthropology that also focuses on magical-religious phenomena in non-Western societies, but analyzes them differently. This trend consists of various arguments regarding ontology (hereafter called ontological anthropology: OA). In addition to criticizing the modern dichotomy of nature and culture, advocates of OA also see it as means of freeing anthropology from the shackles of epistemology. Here, the goal is "taking things encountered in the field as they present themselves" (Henare, Holbraad & Wastell 2007, 2), and its proponents take issue with focusing epistemologically merely on people's worldviews and with the reductionism entailed in describing fieldwork observations through modern rationality.

Accordingly, following OA, rather than elaborating on worldviews, anthropologists should engage with the ontology of the people in the field. Consequently, peoples who are assumed to have different ontologies, such as Euro-Americans and Amerindians, are understood as not just perceiving the same world in different ways, but as living in different worlds (Henare, Holbraad & Wastell 2007, 10–12; Holbraad 2009). In OA, the concept of "ontology" thus suggests a multiplicity of worlds and is inseparable from *difference* and *alterity*. Here, these concepts do not refer to epistemological differences between worldviews, but are reserved for denoting ontological differences between lived worlds. A central tenet is *radical alterity* (Henare, Holbraad & Wastell 2007, 8), which cannot be reduced to modern rationality.

Intending to take seriously the things they find in the field, proponents of OA set out to describe ontological worlds in which magical-religious phenomena such as spirits, deities, and witchcraft can exist. Here, *things* are not merely tangible objects, but also *concepts*. When the distinction between things and concepts collapses, "thought here just *is* being," and "conception is a mode of disclosure that creates its own objects" (Henare, Holbraad & Wastell 2007, 14–15).

Such assertions in OA clearly challenge previous rationalistic approaches to "apparently irrational belief" taken simply as unrealistic fantasy. By reiterating such assertions, however, proponents of OA seek to take each thing and notion encountered in the field into the sphere of *being*. While remaining virtual and indefinite for "us," these things are considered to be extant entities to the extent that the ontographer considers them to really exist *for the people* (e.g., Viveiros de Castro 2014).

It is not self-evident, however, that people connected to spirit possession or witchcraft really regard spirits and witches as given existences, or thing-concepts that can be created by their own thought. As several anthropologists have pointed out, the arguments of OA contain the risk of substantializing magical-religious phenomena that are incomprehensible even for the people in the field, as the reality for *them* (see Candea 2011; Graeber 2015; Vigh and Sausdal 2014). Furthermore, arguments focusing on thing-concepts created by one's thought seem to depend on and strengthen the tradition of the humanities and social science in the modern West, which has attached great importance to the issues of human subjectivity, the ability to think, and being/existence.

The centrality of being/existence of thing-concepts in OA, however, must be reconsidered in light of the inscrutability of the state of *being* as well as the uncertainty of human subjectivity. If we take seriously the fundamental contingency and incomprehensibility of both *being* and subjectivity, then, to understand the magical-religious phenomena we study, it is necessary to shift our perspective from the ontic/ontisch view to the pathisch view, as I will explore below.

Ontisch Being and Pathisch Being

In this section, I will investigate the emergence and mutual interactions of entities and forces beyond the sphere of ontic *beings*. I will do so by examining the ideas of Weizsäcker, particularly the concept of umwelt, which enables us to explore the lives of humans and other organisms in processes of mutual formation within milieus. While Weizsäcker incorporated Uexküll's basic conception of umwelt, he did not accept Uexküll's (1921) characterization of the relation between an organism and its umwelt as harmonious and self-sufficient. Instead, Weizsäcker focused on instability and crisis, that is, the dynamic relations between an organism and its umwelt.

For Weizsäcker, the crisis that an organism undergoes in relation to its umwelt reflects *Pathisches,* which can be glossed as *pathos,* of life. While each organism behaves actively in relation to its umwelt, it also has a pathisch (the adjectival form of Pathisches) aspect at its root, in the sense that it just happens to exist whether it *receives* life or suffers the burden of life (Weizsäcker 1997 [1950], 312–3). In particular, fluctuations in and ruptures of coherence with the umwelt caused by out-of-the-ordinary changes force an organism, at risk of loss of life, to transform its life-form. Weizsäcker characterized this state as Pathisches, which contrasts with the state of *Ontisches,* or the *ontic* (1997 [1950], 314).

In *Anonyma,* Weizsäcker (1946, 9–12) posits Pathisches as a basic attribute of organisms: animate beings are pathisch and inanimate beings are ontisch (the adjectival form of Ontisches). In this schema, ontisch merely denotes pure being, or bare existence (*das nackte Sein*), or, in other words, that someone or something just *is.* Pathisch connotes existence that is *received* rather than assumed.

As we will see later, however, the notion of pathisch should not be considered as synonymous with "passive." In contrast to ontisch being as bare existence, pathisch being receives its life and way of being in relation to, and is affected by, the umwelt, including itself. Pathisch being is thus understood to be in the *middle voice* in the sense that a particular life form, or *life itself* as becoming force, is actualized within itself.[2] This is important when we consider spirit possession as an event occurring in a medium's body.

The above arguments provide us a clue for reconsidering spirit possession. As the proponents of OA point out, in order to understand magical-religious phenomena such as spirit possession, it is insufficient to regard them merely as the symbolic representation of people's sentiments or a protest against modernity. At the same time, it is also problematic to regard spirit possession as an indication of the radical alterity of a particular ontological world. If not by reducing the phenomenon into functionalistic explanations, nor by assuming an existence of spirits for *them* that is never comprehended by *us,* how can we understand the phenomenon called spirit possession?

Here, Weizsäcker's thought leads us to shift our perspective of spirit possession from the ontisch to the pathisch view. As we will see later, we should pay more attention to the pathisch aspect of a spirit-medium's experience, as well as to the relationship between the spirit, the medium, and the mediator who perceives and receives the manifestation of spirits. In the next section, I will draw on the study of Takeshi Matsushima, who examined performers' bodily movements in experimental drama, to elaborate an understanding of spirit possession in terms of the middle voice.

Manifestation of Performance and Spirits in the Middle Voice

Matsushima (2014), who conducted fieldwork on community mental health care in Italy, examines the relationship between self and other emerging through synchronous movements and a bodily mode not totally controlled by the subject. Through his participation in experimental drama, Matsushima argues that when an actor performs in relation with others, his/her body sometimes adopts a state that is neither totally active nor totally passive. According to Matsushima, such a bodily mode can be well understood in linguistic terms: it is neither in the active nor passive voice, but rather in the middle voice—the state in which an event occurs or emerges of its own accord at the site. Drawing on the linguist Takehiro Kanaya (2004), Matsushima defines the function of the middle voice as the expression of *natural momentum* without a subject-agent. The opposition between the active voice and middle voice is thus the opposition between the action of a subject-agent and the event that occurs of its own accord (2014, 340–1).

Based on the work of philosopher Koichiro Kokubun (2017), I will briefly complement the above argument on the middle voice. According to Kokubun, although the Indo-European languages originally recognized the opposition between the active voice and middle voice, gradually the opposition between the active voice and passive voice, which had developed as a derivative of the middle voice, became more predominant (see also Andersen 1989; Benveniste 1966; Macksey and Donato 1972, 151–2). This shows the transformation of most Indo-European languages from languages that *describe events* to those that *determine the subject-agent*.

In languages constituted of the opposition between the active voice and passive voice, it is necessary to identify and determine the agent of action (i.e., the subject of a verb) to whom the action is ascribed. Here, in order to determine the subject of the action designated by the verb, the *will* of the subject-agent is essential. Contrary to this, the middle voice indicates a process in which the action or state affecting the subject occurs irrespective of his/her will. Thus, the middle voice expresses the actualizing process of a natural momentum on the subject as the site. Here, the subject is not a voluntary actor, but rather, is involved in this process. Therefore, the middle voice inevitably contains the image of the *force* that actualizes the process (see Kokubun 2017, 187).[3]

This indication by Kokubun provides us a theoretical background to consider spirit possession as a manifestation of natural momentum in the medium's body as the site. Importantly, if we consider spirits as ontic beings/existences, as do the proponents of OA, we may overlook the perspective of the middle voice and strengthen the opposition between the active voice and passive voice—possessing and being possessed—by regarding the phenomenon as an action to be ascribed to a certain subject-agent.

Keeping the above philosophical investigation in mind, let us turn back to the case presented by Matsushima (2014). He says that when a performer is moving freely and smoothly in a detached state of mind, it leads him/her to leave temporarily his/her status as a subject controlling his/her action and bodily self. That is, a person involved in the performing process experiences himself/herself as the site where the performance occurs of its own accord, and thus leaves the opposition between the active voice and passive voice that demands every action to be ascribed to the subject-agent. Experimental drama can thus offer relief or a breakthrough to the patient who suffers from this modernist obsession with always being a strong subject-agent.

Here, Matsushima discerns another important point. In the practice of experimental drama, when a person is performing, detached from his/her ordinary mode of self, he/she does not always notice his/her altered state. It is in relation to another person—Matsushima calls this person a "witness"—who stays by the performer's side and notices his/her transition, that the performer can realize his/her altered mode of being reflexively. In other words, it is through the encounter of the performer moving in the middle voice with the person who witnesses and receives his/her movements that the event befalling the performer is actualized as a shared, social experience.

This point is suggestive when we consider what happens in spirit possession. As we will see below, the medium who is overwhelmed by a spirit's power is not necessarily being "possessed" by an external subject-agent. Rather, he/she veers toward the pathisch mode of being in this process, as the site where the event naturally occurs. This occurrence, however, does not conclude solely in the medium's body. The coming of the spirit is actualized as a shared experience only when a third person notices and receives it as an actual event. In other words, the spirit is not to be assumed as an ontic being from the first, but rather is a force that becomes a temporary sojourner through its manifestation in the medium's body.

Here, the importance of the mediator who intermediates between spirit, medium, and ordinary participants comes to the fore. In spirit worship, both in Southern Ghana and South India, it is only through his/her practices of waiting for, receiving, and caring for the spirit that the manifestation of spirits becomes part of the shared experience in a social milieu or umwelt.

Spirits, Priests, and Ɔkyeame in Suman Worship in Southern Ghana

In this section, I will examine spirit (*suman*, pl. *asuman*) worship in Southern Ghana, focusing on the relationship between spirits, mediums, and mediators. I conducted fieldwork in a village called Obretema located in the Eastern Region in Ghana.[4] During the fieldwork, I lived in a suman shrine, where a priest called Nana Sakye, born in 1971, served a suman called Tigare. According to Nana Sakye, when he was seventeen, he was spirited away by dwarfs to a bush and remained there for several days. After this event, he underwent the training for suman priesthood under a senior priestess in her shrine near Obretema. During this training period, Sakye experienced spirit possession for the first time and was diagnosed as being possessed by Tigare, said to have its origin at Yipara in the Northern region. In 1996, he visited a suman shrine at Yipara to receive Tigare's sacred objects and built a shrine in Obretema.

Like Nana Sakye, most suman priests first encounter suman in their adolescence, in experiences such as those detailed below:

> When I was around twelve years old, I started to act abnormally. Since I was very sick and always running into a bush, people thought I became crazy. [...] When the elders conducted a ritual for me, the suman finally manifested itself. (Kweku Kwapong, January 5, 2000)

> When I was working in my father's cocoa farm, something small fell on my head [...] When I came back home and saw it again, I found it was a small bead with a hole. That night, when I was asleep, I heard the wind howling and calling: "my

name is Kwesi Jojo. Kwesi Jojo, whooi … " I went out, but nobody was there. After this event, when I was on the farm, suddenly a strong light hit my face and I was overcome with very fierce feeling. […] As my behavior became more and more eccentric, my uncle took me to the elder called Nkwa. He diagnosed that a deity was going to take me. (Kwakye Wiredu, February 7, 2000)

As the above narratives show, most suman priests experience possession as an overwhelming power befalling them. In Twi, the native language of the Akan people in this area, spirit possession is called *akɔm* and a medium-priest is called *ɔkɔmfo* (pl. *akɔmfo*). Entering into the suman priesthood is also called akɔm. The common expressions for possession in Twi, such as "*akɔm no faa me* (the akɔm took me)" or "*akɔm no kaa me* (the akɔm bit me)," indicate a feature of the event, that an unnamed power affects the person involved in the process.[5] Here, though these sentences grammatically take the active voice with an impersonal subject, they designate the state of affairs in the middle voice: some force manifests itself and affects the entity involved in it as the site.[6]

How, then, can we understand the event called akɔm from the perspective of the suman itself? Does it indicate the experience of the subject-agent who possesses the medium as its object? Though it is difficult to answer this question, a narrative of Nana Yakubu, one of the powerful asuman in Southern Ghana, also said to have its origin in the Northern region, provides us a hint. When I met Nana Yakubu, incarnated in the suman priest called Nana Yapale at his shrine, the suman narrated the following:

> Even though you go somewhere and someone tells you that there is only one Nana Yakubu, there are more and more great names for me. I am hot liquor. I am hot liquor. I'm drinking hot liquor and the liquor is myself. If you cook kwakwa to make a soup and put palm kernels into it, you are putting yourself into it. Do you understand what I mean? So I'm sitting here and drinking myself. (Nana Yakubu, October 15, 1999)

Though this narrative sounds puzzling, it demonstrates an interesting feature of the suman, in terms of the middle voice. Namely, the suman is both the initiator and endpoint of its own act. It is thus the subject-agent and, at the same time, the one affected by its own force (see Benveniste 1966). It suggests that not only the medium-priest overwhelmed by the suman's power, but also the suman itself is a sort of pathisch being that receives and is affected by its own power.

Keeping the above features of asuman and their priests in mind, let us investigate the relationship between a suman priest and mediator. As seen in Nana Sakye's case, after training for several years, a suman priest usually establishes a shrine and starts activities such as organizing rituals and treating clients who visit the shrine for care and advice. In daily activities at the suman shrine, the suman is not only worshipped in the figure of sacred objects, but also often manifests itself and interacts with people through spirit possession. A mediator or interpreter called *ɔkyeame* supports the priest's activities and rituals at the suman shrine.

In Nana Sakye's case, an ɔkyeame called Yaw, who was an excellent drummer, lived with Sakye's family and assisted with ritual practices at the shrine. When Tigare manifested itself on one occasion, Nana Sakye's two uncles, who undertook the role of hosts for the suman, were called to come in haste. The elders took off their shoes, came into the shrine, and greeted the suman sitting in the inner room. Tigare, incarnated in Nana Sakye, wearing an indigo-dyed smock and fez, smoked a black pipe with a frowning powdered white face. Though Tigare was taciturn, he sometimes spoke Hausa, and the ɔkyeame interpreted his words to them.

As this case shows, the ɔkyeame is both interpreter and caretaker of the suman incarnated in a priest, and intermediates between the suman and people. The close relationship between the suman/priest and ɔkyeame is more remarkable in the possession ritual. During the festival (*afahyɛ*) dedicated to suman, many suman priests and priestesses gather from various areas and conduct rituals involving dancing, drumming, offering libations, and making sacrifices. During the dance, accompanied by enthusiastic singing and drumming, the priests/priestess are often possessed by asuman, as described below.

As shown above, in spirit possession rituals in Southern Ghana, the ɔkyeame plays a significant role. While the priest becomes the suman itself by receiving its power into his/her body, the ɔkyeame receives the suman as an actual and estimable being by caring for the suman incarnated in the priest and interpreting his/her words. This shows that, through the work of the ɔkyeame, who witnesses spirit possession and mediates between suman, priest, and other ritual participants, the suman's manifestation is actualized, and it becomes a transient sojourner among people. In this sense, the ɔkyeame is an essential constituent of the momentarily emerging social milieu called akɔm.

Case 1: Manifestation of Suman in the Afahyɛ

In the evening around 4 pm, when the singing and drumming reached its climax, Nana Sakye entered the precinct and started dancing in front of the musicians. He swung around on one heel and danced around the precinct with his clothes billowing with the wind. As he turned faster and faster, the singing and drumming became more enthusiastic. When Nana Sakye, still turning, tilted his head, closed his eyes and became absentminded, the ɔkyeame Yaw came forward and sprinkled white powder over him. Following the priest, Yaw was watching his every move intently. After dancing hard, Nana Sakye fell into Yaw's arms. Yaw and other helpers took him into the shrine, changed his clothes, and put him in garments appropriate for Tigare. The suman, now incarnated in the priest, walked around in long strides, demanding to shake hands and hug people around him, and demanding more cigarettes, schnapps, and white powder. Yaw followed the possessed priest, listened to his words, and brought whatever the suman needed. (October 22, 1999, at the suman shrine in Obretema)

Spirits, Dancer-Mediums, and the Gaḍipatināṟu in the Būta Ritual in South India

Next, I will investigate spirit or *būta* worship in coastal Karnataka (South Kanara) in India, focusing on the relationship between būta mediums and the head of the local manor house, who plays a key role in the būta ritual. I conducted fieldwork on būta worship in a village called Perar in South Kanara.[7] Būtas are believed to be spirits of local heroes/heroines or wild animals dwelling in forests. Būta worship at the village level is organized by several manor families called *guttu* and supported by families of various service castes such as priests, dancer-mediums, musicians, and so on.

I will first examine the experience of dancer-mediums who embody būtas in the yearly ritual (*nēma*) in the village būta shrine. As with suman priests in Southern Ghana, during possession, a dancer-medium is overwhelmed by a būta's power (*būta śakti*) and cannot fully control it. After this ecstatic moment, he calms down and behaves more consciously, as Yatish, one of the main dancer-mediums in Perar, narrates:

> At the moment [of being possessed], my consciousness concentrates totally on the deity. This is the moment of *ākarṣaṇe* [attraction]. For about three seconds, my soul goes to the deity ... Then I recover my senses enough to be able to distinguish people. [...] After ākarṣaṇe, a time of *śānta svabhāva* [calm state of mind] comes. When people chant prayers and throw petals and grains on me, I receive *āvēśa* [spirit possession]. After that I know what to do next. (Yatish Pambada, June 16, 2008)

In Tuḷu, the native language of people in South Kanara, ākarṣaṇe means attraction or a ritual to invoke spirits, and āvēśa means spirit possession, subservience, enthusiasm, and happiness (Upadhyaya 1988–1997, 219, 277). Possession is also variously described in Tuḷu as *jōga* (ecstasy), *darṣana* (trembling owing to spirit possession), and *būtapattundu* ("the būta caught ... ") (see Brückner 2009; Claus 1984; Smith 2006, 138). Similar to the terminology of spirit possession in Twi, these expressions indicate the situation in the middle voice in which uncontrollable power befalls the medium's body as the site.[8]

In the būta ritual, a dancer-medium filled with būta śakti dances around the precinct, receives offerings, speaks prophecies, and blesses villagers. These acts of the būta incarnated in the dancer-medium are followed and supported by various ritual workers, such as musicians, other dancers, and carriers of sacred objects. Among them, the person playing the most important role of responding to the deity is the *gaḍipatināṟu*, the head of the first manor house in Perar.

The term gaḍipatināṟu originally indicates a person who takes authority/ responsibility (*gaḍi*), and this duty must be fulfilled to one's dying days. Since the gaḍipatināṟu contacts the deities and mediates the relationship between the people and deities, he should always keep himself pure and clean. The present gaḍipatināṟu of the first manor house in Perar is Gangādara Rai, born in 1931. I will below describe an interaction between the gaḍipatināṟu and dancer-medium called Jayānanda during the yearly ritual in the village būta shrine.

Case 2: The Interaction Between the Dancer-Medium and Gaḍipatināṟu in the Būta Ritual

When the ritual starts, Jayānanda stands in front of the altar in the precinct. The gaḍipatināṟu and other heads of guttus surround him and watch his movements intently. Jayānanda takes a step toward the altar and bows. His body begins to shake at the moment the gaḍipatināṟu offers the prayer, and then the other guttu heads throw rice and flowers on him. Jayānanda, possessed by the deity called Arasu (hereinafter referred to as Jayānanda-Arasu), dances around the precinct and greets each guttu head. Jayānanda-Arasu steps lightly to the sounds of the horns and starts talking to the gaḍipatināṟu through body and hand gestures. He draws close to the gaḍipatināṟu's face to look up at him, holds both his arms up in the air, and leans forward to catch his answers. Through his facial expressions and gestures, he communicates with the gaḍipatināṟu and other manor heads who stand up in respect and watch his every movement seriously. The gaḍipatināṟu looks directly at the deity's eyes, responds to his every word, and walks around with his wrist held by the deity. Jayānanda-Arasu receives a tender coconut from the gaḍipatināṟu, pours its water on the floor, and gives it back to the gaḍipatināṟu with blessings. (March 11, 2009)

During the nēma, the gaḍipatināṟu occupies the position closest to every deity manifesting itself in the ritual. The gaḍipatināṟu chants a prayer to summon the deity into the medium's body. It is to the gaḍipatināṟu that the deity conveys her various requests and indications, often communicating her dissatisfaction and anger over people's faults during the ritual.[9] The gaḍipatināṟu follows the deity to respond to her every movement, treats her hospitably, and appeases her anger. Gaṅgādara Rai refers to his intimate relationship with the būtas as follows:

> Only the gaḍipatināṟu can physically touch the deity—nobody else can do it. Only the gaḍipatināṟu can assuage the deity's thirst. The gaḍipatināṟu has *adikāra* to the deity and the deity has adikāra to the gaḍipatināṟu. To hand a sword to the deity and receive it from her is the adikāra of the gaḍipatināṟu. (July 2, 2008)

As this narrative indicates, people often mention adikāra in relation to the relationship between humans and deities. Adikāra originates from the Sanskrit word, *adhikāra*, meaning authority, royalty, rank, and right (Monier-Williams 2008 [1899], 20). In Tuḷu, this word has a broader meaning, including authority, power, rank, office, administration, governing, and responsibility (Upadhyaya 1988–1997, 96). In the context of būta worship, adikāra describes the mutual rights and responsibilities of humans and būtas. It also indicates the role and prestige of the caretakers who have the right and responsibility to maintain an intimate relationship with the deities.

As with ɔkyeame in suman worship in Ghana, the gaḍipatināṟu welcomes the deity into the human world through waiting for, caring for, and responding to the deity. However, contrary to the ɔkyeame, who devotes himself to assist suman incarnated in a priest, the gaḍipatināṟu—who is the head of the local manor house—plays a more vital role in the ritual as the representative of villagers, by summoning and interacting with the deity.[10]

The complementary notions of jōga and *māya* are also important in būta worship. In Tuḷu, the realm of "reality" inhabited by humans and other beings is called jōga, while the realm of the unknown filled with būta śakti is called māya. In general, jōga refers to the physical world, the human form, existence, and reality, while māya means mystery and disappearance. Also, *māyaka* denotes vanishing, fleeting, passing away, and disappearing. It is thought that while būtas belong to the invisible realm of māya, they temporarily manifest themselves (*jōga āpini*) through spirit possession.[11]

Būta śakti is thus believed to be a dynamic power that flows from the realm of māya to that of jōga, and manifests itself in the būta ritual. Unlike humans and other ontic beings, būtas are not assumed to exist as ontic beings in the realm of jōga. Rather, they transiently come into being as untamed force in the ritual process. Here, similar to the shrine precincts during the ritual stage, the medium's body becomes the site where the deity's power manifests itself. In order to be actualized in the realm of jōga, however, it is necessary that the deity's manifestation is received not only by the medium but also by others as an occurrence beyond human knowledge and will. In the būta worship in Perar, it is the gaḍipatināṟu who becomes the first witness as he waits for, perceives, and receives the būta śakti through intimate interactions with the medium.

Waiting for Deities

As discussed earlier, Matsushima (2014) observed that when a performer acts naturally and unconsciously, he/she transiently leaves the status of subject-agent and becomes the site where performance occurs of its own accord. Here, the performer's body moves smoothly in relation to others, neither totally controlled by his/her own will, nor completely at random. In such a situation, it is the witness who notices and receives his/her altered mode of being.

When we consider spirit possession not as the "possession" of one's subject status by an external subject-agent, but as the manifestation of overwhelming force occurring of its own accord, we notice the similarity between spirit possession and the experimental drama described by Matsushima. When an event such as a spirit's manifestation or performance naturally arises, the medium/performer moves and is moved, not as a completely self-controlling subject, but as the *site* where the event comes into being. While the emergence of such event is beyond one's will and ordinary state, it becomes a shared social experience by being perceived and received by the witness, such as the mediator in the ritual or the director of the experimental drama.

Moreover, both cases suggest the possibility that not only the medium/performer but also the witness tentatively leaves his/her ordinary mode of being as subject-agent, through his/her experience of waiting for, witnessing, and receiving the event. As Matsushima suggests, their attitude of *waiting for* the event is significant. For instance, the attitude of the gaḍipatināṟu, who obeys various ritual norms, carefully prepares for, and waits for the coming of the deity shows not necessarily his active role to make the deity exist, but rather his pathisch relationship with the deity as an incomprehensible force.

The word *sēve* in Tuḷu is key to understanding this point. Usually used in the context of serving deities, this word originates in the Sanskrit word *sevā*. It means to serve or to care for something, and its root *sev* connotes the meaning of "to stay near" (Monier-Williams 2008 [1899], 1247). This word well expresses the gaḍipatināru's attitude, who undertakes the role of witness by serving, caring for, and staying besides the deity.

To understand this intimate relationship between the spirit/medium and mediator, again experimental drama can offer us a clue. Matsushima (2014) examines a practice that leads to the emergence of synchronicity between performers. In this practice, two persons first move together holding the ends of a long rope. Next, they move together without the rope, yet keeping the feeling of holding its ends. When the practice goes smoothly, each performer comes to feel the other's act directly through his/her body, as if they are still connected through the rope, even when they are not. Similarly, the interactions between the spirit/medium and mediator are considered to be ever shifting, flexible, and synchronous movements emerging in between the two that can be conceived neither as the relation between subject and object, nor as a relation of autonomous subject-agents. As Weizsäcker points out on the relation of an organism to its umwelt, it shows that they temporarily create a unique social milieu or umwelt through interacting, and moving coherently with each other and with their circumstance.

Conclusion

As we have seen, spirit possession has long been regarded as the inversion of the ideal image of the rational and autonomous individual in the modern West. At the same time, anthropologists have attempted to explicate magical-religious phenomena in various ways. Among them, functionalistic analyses explicating these phenomena in terms of sociopolitical circumstances or of the desires, agonies, and anxieties of people have prevailed. In line with these arguments, since the 1980s, the trend analyzing magical-religious phenomena in non-Western societies as people's response to modernity has become influential. Although such theoretical trends have changed with the times, the basic tone of arguments seems unchanged: most studies oppose these phenomena to reason and rationality in the modern West, and still attempt to give them meanings understandable for "us" in the West.

Meanwhile, the proponents of OA criticize these functionalistic analyses and present a new perspective by taking things in the field seriously, presuming that things or concepts, including intangible objects such as spirits and witchcraft, conceived by the people, simply exist for *them*. At the same time, they pay deference to these people's reality as a radically different ontological world that cannot be easily elucidated by "us" in the West. These arguments, however, seem to contain the risk of strengthening fundamental differences and incompatibility between "our" ontological world, based on modern rationality, and "their" ontological world, filled with magical-religious phenomena. Moreover, their arguments tend to substantialize phenomena such as spirit possession, magic, and witchcraft that cannot be fully comprehended even by those in the field, by assuming them to exist for these people.

I have attempted to find an alternative way to understand spirit possession, by moving away from the presumption that the manifestation of spirits is merely a metaphor of something else, or that spirits are ontic beings/existences in a particular ontological world. In both cases of possession rituals in Southern Ghana and South India, the medium embodies the spirit's force by receiving it into his/her body. Here, the medium's body moves neither totally actively nor passively: rather, it becomes the *site* where the spirit's force manifests itself of its own accord. Moreover, it is indispensable that there is a third person who waits for, encounters, and receives the spirit's manifestation to make the phenomenon a part of shared social experience. These cases lead us to consider spirit possession as an event occurring in the medium's body, being actualized by the encounter with the other, who receives it as the witness.

This perspective urges us to shift our focus from the ontisch to the pathisch aspect of the phenomenon, and from the opposition between the active voice and passive voice to the opposition between the active voice and the middle voice. The phenomenon called spirit possession, therefore, does not merely indicate "possession" of the subject by external spiritual subject-agents, but rather is a multiple occurrence: it is a force manifested in the medium's body, an event actualized through being witnessed and received by the other, and the social milieu temporarily emerging through interactions between spirit, medium, and mediator. Here, spirit possession is understood not simply as a magical-religious phenomenon in a particular ontological world, but rather as a phenomenon that has something in common with our ordinary experiences. It shows some essential traits forming the basis of our experience of *life itself* that may be acutely sensed in terms of affect, passion, and care.

Let us turn back to the arguments on pathisch being and the middle voice. According to Weizsäcker (1997 [1950]), to live in the umwelt is a pathisch experience for an organism, in the sense that life itself is actualized as an inevitable occurrence for the organism involved. Here, the relation between life itself and the organism is understood in terms of the middle voice: life force manifests itself as natural momentum on the subject as the site. Likewise, in the possession ritual, spirit's force manifests itself of its own accord in the medium's body. Both events contain the image of the *force* that actualizes each process (see Kokubun 2017, 187). Spirit possession is thus not an aberrant state to be described in terms of the opposition between the active voice and the passive voice, where the subject ("I") fails to possess itself and is totally owned by the other. Rather, it is a phenomenon that shares common features with the basic experience of an animate being in its umwelt: a natural momentum with no subject-agent manifests itself in *me* as the site.

As already seen, the possessed have long been regarded as the inversion of the ideal, autonomous subject in the modern West, and spirit possession has also been seen as an abnormal, incomprehensible phenomenon. This may be not unconnected to the history of the middle voice that has been replaced by the passive voice and disappeared from most Indo-European languages including English, one of the dominant languages for the humanities and social science in the West. This decay of the middle voice indicates the transformation of these languages from languages that *describe events* to those that *determine the subject-agent*.

Here, to consider spirit possession as the actualizing process of a natural momentum leads us to retrieve the perspective of the middle voice. Moreover, it leads us to reconsider our relation with life itself from the perspective of the middle voice, as what is transiently actualized in "me" in relation with others. Just as spirit's manifestation is actualized through being received by the medium as well as the witness, the emergence of life as natural momentum can be actualized as a shared social experience when it is received not only by the subject-recipient but also by intimate others who stay besides, witness, and care for the occurrence. It may not be a coincidence that in English expressions such as "spirit manifests itself" and "be born," expressions that indicate the pathisch aspects of these events, still maintain the characteristic of the middle voice. Only when being affected by, and involved in, such actualizing processes, and also being received by others, can one live life as a natural momentum that manifests itself at the site—*me*—in the ever shifting, transient social milieu with others.

The Motion-Power of the Collective, or How Spirits "Come into View" in Cuba

Diana Espírito Santo

Introduction

How can we, as scholars, get spirit worlds to "come into view" (or, we could say, into perception)? This question—inspired by a disquieting inconformity with anthropological depictions of "supernatural beings", especially in Japanese folklore studies—was asked by Jensen, Ishii, and Swift, in a recent article on Japanese spirit worlds (2016). They argue that a possible antidote to the view of spirit beings as reactive responses to broader social realities, or as figments of human cognition, or as symbols of something or another, is to take heed from maverick Japanese scientist Minikata Kumagusu, who lived and wrote in the late nineteenth century to early twentieth century. Minikata stressed the need for "tact," implying a "receptive attitude towards the surprises of (nonhuman) things" (2016, 162), in the perception of *en*, meaning the multiple ties and relations of invisible orders which form webs around all things in the universe (ibid., 160). Minakata said: "At any moment, we encounter enumerable *en*. They can make occurrences happen, depending on how one minds them or how they touch one's body" (1971, 391, in ibid., 164). *En* is, then, in perpetual dynamic formation: imminently affected (and affecting) by their observer, who activates them in their surroundings. In this chapter, I will argue that in Cuban espiritismo, a widespread mediumship practice associated with nineteenth-century spiritualism, spirits "come into view" through various forms of mediumship and ritual; indeed, similar to the activation of *en*, people *activate* spirits by activating fluid spiritual substances in their midst—*fluidos*. Through Don Handelman's analysis of "ritual in its own right" (2004), I argue that we have to look at these forms of activation more carefully, especially ritual, the most frequent rite of which is called a *misa espiritual* (spiritual mass). I argue that *misas* are both the simultaneous opening and the closure of movement—they

I would like to thank Matan Shapiro for his excellent and detailed revision of this chapter and for his many ideas to restructure it from an initial mess! This text is the result of ten years of fieldwork in Havana, and I would like to acknowledge funding from multiple sources: the ESRC in the UK, FCT in Portugal, and the Fondo de Insersión in Pontificia Universidad Católica de Chile. Most of all, I am thankful to my Cuban friends and interlocutors, especially Eduardo and Olga Silva.

specify and enable it, directing it, and in so doing, create the dynamic parameters for the manifestation of *fluido*—which can be heuristically defined, among other things, as spirits-in-becoming, translating them into knowledge. Spirit, then, is contained in movement itself, as *fluido* is never static. But while *fluido* is a constitution of forces that is set in motion by participants, it is ultimately unaccountable to them. There is thus an indeterminate aspect to both the rite and the spirits themselves, which, I argue, creates a "phantasmagoric space," an "imaginal field" that "opens up within itself" (ibid.), and manifests its own emergent logics (Kapferer, 2002, 23).

In his Introduction to the special issue, "Ritual in its own right," Handelman defends the idea that, "if one wants to think about what ritual is in relation to itself, how it is put together and organized within itself, then first and foremost ritual should be studied in its own right and not be presumed immediately to be constituted through representations of the sociocultural surround that give it life" (2004, 2). In this ethnography, I argue that we need to see the possession rite itself (with all that precedes the possession event, but that also includes it) as resulting from a moving form of *fluido*. Think of a three-dimensional wave, in continual motion, of varying intensities and thrusts, and even compositions. This moving *fluido* has constant feedback and feedforward effects; it is *affected* constitutionally, spatially, and in terms of motion, by participants and their emerging visions in the rite. This continual ontological "conversation," so to speak, gives rise to certain things: spirits, powers, and essentially, information that can be passed on to *augment* the self. Spirits "come into view" through the moving *fluido* of the rite itself. This is facilitated by a cosmology that understands spirits as *internal* components of people needing exteriorization, an ethnographic fact that I will explore on in a section below; internal components, externalized as visions, and subsequently internalized as motion. Indeed, in spirit possession this *fluido* becomes momentarily at one with the person's body, before flowing out once more, as knowledge. But this is not to say that *any misa* can become cosmologically productive. The "motion-power" of the "collective" referred to here is instigated by mediums who must conduct the *misa* expertly; they must know when to "push" for possession, or to explore a given avenue of information, giving space for the *fluido* to find its way into becoming the forms it must, including mediumistic visions, advice, and the particular manifestation of spirits themselves. These experts keep the movement forthcoming, and can proliferate communicational links, meta-communications, between spirits and their persons, and to the large mediumistic emerging "screen" of the rite. They must also know when to "cut" forces and close them down. In other words, they must have "tact," to cite Jensen et al. (2016).

In the rest of this chapter, I will do two main things, while deconstructing the main ethnographic example in the very next section. Firstly, I will explore Don Handelman's understanding of "degrees of curvature" in rituals (2004, 12), by which he refers to a ritual's tendency to variously self-organize and gain temporary autonomy from its social environment, or not. I will explain what he means by this with a counterexample of a relatively "flat" spiritist session, which, in comparison with the one described in the next section, has its existence dependent on a sort of mirroring, or representing, of its sociocultural milieu. The "curved" rite, says Handelman, is much like Bateson's example of the torus, a smoke ring "turning in on itself, giving itself a separable existence" (ibid., 12), at least momentarily. The torus is an excellent example here because we can see it as a direct analogy with *fluido*, which is taken by my interlocutors as a substance-thing, not as a metaphorical concept, or figment of the mind. Secondly, and more briefly, I look at a notion of virtuality as explored through Kapferer (2002, 2004), to show that *fluido* can also be described ethnographically as an aspect of the "virtual self," which, when unfolded successfully during rituals, can become objectified aspects of oneself, which includes the spirits or *muertos* one comes with. A spirit may, at the same time, be prevented from becoming a *muerto* with weight and impact in a person's trajectory. One needs to "develop" spirits (*desarrollar muertos*). If the spirit is underdeveloped, it remains a dormant condition in one's life. This also applies to the self, which experiences varying degrees of *itself*. Undeveloped selves find, as Panagiotopolous argues (2017, 949), that "things 'stumble' (*tropezar*), 'deviate' (*desviar*) or become 'heavy' (*pesadas*) and people constantly find themselves in a state of 'struggle' (*lucha*) so as to 'make things walk' (*hacer que las cosas caminen*)." The person is thus a virtual repository of spirit potentials, talents, dispositions, and opportunities. As Kapferer remarks for his ethnographic material in Sri Lanka, "the potency of much magical practice is in its virtuality, which stands outside all reason—even, perhaps, its own. As such it contains its own "truth"" (2002, 23), one not subject to falsification.

Dynamics of the *misa espiritual*

The vignette described here was a *misa* designed to "give the dead knowledge" (*darle conocimiento al muerto*) before the receiving of the deity (*oricha*) of the earth in Afro-Cuban religion, a deity called *oricha-oko*, and was commissioned by Berta, an acquaintance of my two close friends, godparents, and interlocutors, Eduardo and Olga. In Santería, Cuba's best-known religion of African association (Bolívar 1990; Wirtz 2007), one needs to ask permission to one's *muertos* in order to procure initiations. This permission, or "giving of knowledge," is achieved through spiritist rites, *misas*, whose function is to invoke these dead. The *muerto*, as they say, gives "birth" to all other entities, including the majestic Cuban-Yoruba gods, the *orichas*. Among those present was Berta's daughter, also a practitioner of Santería, and some other initiates that were mediums and friends of the family's. The *misa* was carried out in Berta's house. Before it began she placed a glass of water with a single sunflower on top of her cupboard in the living room. She said it was for her Indio, the spirit of a Native American. This cupboard top was her *bóveda*, or altar to the spirits. A candle was lit, and there were two small vases with flowers. A large bowl of perfumed water with flower petals was placed—confectioned so that we could cleanse ourselves before it began. Everyone was wearing a head cloth, including myself, belonging to the spiritual "current" of the person's main *muerto*, her lead protective spirit, as a protective measure. We began the *misa* with prayers and some readings from Kardec's book of prayers. Allan Kardec was the nineteenth-century founder of French *spiritisme*, designed as a scientific-philosophical doctrine. We then sang some ecclesiastical songs, called *plegárias*, and, as is custom with singing, this seemed to open the door to "sight." These songs tell of racially, ethnically, and religiously differentiated casts of spirits (Pérez 2012, 368), evoking different qualities of *fluido* in turn, from most elevated and ephemeral (saints, orichas), to the coarsest (one's ancestors, African spirits). This hierarchy is in complete alignment with a model of racialist spiritual "evolution" in place since the Republic (Román 2007) and before it, which rendered the blackest spirits in need of "refinement" and "civilization." We each took our turn to "cleanse" ourselves with a bottle of cologne, in front of the altar, and with water from the pail with petals (*umiero*). This procedure is not incidental. Leonel, one of my oldest interlocutors, says that *fluidos* can come to take form and depth with both the initial prayers and singing, and with an attention to the *bóveda* itself as the space for the "descent" of spirits. Without it the entry of *fluido* into the space of the *misa* is impossible. Eduardo took the floor.

"As we were singing, there was the spirit of a nun that came with the *plegaria*. She lets me see an altar, and is kneeling before it, with her hands up to the sky, pleading. But while she's kneeling, other nuns arrive and there is an entire *comisión de monjas* that seems to be part of your *cordón*." The "cordón espiritual" is the set of spirit guides the person is thought to be accompanied by, even born with. *Luz y progreso*, light and progress, participants said, signaling an acceptance of these nuns to the *misa*. Eduardo asked Olga, his wife, whether she wanted to add anything to the *cuadro*, literally meaning "painting"—and referring to a vision unfolded in an emergent way in a collective domain. She did. "This spirit comes with the thread (*hilo*) of Obbatalá," one of Santería´s most respected oricha-gods. Olga also said she thought this spirit used to work with children, to care for them, as if she were some sort of Mother Superior in an orphanage. "When you can, to go to church and attend to her." Attending, in this case, means leaving flowers, praying, or lighting a candle.

Olga then began to describe another *cuadro*. She said she saw a "*sombra*" (shadow) of a dark man who comes with a curled snake, sometimes known in Cuba as a "21" (a *maha*, associated in religious Cuban consciousness with diabolical forces or witchcraft, and also a number-image from a popular lottery). "When this 21 retreats, is when this dark *muerto* lets himself be seen. However, this is a spirit that protects you." Berta told them it was the spirit of her father. Olga said that sometimes she felt endowed with special strength, "as if you were a man," and this is due to this spirit's influence. Eduardo came in at this point saying that with the spirit came another one, of a *negro con caldero*, a black man who works "magic." Berta confirmed that this was a spirit of her father's in life—that worked with him in his Afro-Cuban religious endeavors. He said that this was not one of her spirits, but that she benefits from his protection. Several other spirits were subsequently described. Olga told Berta about the spirit of a *negra Africana*, an African woman, who worked with *palos*, literally meaning sticks but also referring to a kind of medicinal botany and magic. She told Berta do a *canasta* (hamper) for her so that she can work, because "it's a weapon she has to do her magic." Eduardo added to this *cuadro*—he said he even saw her working with this *canasta* near the cliffs and the ocean, as if she were throwing things into the sea. Berta said: "*Luz!*, confirming his vision. Olga also described the spirit of an Indio, like a chief, and told her she needs to represent him, and place him 'facing the door', so that he can battle for her better. Rodrigo, a *santero* who was participating in the *misa* confirmed this vision, saying that she should represent him in an icon because the Indios are the ones 'who defend you, the true guardians'. He said that she should offer him irises and sunflowers, to which Eduardo and Olga said, *luz!* The spirit comes with the *hilo de Changó,* meaning associated with the *oricha* that has to do with war and virility, and also irises and sunflowers, adding that she should work with this spirit to strengthen her power for battles. Eduardo said: 'She's religious and she's stuck deep in all this, so she needs strong things, big things', referring to the fact that she needs a proper statue of an Indio," namely, that this needs to be a proper statue, something that can stand, not just a small icon or bust.

Later that day, Eduardo confessed that sometimes in *misas* things don't quite turn out as expected, especially when one is working with neophytes, for instance in rites for the development of mediumship, called *escuelitas* (little schools). He complained that the problem with doing *labores* where there are only a couple of developed mediums is that the *corriente de fluido*—the current or momentum of *fluido*—is easily lost; if the *plegárias* aren't known well by the participants and important rhythm and repetition is lost during the work, the spirits cannot materialize, or pass their messages. The unity in the group is easily dispersed. Concentration is key. He complained that some of his new people were still shy and were reluctant to work on their *cordones* and induce trance, or be induced, and many of them just sat like observers. When the neophytes are the minority, then fluidity and integrity can be maintained. In this *misa,* there were no neophytes, only myself, and I concentrated hard, while trying to keep up with what was occurring. The *cuadros* continued for a while longer. At one point we began to sing a very repetitive song. And Olga, a veteran of spirit possession, was preparing herself for trance. She took her shoes off and her glasses, shut her eyes, and kept singing, although she seemed more and more flustered, unbalanced. Her trance transition was relatively smooth, and soon she was possessed.

At first I thought it was Eduardo's witchcraft spirit (*espiritu de prenda*), Ta Julien, with whom he works regularly, and whom Olga is often possessed by, but then later I understood that it was Olga's. Both Eduardo and Olga are experienced practitioners of Palo Monte, a constellation of ritual practices of Bantu-Congo influence centered around a personalized magical recipient (the *prenda* or *nganga*) thought to contain the bones of a deceased person (Figarola 2006; Ochoa 2010). The *espiritu de prenda* would be the *muerto* of their *cordón* "in charge" of their Palo activities. Each of these would also bear a relation with the *corrientes santorales,* namely, an affinity to one or another *oricha* in the domain of Santería. Their respective *espiritus de prenda* often work together, like a married couple, taking turns to come down on Olga. The spirit commented for a long time on Berta's concerns. He made puffing and growling sounds and was on its feet all the time. He told Berta that she had done almost everything to compliment with the *santio,* a chronotopic linguistic creollization of the African dead referring to *santo* (Wirtz 2016), but that one thing was missing for this to have complete *firmeza,* firmness. With much difficulty in understanding him, I caught something about having to "refresh" her "*krillumba*." Krillumba literally means skull, but in this context seems to refer to Berta's own *nganga.* The spirit made kissing sounds and had its hands on its hips. At one point, he grabbed the *umiero* and began wiping our faces with water, with his hand. The spirit prepared to leave and soon Olga's principal spirit guide, the Indio, came. This was standard procedure in a possession ritual: that a *muerto* from within one's own constitution came to "clear" the body after trance with one from its outer layers, so to speak. She shook quite a few seconds and suddenly the spirit did the prototypical Indian (Native American) salutation sound with his hand on his mouth. Then he left quite violently, leaving Olga shaking and disoriented. She stood for a minute at the *bóveda*, recovering from the trance.

Cosmology and Curves

In an article that explores the "theatre" of *misas espirituales* among a Lucumí community in Chicago, Elizabeth Pérez argues that much of the energy of the rite she analyzes went toward *representing* or *simulating* the spirit guides, whereby "participants assumed the spirits' postures in pursuit of a self-transformation that would collapse the distinctions between actor and audience, living and dead" (2012, 368). While she recognizes that in this ethnographic setting, "one is comprised of many selves, some in accord, others in contention," and that, beginning as "ideal types," such as the Indio, or the Africano, spirits come to distinguish themselves little by little in a buildup of biographical data (ibid., 371), she understands mediums' behavior as a "modeling" of what "they deemed to be the proper coordination and expression of these selves in varying contexts" (ibid., 370). Indeed, Pérez suggests that *misas* set in motion "not only an *imitatio* of the spirits, but also emulation of the mediums" (ibid., 380), in their respective modes of experience-based expertise. Elsewhere (2013), I have also argued that simulation is necessary, if for nothing else than to enable the spirits, as Pérez says, to "recognise themselves in their supplicants' mimicry," and to "materialize in their midst" (ibid., 379). But here I call attention to another fundamental, intangible, often ignored, but phenomenologically central aspect of the *misa*, which is *fluido*. A description of liturgical structures and procedures for interaction falls short of an ethnographic understanding of the all-encompassing moving, metamorphic structure that is *fluido* itself, and the methods for evoking and controlling it.

For instance, in a espiritismo session I was once witness to outside of Havana, in 2005, the importance of bodily posture and movement to the synchronization of collective thought and the invocation of spiritual energies became patent. Mediums wobbled their heads, bodies bent, breathing heavily, stomping on the ground, and waving their arms. This was not an ordinary session. I was with one of the capital's few *espiritismo de cordón* groups. *Cordón* is an especially physical form of espiritismo (most mediums were dripping of sweat by the end of the night), mostly seen in eastern provinces in Cuba. Enrique, the group's leader, told me that these collective exercises unify mediums' minds, allowing for *fluido* to manifest as spirits; they are also a way of controlling the energy of the *muerto* so that it does not damage the medium. This is particularly important when one is first developing one's skills, because *fluido* here is experienced in the body in a totally new way, and some do not know how to "breathe" with it. There is a sheer force of energy produced and moved in a ceremony, or *misa*, he said, that must be managed well. The movement of bodies in turn facilities this flow and reduces the possibility of injury, physical or spiritual.

But this flow cannot just be seen in terms of enactment, simulation, or dramatization, even if these are imperative to its appearance in the first place. In an article published in 2015, I argue that *fluido* can also be conceived as knowledge, one that can accrue, diminish, be blocked, hang suspended, and be sensed and absorbed by bodies that must communicate it (2015b, 518). Impasse in *misas,* the curtailing of messages or spirits, is akin to a collapse in the intensity and flow of *fluido* (ibid., 583). *Fluido* is thus many things: knowledge, spirits and selves-in-potential, information, sensation, and a potential catalyst for spiritual prophecy and healing. My proposal here is to look more deeply at the turns of this *fluido,* which, I argue, are dynamical, complex, and self-referential, and to look at how possession is constituted by the directed movement of *fluido* through particular bodies. However, contrary to Pérez's ethnography, while *misas* are not processes of hapless self-becoming or unbridled improvisation, neither are they bound by ritual structures or norms; rather, the latter tend to serve an initial purpose, after which every *misa* takes its own tone, and form, becoming relatively indeterminate. The more experienced the mediums involved, the more indeterminate, within the parameters of the *misa's* aims, it gets. The structure of the *misa* provides a scaffold for the turns and curves of *fluido,* but it does not contain its content or expression. Only the expertise of the head mediums can ultimately bring it to an end. I continue this section with a brief description of Don Handelman's revolutionary model of ritual, where we can understand *misas* as generating their own interiorities, forming and reforming on their own.

Handelman begins his Introduction with a look at the kinds of modalities he wants to avoid. Firstly, the notion that ritual *represents* social and cultural order; secondly, ritual understood as functional of, or *for,* social order; and thirdly, ritual understood as "yet another arena for the playing out of social, economic, and political competition and conflict" (2004, 2). These are the anthropological models of ritual of Geertz, Levi-Strauss, and Leach, among others. He does not refute that these modalities might work, somewhere, at some point. But he wants to look first at what can be learned from ritual *itself,* before turning to the "connectivities between ritual and wider sociocultural orders" (ibid.). For particular instances, ritual "may be a treasure house of culture and society, epiphenomenally shaped to reflect and to reflect on the latter" (ibid., 3), but this is not something knowable beforehand. In order to reflect upon ritual "in own right," then, no assumptions need to be made in the first instance about relationships obtaining between orders. Handelman's two steps for thinking about this are, first, a separation of the phenomena from its environment, and second, a reinsertion of it into this surround, with the added knowledge of what has been learned about the inner dynamics of the ritual itself (ibid., 4). This second step would then illuminate whether there is some sort of interiority or integrity of the ritual, a space whereby the rite is somewhat autonomous from its surrounding, and would then clarify the exact nature of this relationship (ibid.). Handelman posits the self-organization of a ritual as a key factor in ascertaining whether it does have this autonomy to degrees, or not. Self-organization itself implies emergence, which allows for something *new,* something unpredictable, to be produced from its dynamics. The greater the degree of self-organization, the greater the "curve" is in a ritual, and the less it can be seen as a simple representation, or mirroring, of its social surround: it "arcs away from the immediate embrace of its sociocultural surround and moves towards self-enclosure and increasing self-integrity" (ibid., 12). The torus is the perfect example of this, itself existing through a curving inwards, "through form recognizing itself within itself, and on the basis of this self-integrity moving outwards, driving into broader cosmic and social worlds" (ibid., 13). It is separable, yet inseparable from its environment.

Handelman himself thinks through several examples in his article. His first one betrays a minimal self-enclosure, and is the conversion of Maria Antonia, an Austrian princess, into Marie Antoinette, the wife of the future king of France (ibid., 17). The exchange of identity took place in a pavilion on the Rhine, in a hall that faced France and that also faced Austria on other side. Maria Antonia shed her garments and was dressed in a French trousseau, every gesture "carefully rehearsed" (ibid., 18). Back in France, the Versailles, her new home, architecturally embodied the king. According to Handelman, "the ritual in mid-Rhine has no self-organizing properties. The ritual lacks complexity in relation to itself" (ibid.). Handelman deals with what he calls "bureaucratic" state rituals, such as Nazi parades and Soviet marches, in his book *Models and Mirrors* (1998), whereby these ceremonies are characterized by "regimentation, standardization, and displays of power" (1998, 43), and where the internal dynamic of the rite is one where "nation sees an incisive vision of itself stand forth" (ibid., 44).

The second example demonstrates more curving, and it is taken from Jean Jacques Rousseau's account of a military regiment's dance in eighteenth-century Geneva (2014, 19). It goes as such. In the evening, officers and soldiers gathered around a fountain, holding each other's hands, and dancing to the sounds of drums and fifes. Women and children were already retired, but with such jovial sounds, came to the windows and eventually out onto the street, interrupting the dance. Embraces, laughs, wine-drinking—all this ensued at this point. Rousseau commented how the men wanted to pick up the dance once more, but their heads were spinning with joy and drunkenness, and they didn't know how. Handelman says that the "aesthetic recurrence of rhythmicity and its movement generate their own space/time. Effectively, the dancers and musicians existed in their ritual reality, quite autonomous of the immediate surround" (ibid., 20). The "curves" are evident, from the serpentine line of dancers, the togetherness of the men in physical unison, the winding around (ibid., 19)—the ritual curves into self-enclosure. But then it also *torques* out, into its exterior, into the village, and its other female inhabitants who listen from afar but who then join their men in embraces. "The self-sustaining fold of the dance did not withstand the social surround torqueing into the dancers" (ibid.); instead, the regiment turned into a microcosm of family. This self-referential curvatures can also be gauged, for example, in jazz players' improvisation sessions, where an initial melodic line becomes a cacophony of individual melodies by performers that all somehow respond to another, leading to further disruptions in direction, which are responded to again, and creating a feeling of emergence, not predetermination, in the outcome.

Misas such as the one I have described in the last section create their own curvature—but they do so collectively. These rites work with the motion-inducing power of a group of people, who synchronize to each other's actions and moods. Singing is one aspect of this collective effort that enables sustained involvement, creating what Handelman calls a "boundary loss," a "collective feeling of oneness" (ibid., 41). A participant *participates*—aids in the self-propelling of the ritual—through a dedicated attentiveness of some kind. Song and prayer is one such way—repetition creates conditions for concentration as a group. Repetition itself thickens and deepens the emerging form. Indeed, lack of focus in the group in these situational, participative, and repetitive aspects can lead to the dissipation of *fluido*. I was once in a *misa* in the Cuban summer in 2011, when it was so hot in the room that people found it hard to be continually focused, and began to drift into private conversations. Like Eduardo, whom I mentioned telling off his neophytes, the lead singer chastised the audience, saying, *pónganse para eso para que esto todavía no se vaya* ("put your mind in this so that this doesn't go away yet"), referring to the *fluidos* in the space; the chorus is not that difficult, keep singing, she urged, "so that they may come and tells us things." This collective push toward vital forms of connectivity also implies a kind of posture of receptivity, which includes what Inger Sjørslev has called an "unfocused presence" (2013), which does not discount cognitive focus but instead makes salient a phenomenological one. Attentiveness to the affectations of one's body is central. This is not just about chills; but about images and words becoming suddenly available, emotions that surge unexpectedly, or waves of other forces that become manifest. The inextricability from the movements of others (be they human or not) is what "opens up" perceptual faculties, to paraphrase Kapferer (2002). Possession is the intensive culmination, so to speak, of this *fluido*—its appropriation in a time frame of a moving body in open communion with the *misa's* forces. These forces can come with such intensity that they can dislodge their medium, causing violent and convulsive reactions that can be uncontrollable, even stopping their breathing for moments. It is no coincidence that spiritist experts recommend that neophytes "educate" the spirits that come with the most forceful and patent of *fluidos*. Classifications of the varying kinds of *muertos* come into play here, with an emphasis on those closest, or further, to "matter." Not all possession is the same; the qualities, vibrations, sensations, pains, or aftereffects of different *fluidos* leave their marks, even in trained bodies. In some cases, these consequences are purposeful and the medium embraces them. One elderly, deceased medium I had sporadic contact with, Enriquito, used to "die" when he caught *fluidos* from disruptive *muertos,* such as ones sent by witchcraft. Once incorporated in his body, he would stop breathing for a couple of minutes, before coming to again, recovered, and safe. His assistants told me this was necessary in order for the afflicting *muerto* to "die" for their victim.

Handelman says there are two steps involved in understanding "ritual in its own right." The first is to separate the phenomena from its social surround, and to take this heuristically as far as possible; the second is to reinsert the ritual back into its surround, without slipping into a functionalist understanding (2004, 4). There is firstly a self-enclosure, "organizing the temporary existence of the rite" (ibid., 9), in which we can gauge the curvature of this enfoldment. Curvature here, according to Shapiro, also follows from the depth of the "ecstatic sensory alteration" (2016, 54) people experience in possession episodes. In espiritista *misas,* my argument is that possession is the point at which the curve gets deeper within itself, but where it simultaneously enables the torquing "out" into its surround. It is the ultimate point of communication between the differing aspects of the self. *Muertos* come, as in Olga's trance, to verify, condone, condemn, suggest avenues for self-improvement, which gets taken up by the recipient, who may (or not) take this advice in its stride. *Fluido* here becomes workable information, advice, prophetic speech. It is the moment at which what Handelman calls the "looking inward" becomes the "looking outward" (ibid., 11), literally *into the future*. In Olga's spirit's case, the "outward" element was in the recommendation that Berta "refresh" her "kriullumba," meaning her Palo *nganga*. The torqueing out in espiritismo tends to take material form; it is a material unfolding of interior relations, which has consequences not simply for the integrity of the self and its spirits, but in terms of spatiality (it is an outward-moving cosmogonical project). Spirits become *objectified* as actions (say, ritual modifications, or spirit representations) in their environment. Getting the "spirits into view" thus requires both of these steps.

But there is an order to events in a *misa*. As Handelman notes for a further example of a curved rite in his article, Slovene butchering of pigs (Pig Sticking), the segments in a rite are not interchangeable, or modular; the order cannot be switched (ibid., 23). In the *misa*, this order means an initial preparation to invoke and subsequently manage *fluido*, for instance at the *bóveda*, and with songs. A closing of the ritual is also imperative, lest participants take home with them the "substances" worked in the context of the rite. An interlocutor once told me that, when the messages or the *fluido* begin to harm the medium, then these are "illicit" or "non-authorized" manifestations. They become *perturbaciones*, perturbations. One concerned medium even told me that *fluidos,* especially ones that come from "sick" spirits, can cause the same ailments in the mediums incorporating them. Expertise lies in dispersing these kinds of *fluidos* after the *misa,* as well as in creating the possibilities for group-flow and concerted action around *productive* kinds of fluids, rather than destructive ones. Indeed, self-organization does not preclude, but is *dependent* on such expert guidance. Engaged interaction is what allows for curvature in the first place, and this is enabled in this case by certain previous synergies between the main players, and others constituted in situ.

We find emergent interaction between several actors in this *misa*. Eduardo and Olga would be the obvious synergy, a historical partnership that extends to their respective *nganga* spirits that tend to work like a "couple," as they describe, and rhizomatically with their respective mediums, skipping bodies, so to speak. Another synergetic connection forged was with Rodrigo, who intervened because the *cuadro* under construction suddenly became visible to him, and he was able to "add" to it, with comments on forms of representation and homage to the Indio. Brush strokes onto previous marks and forms on a canvas. This is no small matter. The *cuadro* here encapsulates the rite-in-movement: it changes configuration according to participants and their contributions to its perpetual formation (see Espírito Santo 2015b); it deepens the ritual. This means knowledge in the *misa* cannot be regarded in pure propositional form; instead, it is substantial, something felt physically as a measure of spiritual mobility, a curve turned inward, *into bodies*. Knowledge, in espiritismo, is indeed *felt* as *fluido,* fluidity and fluid, namely spirit presence. Hairs on one's arms stand on end, and a sensation of pure electrical impulse flashes through one's body, indexing a *potential* for knowledge, to be "transduced" (Keane 2013) into propositional, tangible form. As one of the reviewers of this text noted, the *cuadro,* the collective, composite vision, constructed during the course of a *misa,* curves into itself to varying depths, enabling communication between various "deep" actors in the rite—the spirits of those involved in the explicit message making, for instance—but also in the emerging image, which, in fluid form, exemplifies perfectly the aims of a *misa*: to give concrete form to virtualities of various kinds. Both the *cuadro* and the *possession* episode present instances of "torqueing," of absolute openness and service to the "other," of *output*, where interiorities transform into sound forward-thinking advice, or materialities; but they are also shifting boundaries between an inside and outside of a cosmology, and thus must never sit still. They are paradoxical in the sense that they are both constituted by and *permit* movement.

In order to understand this better, I will now look briefly at an ethnographic instance that does not enable spirits "to come into view" in any emergent way. The forms of this ritual are relatively shallow and they do not self-propel, and while they may yield novelty, they do so in ways that do not "fold back into their surround" (2004, 13)—there is no "surplus" to be gleaned, so to speak, no movement toward the restoration of selves. For me this could mean taking a closer look at a *misa* dominated by a single person, where oracular statements from spirit visions are authoritative, top-down, linear. But we should perhaps look at where the curve is truly flat, and there is a clear separation between realities of persons and of spirits. This would be sessions within certain "scientific" spiritist circles in Havana, which I have also studied (2015a). The spirits in the following session are summoned, not interacted with, and leave propositional messages of their whereabouts, missions, or indeed, descriptions of future events. There are no meta-messages or paradoxical boundaries. The episode in question is a session in one of Havana's elite traditional spiritist societies, *Misioneros de Jesús,* a society that sees its birth in early twentieth century with an Independence War veteran, a tailor, who was also a medium. When the session began, the director of the Society, Pastor, gave an introductory speech. Among what he said was that spirits often inspire people during their work, or their speech, even though they don't notice it. "We feel them when they are with us, undeniably, we don't need dramatic demonstrations, like there were in the nineteenth century." This abstraction, so uncommon in spectacular Cuban creole espiritismo, set the tone for what would be perhaps the most somber spirit mediumship sessions I was to witness. Five female mediums sat around a dining room table, with spectators seated with their backs to the walls of the room, away from distraction. The mediums prayed, under their breaths, for a few minutes. Their eyes closed, they "tuned" into what was described to me as the "transmissions." "Good evening, I come from Japan. Goodbye," said the first medium almost imperceptibly. "Good evening, from Miami, I am the unexpected. Goodbye." "Good evening, I am an explosion in the air, on a plane." "Good evening, I am an international survey," and so on, for about thirty minutes. At the end of this, the mediums went quiet again. Then opened their eyes, and got up to leave. The messages here are "ontological inaugurations" (2008, 101), to cite Martin Holbraad, taken authoritatively. Spirits are not emergent; they are nowhere to be found in this linear motionless cosmology. And the people involved in the rite, which can be likened to a cosmic radio of sorts, are exactly the sum of their parts. Spirit and person collapse in the act of parsing single, disconnected sentences of worldly dispersion.

Virtuality and the Self

One does not simply take a religious *camino,* path, because one desires it (Panagiotopoulos 2017). There are multiple agencies that form their own *caminos* in and within one's self and destiny and that create continual chambers of resonance, sometimes "turbulence" (Ochoa 2010), in the furniture of one's life that one must respond to. This turbulence can be felt physically, *inside* one's body, as chills, electric pulses, dreams, visions, or forceful illnesses, or lie beneath the surface of sense-perception or spiritual discernment. Acknowledging "affinity" is one of these responses (Panagiotopoulos 2017), among other things, by giving material and physical-actionable *form* to this alter layer of agency, or in the words of Beliso-De Jesús, of spirit "co-presence" (2015). Form means creating objects to "represent" spirits, receiving initiations or undergoing rites, carrying out certain favors for deities, placing certain ingredients in specific places (such as the river, or the crossroads) to elicit magical efficacy, and a host of other personally relevant activities voiced by the spirits during *misas.* There is no pure division between "realms" of the living and the dead; it is inherently "fuzzy" (see Nielsen 2012). Indeed, in a broader Afro-Cuban religious cosmology where even material "objects," such as the *ngangas* confectioned by Paleros, must be understood as "assemblages" (Palmié 2006), or "entities that revalue" in "networks of becoming" that seek to extend themselves (Ochoa 2010, 405), selfhood must itself be reseen as cosmogonical, world-producing, not substantial, or representational. This means that differentiating between interior and exterior aspects is moot in relation to understanding how selfhoods arise, even though *materiality* is fundamental to the exteriorization and expression of self, with corresponding effects (Espírito Santo 2015a).

Kapferer argues that the force of magic, sorcery, and witchcraft is not directly connected, as many have understood, to social and political life: "Not only is their practice or occurrence motivated in spaces of disjunction, dislocation and discontinuity—in the breaks, blockages and resistances in the flow of everyday life— but also they elaborate their power and potentialities in such disjunctions" (2002, 22). There is a "phantasmagoric space," an "imaginal field" that "opens up within itself" (ibid.), and manifests its own emergent logics (ibid., 23). Kapferer sees Deleuze and Guattari's concept of virtual here as imperative to conceptualize this. They describe the virtual as an "entity formed on a plane of immanence" (1994, 156), which they call the "event." "But the event is pure immanence of what is not actualized or of what remains indifferent to actualization, since its reality does not depend upon it. The event is immaterial, incorporeal, unlivable: pure *reserve*" (ibid.). In a *misa*, there are multiple spaces of virtuality, realms of a "different temporal structure, in which past and future brush shoulders with no mediating present," as Massumi says, paraphrasing Bergson (2002, 31). The "virtuality," or Kapferer's "imaginal field," of a specific ritual, undetermined by environmental factors, creates a space for its own workings, its own imaginings. But while for Keane, when divine worlds are rendered "material," scriptural, they radically transform, materializing across "semiotic modalities" (2013), in espiritismo this materialization must be seen in gradations of "reality"—there is no absolute transduction, which is also what the *misa* shows. Berta's spirits—say, the Indio, or the "shadow" African man – are as virtual as they are real. They must be *pushed* into existing *for her*—this push implies being put to "work" (rather than worshipped), strengthened. Acknowledgment (say, people telling you that you have one or another spirit and you *knowing it*) is only one facet of this "push" into existence; materiality is its flipside, with corollary for the self—*muertos* need to be "known" in the material world. Without their exteriority, then, interiorities, whether we conceive them as selves or as spirits, do not achieve fruition. This existence is achieved by bringing them into the folds of one's consciousness of oneself and then giving them *material* form. These new forms will then have recursive effects on this same self; for instance, once an "African" spirit is constituted as a doll, or icon, he may not simply ask for consumables, such as cigars or sugar-cane liquor, but an initiation of some kind on the part of the person that has represented him. Thus, as Handelman says, the "very forming of selves may become part of the form itself" (forthcoming, 7).

In an article published in 2014 I argued that psyche and spirit are simultaneously encompassed by a self that manifests them simultaneously, plastically. I took my definition of plasticity from Catherine Malabou, for whom "plasticity is the form of alterity without transcendence" (2010, 66). Something "plastic" is at once capable of giving and receiving form. Movement, in the *misa* described above, is equivalent exactly to this dynamic of self/spirit in which there is an "absence of exteriority, which is equally an absence of interiority" (ibid., 67). In espiritista rituals and everyday life more generally, spirit is not other to but *of self*. This is a systemic model, rather than one that discriminates a priori between persons and spirits. But people do not take the "reality" of their spirits in any way for granted. We are not just talking about how "strong" or present one's *muertos* are, but also *who they are*, or have the capacity to *transform* into. In an interview conducted in 2011, Eduardo told me that the spirit can come in "different stages of itself, according to the needs of the situation," for example, as young, or old, or a different identity altogether (*desdobles*). These transformations enable the spirit to have access to different *potestades*, powers of intervention, and knowledge. "The spirit has no form; it can come as anything, even snakes and animals." This means that there is an added level of virtuality in each ritual instance. We must, thus, refrain from regarding even a *muerto* as something static in time or space. The *misa* is an imminently unstable place, one in which all of its elements are in constant motion—across time frames, knowledge spaces, identities, and selves, unfolding themselves in myriad directions. In Berta's case, she understood that she *inherited* one of her father's spirits—the *negro de caldero*. This spirit, in turn, can unfold itself into a whole other "commission" of similar African *muertos* who work magic. There are added layers of virtuality, then. But this also means that the logic of this unfolding has certain rules. It is not a hapless process of endless self-becoming. Instead the ritual itself demarcates the boundaries and thresholds through which spirits on the one hand, and people, on the other, emerge. The specific task at hand—to ask *permission* for a Santería initiation—becomes the driving force for what is "allowed" to manifest as *fluido* in the *misa*.

We can explore Kapferer's work with Singalese rites of exorcism to understand this notion of boundaries more deeply, as well as the essential cosmogonical role of specialists. Kapferer (1997, 15) complains, in a similar point made by Abramson and Holbraad (2014), that "the appearance of cosmologies and social structures as integrated systems is true only if they are abstracted from practice and regarded as coherent wholes, as scholars do but not human beings in routine life" (ibid., 19). Sorcery, like spirit possession and its symbolism, addresses the existential problematics of people, but "take form not as coherent, integrated wholes"; "their meaning is always in the dynamics of their situational production" (ibid., 20). Indeed, sorcery is "internally unstable," "inherently transgressive" (ibid.). It is perhaps no wonder that the Suniyama, the most comprehensive antisorcery ritual, manifests in the ontologically regenerative way that it does. Experts create realities in the exorcistic drama that enfold their victims; major narratives, of the power of kings and conquering heroes in Sri Lanka's history take center stage. But "Suniyama is not a model of or for reality"; it is its own reality, "the dynamic play from which the constructions of reality take form" (ibid., 180). While it is ultimately oriented to the capacity of victims to deal with their actual circumstances, "as a virtuality, the rite does not simply dissolve into reality but brings it forth" (ibid.). Indeed, the ritual activities "open up the perceptual faculties" of victims (ibid., 181) and enable a "slowing down" of time so that the victim can redo his or her world anew. There is a reset of space-time during the rite. The *misa* itself also obeys a different temporality to the world "outside"; *fluido* contains its own historical and futurological seeds, its own virtualities, which furnish the raw material from which the constitution of alter-realities occurs.

Final Note

Possession and a deep collective engagement with *cuadros espirituales* in *misas* are what enable a particular virtuality (*fluido*) to translate into its exteriors—spirits, new elements of the self, information. They are points of transition *between realities*. Both possession and the elaboration of *cuadros* are these transitions, the paradoxical boundaries, where inside becomes out. But they also rely on a simulation of an outside: a performance of, or preparation for, this manifestation. This is where we can observe what Kapferer has called "the volatile site of structuration, neither essentially sacred nor profane" (2002, 23). It is in this virtual space that people meta-communicate, building their own relations to themselves via the myriad objectivations enabled by movement. What is crafted in this reality is not simply free-flowing but dictated by the designs of the *misa* itself and its gatekeepers, whom are, needless to say, not just human. If we take Handelman's understanding of rituals as a starting point, following the previous discussion on self in creole espiritismo, we can argue that spirits "come into view" exactly and simultaneously as selves do as well. The degree of recursivity of a possession rite is related in direct terms with how it incites the actualization of the self's possibilities—*muertos*.

(EN)Spirited Pedagogy: Learning and Simultaneity in Pentecostalism

Bruno Reinhardt

In their introduction to this volume, Shapiro and Espírito Santo propose to engage with possession as an opportunity to reflect about paradox and movement cross-culturally. Their definition of possession is purposively broad, "the transformation of one's own body and self (along with the social relations that constitutes that body-self) by (and to) an Other." The very term possession is eventually displaced by the less specified notion of simultaneity or "the co-presence of two distinct things at the same time in the same frame of reference (or body)," which they establish as a baseline to think about a range of movements fueled by the experience of alterity.

By doing so, I believe Shapiro and Espírito Santo align themselves productively with other scholars of possession (Boddy 1994; Crapanzano & Garrison 1988), who, by recognizing this concept's inherent fluidity, have opted to approach it through a midrange scale of analysis. By midrange I mean definitions of possession that evoke an unspecified permeability between spirits and bodies and accommodate to various inner distinctions, including "central" and "peripheral" (Lewis 2003) cases, "exorcism" and "adoricism" (De Heusch 2007, 151–64), as well as multiple dynamics of cohabitation between non-human agents and human mediums: from African and African-American traditional religions to shamanism, spiritualism, and axial traditions that insert a moral divide between *pneuma* and *daimon*; "clean" and "impure" spirits, such as Islam or Christianity.

Midrange definitions are broader than the restricted uses of possession that associate it exclusively to religious experiences of absolute Self-erasure or "trance," when spirits take "temporary control of bodily and mental functions" (Lambek 1981, 40) and allow mediums to "become a deity" (Stoller 1989, 31). But they are narrower than highly extended uses of this concept, more famously, Gabriel Tarde's approaches to possession as a "universal fact" (2012, 54) and to society itself as "each individual's reciprocal possession, in many highly varied forms, of every other" (51)[1]. Rather than "dissolving the social" (Latour 2002) *a priori* by portraying humans as monads possessed by faith and desire, midrange definitions start more humbly, from within "the religious," despite all its contradictions. But different from restricted definitions, they still allow scholars to trace ethnographically *how possession widens out* as both concept and phenomenon, for instance, how it saturates secular modern compartmentalizations of religion vis-à-vis art (Kramer 1993), politics (Comaroff 1985), or history (Taussig 1987).

Midrange definitions, in sum, enable comparison by recasting possession primarily as a space of problematization inhabited by anthropologists and "natives" alike, rather than a stable phenomenon waiting for an ostensive academic definition. I find this prudent, considering that, as a negative mirror genealogically bound to "possessive individualism" (Johnson 2011), the concept of possession is always politically and ethically charged. Anthropologists might represent Pentecostals or Candomblé practitioner as "possessed" by the Holy Spirit (Robbins 2004, 131) or Orishas (Goldman 2007). Yet, both groups avoid this term, Pentecostals reserving it to demon-subject simultaneity, and Candomblé practitioners preferring incorporation (*incorporação*) to describe Orisha-subject simultaneity, probably for the same reasons.

In this chapter, I would like to explore exactly the differentials in translation (Asad 1986) between anthropological and religious approaches to human/non-human simultaneity. I am especially interested in how Pentecostal simultaneity requires of Holy Spirit-filled subjects to thematize the boundaries between Self and Other *ethically*, and how this may push secular observers to rethink *theoretically* the relation between embodied learning and spiritual agency. In her classic review of the anthropology of possession, Boddy (1994) provides me with a good point of departure. After noticing a paradigmatic shift in this scholarship toward the notion of embodiment (Csordas 1997; Lambek 1993; Taussig 1993), she concludes with a provocation: "Yet, do we not, even here, in attending so fully to embodiment, risk denying the whole of the possession experience, which our informants insist is embodied and disembodied at one and the same time?" (Boddy 1994, 426).

Indeed, since the 1990s, embodiment theories have only expanded their reach in anthropological theory, from phenomenological and cognitive approaches to apprenticeship theory and post-structuralism. In the anthropology of ethics, embodiment and related concepts, such as *habitus*, have been disconnected from Bourdieu's primary concern with social reproduction and explored more immanently, in terms of ethico-religious enskilment or autopoiesis (Faubion 2011; Mahmood 2005). But embodied representations of religion have also been recently questioned, and in terms quite similar to Boddy's earlier insight. Addressing the work of Saba Mahmood, Mittermaier (2012) argues that the pedagogical motif of self-cultivation cannot account for "the otherworldly," an axis of religiosity "that valorizes being acted upon" and includes "dreams, visions, apparitions, spirit possession, prophecy, revelation, the miraculous" (2012, 250). In a more reformist tone, Espírito Santo (2018) argues that in order to consider the dynamics of intra-action between medium and spirits in Cuban Palo Monte, one needs "a concept of discipline that includes entirely novel ways of conceiving 'the self' in 'self-discipline', one that expands the realm of the social to host a sundry array of both human and non-human entities" (2018, 70). The impression that embodied approaches to religion have projected a sense of self-mastery that elides other equally constitutive aspects of religious lifeworlds, such as ethical paradoxes and contingencies, the ungovernable agency of spirits or the uncultivated strata of the human body, has become a diffuse consensus connecting otherwise heterogeneous paradigms in this field, such as ordinary ethics (Lambek 2011), the ontological turn (Holbraad & Pedersen 2017), and affect theory (Bialecki 2015).

In what follows, I draw on my broader research on pastoral training in Ghana and trace the overlapping of embodiment and transcendent excess that characterizes Pentecostal simultaneity. I reconstruct some of the methods whereby converts become competent, or, as they prefer, "mature" vessels for the Holy Spirit, a process in which operations of practical learning follow closely spiritual co-presence, composing an (en)Spirited pedagogy. I argue that Pentecostals do not disavow embodied learning in order to make room for divine agency. However, they do problematize its synonymy with self-mastery. I compare and contrast different set of analogies mobilized by anthropologists and Pentecostals to understand religious learning and highlight how the latter circumvent the apparent paradox between embodiment and being "acted upon" through an atmospheric (Eisenlohr 2018; Reinhardt 2020) sensibility to Self-Spirit simultaneity, closely followed by a metapragmatics (Silverstein 1993) that frames learning as "yielding" to and "flowing" with an exogenous Other. I conclude by proposing two alternative templates for skilled action whose ecological components shed light on (en)Spirited pedagogy's uncoupling of learning from anthropocentric control: orchestration and navigation.

The World as a *Medium*: the Problem of (Atmospheric) Presence

"The shrine is broken, but the spirits are there." This is how Priscilla, aka "Sweet Mother," a Pentecostal prophetess summarized the status of "territorial spirits" during one of our conversations at Atwea Mountains, a famous prayer retreat close to Kumasi. I had asked her about the popularity of "deliverance" or exorcism sessions among popular charismatic churches in Ghana, which may sound paradoxical, given the Pentecostal focus on spiritual rebirth as "breaking with the past" (Meyer 1998). In her response, Priscilla lent an interesting twofold meaning for rupture, as the image of the broken shrine points to both a discontinuity with spiritual agents now considered demonic and their modern overflow beyond the traditional ritual techniques that once kept them under contractual boundaries.

According to Priscilla, demons have been widely unmasked in Ghana since the last and most cogent wave of revival hit the country in the 1980s (Asamoah-Gyadu 2005), but their agency is now even more dispersed into the world, from hidden "family covenants" that transmit deleterious effects across kinship networks to deterritorialized "Internet demons" mobilized by occultic cybercrimes like *sakawa* (Oduro-Frimpong 2014) or the "spirit of masturbation," transmitted through pornographic websites. She told me that spiritual rebirth does prevent Christians from being possessed by demons, but they do not prevent demonic "attacks on their destinies," attempts to sabotage divine blessings.

Priscilla further illustrated her point as follows, extending to the Holy Spirit the same environmental properties she had attributed to demons:

It's like in America or Europe. When it's winter, they turn on the heater. When you switch it off, the heat is still in, but for some time. When fresh air comes, it takes the heat out. You have to be enclosed to enjoy the heat longer. The fresh air will occupy the place. That's the natural flow of things. It's like when you switch the light off. When there's no light, the darkness will take over. The power must be on. If there's a power break, the light is off. [...] You have to keep the zeal: praying and fasting. Also, if you don't obey god, work on your righteousness, the devil will sabotage your covenant with God.

Priscilla's techno-spiritual analogies between the Holy Spirit and an air conditioner or a light switch underline the ecological quality of spiritual agency for Pentecostals. By ecological I mean that she avoids approaching the spiritual world as a transcendental beyond that Christians either "reach out to" or are "attacked from," as if the Holy Spirit, demons, and humans lived in alternative strata of reality ("supernatural" vs. "natural").

Pentecostals' tendency to fuse immanence and transcendence while rendering spiritual agents coeval with life itself requires a specific notion of the medium, which, as I argue elsewhere in more detail (Reinhardt 2020), evades the dominant approach to "the problem of presence" (Engelke 2007) in the anthropology of Christianity, focused on representational economies and semiotic ideologies[2]. According to Priscilla, material entities (including the human body) do not "mediate" otherwise immaterial beings. She posed the world itself as the foremost religious *medium*, a term I use in James Gibson's (1979) ecological sense of something humans dwell in, belong, and relate to, rather than a circumscribable material or linguistic entity. The most fundamental medium for Gibson is the atmosphere (1979, 16–31), a condition of possibility for any kind of perception and communication. Bodies, words, materials, and things matter in atmospheres "not because of how they are represented, but because they have qualities, rhythms, forces, relations, and movements" (Stewart 2011, 445). By charging the world-medium with spiritual agency, Pentecostals endow these atmospheric properties with various religious affordances, which reflect a modular approach to Spirit-subject simultaneity (Reinhardt 2015).

Thomas Kirsch notes that, for charismatic Christians, "the Holy Spirit (...) comes in various 'sizes' and 'shapes', sometimes concentrating its beingness on the most minuscule location, at other times expanding its perimeters over large spatial areas" (2013, 36). He proposes that debates about this spirituality's social portability should take into account the Holy Spirit's own kinematics. Indeed, the simultaneously embodied and environmental qualities of *pneuma* for Pentecostals (de Abreu 2008) often lead them to differentiate God's "presence," which they deem to be everywhere, all the time, from his heterogeneous and dynamic "manifestations," understood as the crossing of a threshold of intensity, rather than an apparition "from beyond." It means that, for this spirituality, semiotic deferral of presence through mediation gives room to an intensive modalization of presence, meaning that The Holy Spirit unfolds in the world as well as within, upon, and across believers, most of the times jointly.[3]

The *Spirit in the world* is the Holy Spirit's first and wildest mode, given its extemporaneousness. It does not pertain to born-again Christians only, since its main driving force is evangelistic: to draw converts through healings, prophecies, and visions. As the charismatic movement expanded in Ghana, this mode of presence became a true magnet for "free riders" (Asamoah-Gyadu 2005, 89), people willing to receive the bonus of spiritual intercession without committing to the onuses of "giving their life to Christ." It propitiates ongoing tensions between the charismatic and the ethical (Faubion 2011, 80–90), which are solved by committed believers (albeit precariously) through formulas like "You cannot keep your miracle without becoming born again," followed by testimonies about blessings that have been "withdrawn" after receivers did not submit to the Christian life.

Conversion entails being filled with the Holy Spirit and cultivating a personal relationship with this agent, accepting it as a teacher, friend, and companion. It includes the duty of living "a Christian life" and the right to reclaim charismatic promises, such as spiritual gifts: speaking in tongues, healing, prophecy, and deliverance. For analytical purposes, I organize post-conversion manifestations into three basic modes, classified by the directionality of the atmospheres they co-gestate (Reinhardt 2020). The *Spirit within* is individualizing, a "still small voice" that emerges from within the vessel, amidst atmospheres of intimacy engendered by techniques of introspection (Luhmann 2012; Reinhardt 2017a). The *Spirit upon* is co-performatic, and falls upon believers during the ecstatic atmospheres of corporate prayers and praise and worship (spiritual songs and dances) (Bialecki 2017, 28–37; Robbins 2009). The *Spirit across* is a transpersonal flow of presence with discernible circuits, often having charismatic leaders as resonance boxes for the transmission of blessings, healing, prophecies, and gifts (Coleman 2009; Reinhardt 2014). I take all these atmospheres and spiritual manifestations as modulations of presence, meaning that they *are* the Holy Spirit, but in self-differentiating motion.

Given their ecological quality, spiritual modes are recursive and concomitant. One may be the target of a public prophecy from a man of God (*Spirit across*) while receiving (or not) an intimate "confirmation" of its authenticity from the *Spirit within*. Such property is best exemplified by what Pentecostals call "discernment" (Luhrmann 2012, 39–71), the Spirit-led capacity to judge if a feeling, an emotion, or a behavior from oneself or from others is "from God" or not. It is Spirit judging the authenticity of Spirit. The fusion between Spirit and Self in discernment often leads converts to "privatize" the first as coeval with themselves: "I felt in *my Spirit* that the preaching was not sound" or "*my Spirit* told me she is a true woman of God." Processes of individuation are constantly interrupted by reassertions of God's transcendent wholeness. For instance, during a lecture on spiritual healing at a Bible school, the reverend warned students that: "God is not a feeling, an emotional thing. But when people don't have it, usually the worship is dry. The presence of the Lord is not only felt by the body. To be in an emotional mood is not God's manifestation." Her intention was to urge students to differentiate humanly produced or induced emotions from divine affects like spiritual "joy."

We realize that embodied sensations do not grant veridiction for Pentecostals. Their triadic personhood of mind, body, and Spirit (in multiple modes) values consciousness as an index of authentic manifestation of *pneuma*, while demonic possession is characterized by lack of consciousness, a mode of unwilling submission compared to slavery. But consciousness also means that the Holy Spirit can always be impersonated or misrecognized, which makes of skepticism a desired ethical disposition internal to this spirituality (Reinhardt 2016). Another major source of critical reflexivity is the Bible. Pentecostals constantly oscillate between valuing the sensorial directedness of the Spirit and the solid truth of the Bible, which they define as "the most perfect prophecy." Formulas like "the Holy Spirit would never contradict the Bible" operate as tools of reflexivity that articulate embodiment and objectification (Lambek 1993). For instance, the Holy Spirit is widely characterized as "gentle and kind" (1 Peter 3:4) in opposition to traditional spirits, which use fear to influence human action.

Finally, Pentecostals' agonistic "spiritual battle theology" has the effect of establishing contingency as the rule, making of Christianity something closer to a state of activity than to a stable religious identity. We recall that prophet Priscilla compared artificial heat and light to the Holy Spirit and natural cold and darkness to demons. According to her, demonic opposition is "the natural flow of things." She characterized the relation between vessel and Spirit as fundamentally artificial, in the sense of anti-entropic. It is swimming against a "natural" demonic tide.

I underlined above how Pentecostal presence saturates the atmospheric medium while borrowing its capacity to be simultaneously visceral and evanescent, ubiquitous and modular, hence embodied and environmental. Far from homogenous, such lifeworld carries multiple inner distinctions and latent action possibilities, including moral and spiritual perils. It requires from converts a good dose of expertise to be properly inhabited. In what follows I address the particularities of learning religion (Berliner & Sarró 2007) for this spirituality.

(En)Spirited Pedagogy: Self-Cultivation as Submission and Attunement

Although Mittermaier's (2012) criticism of the trope of self-cultivation points to an important gap in embodiment-centered approaches to religion, it risks incurring in the mistake of assuming that "being acted upon" and "the otherworldly" are entirely alien to the problem of religious competence. Similar to other religious traditions (Goldman 2007; Halloy & Naumescu 2012), Pentecostals recognize both the ontological self-determinacy of the spiritual world and the fact that converts vary in their charismatic propensities and capacities. Whereas this is partially the effect of grace, of God's distributive decision to empower Christians according to their role in the body of Christ, it is also deemed to reflect different levels of practical knowledge acquisition, hence of commitment to a normative life style, which was the core of Pastor Priscilla's argument.

Having this is mind, my intention is not to overcome the problem of religious pedagogy, but to think about it differently, especially because learning, like any other practice, is accompanied by higher order (metacognitive) frames that establish what is to learn for practitioners, alternative ways of learning to learn (Bateson 1972: 279–308). In this section, I compare some pedagogical templates for religious pedagogy mobilized by anthropologists with emic templates mobilized by my interlocutors, tracing commonalities and frictions.

Following Aristotle's parallel between ethical development and musical craft, Mahmood compares the learning process of pious Muslim women in Egypt to a pianist, "who submits herself to the often painful regime of disciplinary practice, as well as to the hierarchical structure of apprenticeship in order to acquire the ability— the requisite agency—to play the instrument with mastery" (2005, 29). Mahmood brings to the fore aspects of religious pedagogy slightly distinct from Luhrmann (2012), who compares American evangelicals' techniques for hearing God's voice to wine tasters: "Just as in tasting wine, there are categories and rules that help the Christian to sort out what is God from what is not," although "unlike wine, God has no label that can be examined when one pulls the bottle from the paper bag" (2012, 60–61). The two approaches agree that religious enskilment is the embodied effect of rule-governed behavior amidst communities of practice and recognition. However, they also present alternative framings for "self-cultivation," which I will call submission and attunement. I believe both of them are not only present, but also merged in Pentecostal pedagogy.

Mahmood's analogy between the piano and the human body portrays self-cultivation as the embodiment of virtues or "internal goods" (MacIntyre 1984) embedded in prescriptive practices. Such focus on the ethical generativity of religious practice is certainly a component of Pentecostal pedagogy, as underlined by pastor Moses, during one of our conversations at Achimota forest, a prayer retreat in Accra:

> Every Christian must be filled with the Spirit, in-built with the Spirit, and then led, follow the spiritual ways. Now, being a follower of the Spirit of Christ is not something you do at your own free leisure, or free will or free way. Why? You are being led. If somebody is leading you, you must follow the person. As a follower, you don't do what you want. You do what the person being followed desires. So technically, it's being 24 hours with the Spirit. With it, you have to have a prayer life, knowledge of the Word, and also a dedicational life [he meant practicing evangelism, charity, attending church gatherings]. These things go together.

Similarly to Mahmood, pastor Moses framed disciplinary submission as the reshaping of desire (Foucault 1997), understanding the latter not as a force to be constraint, but one to be ethically molded and channeled toward God. Both cases represent a shift from conventional notions of "asceticism" as self-restraint to *askesis* as self-formation (Foucault 2006).

But the Pentecostal body is not only a "self-developable means" (Asad 1997, 47). It is a vessel for God's living Spirit, which also disallows sharp scholarly distinctions between "asceticism" and "mysticism" (Bynum 1991, 53–78). This aspect makes Pentecostal pedagogy closer to Luhrmann's approach, which, different from Mahmood, frames religious learning as attentive sensitivity to an Object or an Other (wine/God), whose properties are deemed "objective" by believers. We could claim that both God and wine "act upon" believers/consumers, but their affective force is actualized with variable degrees of complexity, according to the subject's sensorial competence. Whereas uncommitted wine consumers might be able to distinguish good/bad or sweet/dry wine, oenophiles can distinguish more refined tastes like leather or cherries in the same substance. Pastor Moses stressed this aspect while commenting on God's voice:

> God's voice is sweet and tranquil. You need silence and time to meditate to hear it. God talks to me in many ways. Most of the times it's in the form of dreams. I dream and they come to pass. [...] I anticipate things; people's names and all that. These are all spiritual manifestations. If you believe and receive God, you can feel him practically [...] If you dedicate yourself to him, he'll always be there with you. He said "I will not leave you and not forsake you, and I'll be here until the end of ages." You can invite him. [...] God speaks to his people, but in peaceful, still, gentle manner. So if you want to perceive God's mind, his speech, you have to know how to differentiate cool breeze from rough breeze.

Pastor Moses stressed that "God can be shouting at you," but it will come to no avail if your ears are "deaf" to his voice. He evoked the importance of settings (quiet atmospheres) and mobilized ecological metaphors (cool/rough breeze) as embodied sensorial maps that assist him in the everyday work of discernment, including the capacity to "taste death" or anticipate demonic attacks. Here, disciplinary submission is conflated with spiritual attunement.

The same duality can be found in the "background metaphorics" (Blumenberg 2010, 63) used by Pentecostals to address directly the problem of religious expertise[4]. On the one hand, organic images of nurturance and growth—the difference between "spiritual babies" and "mature Christians," the prescription to "feed in the Word" and exercise one's "prayer muscles"—highlight the centrality of submission to the Christian life. On the other, popular analogies as those between Christians and radio sets emphasize sensitivity to the Spirit's co-constitutive otherness, recasting prescribed practices like praying, fasting, reading, and memorizing the Bible as ways of "tuning in" to the Spirit's frequency.

We realize that, instead of rejecting constructivism defensively, through claims of pure immediacy or incommensurability, Pentecostals develop their own style of constructivism as an attempt to reckon with potential tensions between the technicalities of religious pedagogy and God's sovereign decision to manifest. Such constructivism is not theatrical or linguistic, based upon the opposition between real and representative. We could compare it to the arts of the potter, whose objects are as construed as they are real, although, in this case, subject and object coincide in the pedagogical project of shaping oneself as an apt vessel for the Spirit to "flow," a term I analyze later.

Here, I would like to focus on the emic notion of "yielding," which I consider the most privileged ethnographic entrance into the metapragmatics (Silverstein 1993) of (en)Spirited pedagogy. As Brahinsky rightly notices, "Pentecostals don't speak of cultivation, preferring 'yielding' as a more God-centered depiction of spiritual experience, one that can open to an experience of rupture" (Brahinsky 2013, 405). Learning in (en)Spirit pedagogy is ultimately yielding to God, that is, making proper room for the Spirit to manifest, whenever he wills so. It is the proper frame for the atmospheric articulation (intimate, ecstatic, inter-personal) between modes of presence and types of ritual activity I stressed in the previous section.

Yielding unfolds in a particular temporality, akin to what Bialecki (2017, 22–47) calls the "already/not yet time." This is a time of virtuality, pregnant with real but latent divine events that already impinge upon the present. The gap between "receiving" and "manifesting" spiritual gifts exemplifies the peculiarity of such temporal economy. Most of my interlocutors understood that God had already given them a specific set of spiritual gifts after conversion, but in order for them to manifest, they still had to "yield" to those gifts, which may happen immediately or years after conversion. Such logic of anticipation lends agentive force to pedagogical submission by framing it as yielding, a metapragmatics that accommodates the sovereignty of charisma to practical commitment, including basic pedagogical operations, such as imitation and repetition.

The method of learning how to speak in tongues "out of faith" exemplifies the role of imitation in (en)Spirited pedagogy (Reinhardt 2017a). The convert is expected to mimic glossolalic speech until the Holy Spirit eventually "kicks in" and authenticates the copy. Once infused by spiritual presence, glossolalia is deemed to "mature" or "grow," a process often indexed by increase in complexity, variability of rhythms and sounds. Practitioners do not see any contradiction in the method, since they are not imitating the Spirit, but yielding to it, expressing mimetically their desire to speak in tongues[5]. As part of Pentecostals' "meta-language of mimesis" (Lempert 2014, 314)—their "conventionalized, publicly available resources for reflexivity" that "cast behavior as mimetic and give it value" (2014, 390)—imitation is encompassed as yielding. It allows *mimesis* to become (or not) *methexis*—participation of the copy in the original (Taussig 1993)—because it recasts the technicalities of self-cultivation as attunement to an Other.

Similarly to imitation, repetition becomes authorized and cherished by Pentecostals as a modality of yielding, which allows them to embrace its powers while still holding to a Protestant rejection of "ritualism." This is accessed through my interlocutors' most common opinion about Muslims: their thorough ritualization of everyday life is deemed commendable but "cold," that is, devoid of life and Spirit. The climatic difference between "cold" and "warm" repetition is illustrative of how, whenever framed as yielding, repetition infuses habituation with the affective capacity to elicit qualitative changes by crossing intensive thresholds (DeLanda 2005). This particular fusion between disciplinary submission and spiritual attunement is reflected in how Pentecostals value repetition mostly when it articulates habituation (daily cycle of activities) and length (the intensification of a single practice).

Mature Christians are recognized in Ghana as "prayerful" subjects (Reinhardt 2017a), that is, subjects who have developed an embodied disposition to pray habitually, hence to be ethically molded by its internal goods, such as humbleness, temperance, and fortitude. But "prayerful" subjects are also "prayer warriors," individuals able to pray in tongues at great length while developing their "prayer muscles" and "prayer stamina." They acquire such skills quite systematically, by joining a prayer team, going repetitively to "all-night" prayer meetings, or even collecting "prayer points" with friends in order to intercede for them while extending this spiritual exercise in length, for two, three, or four hours. If habituation infuses so-called "rote repetition" with ethical generativity (Mahmood 2005), length amplifies the time the subject spends "in the Spirit," a logic of saturation by presence that catalyzes charismatic experiences, such as visions, prophecies, or be "slain in the Spirit," a peak of spiritual intensification marked by peaceful unconsciousness (the mirror image of fearful demonic possession). Similarly to imitation, repetition can be both disciplinary and alive, habitual and Spirit-filled whenever framed as yielding.

I have argued that (en)Spirited pedagogy embeds a specific conception of learning religion, in which self-cultivation is framed simultaneously as submission and attunement to an Other. By promoting such synthesis, yielding corroborates this spirituality's ontological assumption that presence is modular, that is, embodied and exceedingly environmental, corporeal and atmospheric, while still providing converts with normative tenets on how to dwell in such lifeworld. Yielding postulates the constructedness, hence the variable competency of the human medium, without having to postulate the constructedness of spiritual agency itself, allowing Pentecostals to understand spiritual manifestations in line with Boddy's depiction, as "embodied and disembodied at one and the same time" (1994, 426).

Learning How to Flow: Skill, Performance, Charisma

In the previous section, I showed how, as modalities of yielding, mimesis and repetition are aligned non-contradictorily with charisma, becoming ways of learning how to be "acted upon." In this section, I examine the charismatic *telos* of such practices: to "flow in the Spirit." The technicalities involved in methods like "speaking out of faith" or the rationalized routines of prayerfulness are authenticated a posteriori by the experience of "flowing" they gestate. I argue that "flow" reiterates the synthesis of submission and attunement that characterizes (en)Spirited pedagogy and thematizes reflexively the very gap between embodied skills and eventful performances.

On the one hand, to flow while praying marks the anthropocentric transformation of an "as if" actor, for whom "to have an intention is to prefix that behavior with a thought, plan, or mental representation" into a "skilled practitioner," for whom intentionality "is launched and carried forward in the action itself, and corresponds to the attentive quality of that action" (Ingold 2001, 415). A prayerful subject is the master of an art, and the feeling of flowing indexes the practical sedimentation of a Christian habitus in the believer. Most prayerful converts I interacted with told me that, in their immature years, prayer was an external obligation, a duty they had to constantly be reminded of. Once they started "flowing," prayer became a way of desiring, a disposition, for some, even an addiction (Reinhardt 2017, 57). From this angle, flow can be understood as Pentecostals' version of what Mahmood (2001) calls "rehearsed spontaneity."

On the other hand, to flow while praying also means reaching an optimal experience of attunement to spiritual presence, in line with Luhrmann (2012). From this angle, it also shares many qualities with performance flow (Turner 1974; Csikszentmihalyi 1990), which is slightly distinct from skilled action. In performance theory, flow is the eventful experience whereby a skilled performer becomes one with a practice not habitually, but in motion: "Players in flow may be aware of their actions, but not of the awareness itself. 'The dance danced me'" (Schechner 2003, 97). For Pentecostal, flow is also used to refer to the situated overcoming of the trained body by spiritual agency. Performance and charismatic flows coincide in the experience of exceeding embodied skills through their optimal use or acceleration, something also found in the phenomenon of improvisation.

The gap between embodied skills and contingent performance is key for Pentecostals for additional reasons. The fact that felicitous performances are not granted by skills, which may always misfire, ultimately validates this spirituality by sustaining the transcendence of the Spirit, its disembodied sources. This comes out quite explicitly during the corporate practices and atmospheres I associated above to the *Spirit upon* and the *Spirit across*, given their co-performatic nature. I refer below to the cases of preaching and healing.

Pentecostals consider preaching a Spirit-led practice. However, major churches, such as Lighthouse Chapel International, have no restraint in prescribing to their neophyte minister that imitating their mentors, especially the denomination's founder, is the most efficacious way of learning how to preach (Reinhardt 2017b). Bible school instructors compared the learning of preaching to mundane skills, such as cooking. Similarly to cooking, one learns how to preach by copying familiar figures, those who cook for you, before finding one's own style and "taste." During preaching classes, basic rhetorical techniques were objectified, dissected, and transmitted methodically to students, which were also submitted to "preaching exams" and graded in terms of competence.

Despite all this rationalized training, preaching remained a Spirit-led practice for all involved, which was granted by the difference between skills and performance flow. It is common knowledge that all preachers, including the highly experienced and "anointed," do not flow all the time. After all, the felicity of preaching performances depends on the Spirit's willingness to manifest as well as on environmental conditions that also exceed the preacher, from an adequate setting to a good musical session and a responsive audience. Instructors warned students who did not flow during their exams that their preaching looked like theater or mimicry. It was "dry," lacked life, hence also Spirit. Contrarily, students who had "flown in the anointing"—the oily modulation of charisma deem to animate ministers' performances—were those able to establish conducive atmospheres for spiritual power to flow *through* the techniques they had learned and embodied.

Most well-graded students told me they started preaching to themselves, monitoring their rhetorical decisions, and associated the rise of "the anointing" to both a decrease in consciousness while preaching and the feedback energy released by the responsive audience toward them. Indeed, the final aim of all techniques of persuasion copied from mentors or transmitted in classrooms—eye contact, mobility, call-response formulas, shifts in intonation, and so forth— is to give shape to this synchronized corporate body, a body that flows with the preacher as a conduit for spiritual power. It means that the "preaching anointing" both necessitates and bridges the gap between inactive embodied skills and their concrete enchainment and acceleration into a felicitous co-performance (Reinhardt 2017, 94–8).

A similar process can be found during intercessory practices like healing. During a class on spiritual healing at International Central Gospel Church's Bible school, the instructor warned students that a successful healing ministry requires submission to "a life of prayer and fasting," presenting a morally "clean" vessel for the Spirit, and engaging unashamedly with trial and error, in order to "sharpen" one's healing gift. But he also mentioned conditions entirely alien to a minister's self-cultivation, such as the fact that "the flock is also supposed to help."

He illustrated this by recalling a crusade he organized at an Ewe town. "We brought a lot of people from our church. But they were the only ones singing the songs. The attitude of the locals was like: 'Come on! Prophecy!'" According to the reverend, the crowd's impatience and lack of involvement during worship were "blocking the anointing," which led a student to interrupt him: "Yes, reverend. 'I feel the presence of the Lord'. 'The presence is here'. All this has become a jargon. People have the hallelujahs, the jargons, but don't know what is the presence." The instructor agreed with the student, but also recognized his own responsibility in the ritual misfire: he was singing worship songs in English, which the local audience was not familiar with. He then presented the strategies that enabled him to "unblock" the anointing flow that night.

First, he expanded the praise and worship session beyond its initially set limits and introduced some classic songs in Twi, which increased co-participation. Then he invited an Ewe man from his congregation to sing songs in his native language, which "fired up" the audience. His diagnostic about the crowd's initial indifference and his decisions on how to overcome it were fast and successful, and he attributed them to the Holy Spirit's guidance, to discernment. After the musical section was over, everyone could "feel in the air" something had changed. "The anointing was there." After that he was "flowing mightily" in his healings ministry and was able to cure the sick and save souls.

The two cases above illustrate how the persisting gap between acquired skills and eventful performances is absolutely necessary to a spirituality in which the experience of Self-Spirit simultaneity is both individualizing and atmospheric. In the first section, I qualified the *Spirit across*, the mode of presence exemplified by "the anointing," as interpersonal. I purposively chose this term over intersubjective because it indicates that the Holy Spirit manifests amidst collective arrangements based not upon reciprocity of perspectives between minister and audience, but upon a shared overcoming of these multiple selves vis-à-vis a common Other in motion. It is an atmospheric identity vis-à-vis a disembodied Other which exceeds them simultaneously. Although views about the power of men of God vary greatly in Ghanaian popular culture, experienced believers often portray "anointed" ministers as "plugs" (Reinhardt 2020), that is, not as sources of spiritual presence, but as conduits, amplifiers, and scale transformers.

Concluding Remarks: Religious Orchestration and Navigation

In this chapter, I approached possession as a field of problematization and strove toward an anthropological translation of Pentecostal simultaneity that acknowledged, rather than opposed, its embodied and disembodied, cultivated and extra-human facets. I pursued that by articulating this spirituality's atmospheric engagement with spiritual co-presence with the practices and frames mobilized by believers to couple and distribute perception and agency. The task of conveying how (en)Spirited pedagogy constantly conflates disciplinary submission and attunement to a "quintessential other" (Boddy 1988) led my argument to oscillate between various etic and emic models for learning religion, analogies that ranged from piano players, wine tasters, and potters to warriors, athletes, radios, home cooks, and plugs. This repertoire corroborates Wagner's (1981 [1975]) argument that culture is represented and produced by both anthropologists and "natives" through ongoing analogical labor. My intention was to approach the problem of simultaneity as an opportunity to think through the fertile frictions between these different scales of inquiry and creativity, which also underlines how "paradox" might have different implications whenever approached through propositional or performative, cognitive or ethical stances (Lambek 2016). I would like to conclude by pointing to two other secular analogues whose ecological attributes add clarity to how Pentecostals' circumvent the apparent paradox between charisma and enskilment.

Experienced men of God display the disciplinary vigor of virtuosi pianists, fierce warriors, and resilient athletes, but a good part of their métier is closer to that of a *maestro*, someone who draws others skillfully into co-performance through a suggestive rather than controlling influence (Ivakhiv 2003). It means that a minister's relation to settings and audiences is as visceral and fragile as his relation to the Holy Spirit. Both are fundamentally atmospheric. Ministers' orchestrating techniques simply set the conditions for the Spirit to "kick in" and assume protagonism. They move one step forward to invite or usher in divine presence submissively, and two steps back to let it flow. This is what yielding means at both individual and collective levels. The purpose of Bible schools is basically to teach neophyte ministers how to orchestrate "atmospheric attunements" (Stewart 2011). They objectify and transfer to apprentices highly standardized techniques that, once orchestrated effectively in practice, have the curious capacity to dissolve their very artificial "foregroundedness" into the pervasive "backgroundness" of the ecological and spiritual medium. As I showed, this is not fundamentally different from learning how to speak in tongues "out of faith."

Repetitive spiritual exercises also render mature Pentecostals well-working spiritual radios, constantly in tune with the Holy Spirit's frequency. They cultivate a refined sensitivity to God akin to that of oenophiles, discerning "cool" from "rough" breeze or "tasting" death. But the object of their attunement is neither a stable frequency nor a bounded substance, like wine. It is a mobile miraculous agent that suffuses the rhythms of the everyday, rather than interrupting it as "the exception." Embodiment in this case must have the ecological quality of skills like *navigation* (Pálsson 1994), the acquired capacity to match perceptual information to a cognitive map while traveling, that is, while taking decisions, changing course, and updating dynamically one's references to what is happening. Again, navigational skills can be seen operating in Pentecostalism at both individual level, as "discernment of spirits," and at a corporate level, when a preacher or a healing minister rapidly fine-tunes her pulpit repertoire in order to rescue their audience's attention and "unblock" the anointing.

Similar to individualized spiritual gifts like discernment and healing or corporate Spirit-led practices like praise and worship and preaching, orchestration and navigation are inherently contingent. They evoke rather than invoke, yield rather than produce. Orchestration and navigation are certainly acquired skills, but they operate not despite, but through shifting environmental contingencies, be those "social" or "natural." By doing so, they help us avoid posing a stark opposition between religious pedagogy and the ontological self-determination of the "otherworldly." They do so by releasing embodiment from its supposed synonymy with anthropocentric control, hence allowing us to grasp analogically the importance of both the embodied and the disembodied aspects of religious pedagogy for Pentecostals.

A Theory of Passage: Paradox and Neo-Pentecostal Expulsion of Demons in Brazil

Matan Shapiro

Introduction

Brazil has for long been regarded a "spiritual marketplace" for religious doctrines, which compete with one another as they promote different theological and cosmological modalities (Chesnut 2007). In this context, spiritual entities frequently take different kinds of ritualized passages within and through the bodies of human mediums. Think, for example, about witchcraft in Afro-Brazilian religious traditions, which is done specifically in order to open passageways wherein spiritual entities of different kinds can flow in order to attack human foes (cf. Shapiro 2016b). Sometimes entities even cross between doctrinal lines to uphold such passages in contexts that are explicitly opposed to one another on political, moral, and spiritual grounds (Birman 2009; Espírito Santo 2016; Selka 2010). The example of practitioners of Afro-Brazilian doctrines whose entities posses them during effervescent neo-Pentecostal rituals may elucidate this point even for those readers who are less familiar with the Brazilian cultural universe (cf. Burdick 1998, 83–8; Fry & Howe 1975; Selka 2010; Silva 2007).[1] In all these cases, "passages" do not only bring into focus new sociological categories, such as those of initiated dancers in Afro-Brazilian religious contexts. Rather, they are also conceived and felt as embodied sensations of movement, a tremor, or a dynamic rush, which have a cosmological context and meaning.

Building on this notion of movement, in this chapter I explore Brazilian neo-Pentecostal exorcism ceremonies, which participants often heuristically call "rites of liberation" from demonic influence. I will show that the expulsion of demons in neo-Pentecostal circles includes two kinds of mutually inclusive passages, which together constitute not only a personal transformation at the psychological level, but also a regeneration of the eternal battle between good and evil; of which the

I wrote this chapter with the financial support of the ERC Research Project *Egalitarianism: Forms, Processes, Comparisons*, at the Department of Social Anthropology, University of Bergen, Norway. I am grateful to Don Handelman, Martin Holbraad, Hanna Skartveit and Diana Espírito Santo for their comments on earlier drafts of this paper.

intermittent opening and blocking of certain passage is a crucial aspect. The first passage dispels the demons out and away from the body while often also replacing them with the power of Christ or the Word of God. An explicit "closing" or "sealing" of the external surface of the body guarantees that the passage of demons from their cosmic domain into the space of mundane earthly reality is now blocked. The second and consequent passage is defined in moral terms. Here, the once-possessed person literally steps out of a space and time characterized by a moral vacuum—in which there has been no difference between good and evil—to the possibility of making conscious choices and living under the Word of God in a state of moral accountability. Taken together, these two passages create a linear boundary that separates schematically between God and His eternal benevolence to the devil, demons, and other total evils, which remain excluded from the lives of the faithful. It is this cosmic dimension that I will seek to emphasize methodologically, thus also assuming that the ontology of the divine in Brazilian neo-Pentecostalism is something moving, or shifting, rather than something that exists solidly in a predefined way.

Based on the analysis of multiple exorcism rites online—as well as rites I have observed in person during my intermittent studies in the Brazilian state of Maranhão (2007–8; 2009–10; 2016) and with Brazilian neo-Pentecostal devotional travelers in the Holy Land (2015–17)—I develop this argument in three stages. First, I explain how Brazilian pastors exorcise demons, a process that is seen at the grassroots level to purify persons internally while sealing their bodies externally against further evil infiltration. I will survey three main stages, which include (1) the identification of demons, (2) a confrontation with them that results in expulsion, and (3) public testimonies verifying that a novel moral code has indeed been reinstated. Second, I will show that during these expulsion rituals, Brazilian pastors generate a space for non-human forces to move across visible and invisible spaces of cosmic topography. In a dialogue with Tania Luhrmann (2012), whose thoughts on Theory of Mind have been influential in recent academic discussions of possession, I will introduce the term "Theory of Passage" to refer to such actions. In the third and final part of the chapter, I will examine this term in light of this volume's focus on paradoxes.

Neo-Pentecostal Rites of Liberation from Demons in Brazil[2]

The expelling of demons from bodies is a disputed sacramental territory in the vast Christian spiritual landscape in Brazil, which boils down to three main doctrinal approaches: (1) the so-called "historical" Protestant stance, which generally rejects exorcism as a form of idolatry (Burdick 1998); (2) the Catholic Charismatic Renewal movement (CCR), which uses the term "exorcism" (*exorcismo*) to refer to structured rituals exclusively enacted by trained priests under episcopal authorization (Chesnut 2003), and (3) various neo-Pentecostal churches, which actively encourage practitioners to engage in spectacular rituals aimed at the expulsion of malignant entities from their bodies (Birman 2012; Oro 2005). I will focus on this third type of demonic expulsion, which charismatic pastors articulate as a full-scale spiritual warfare between the forces of good and the forces of evil (Giumbelli 2013).

The term "possession" (*possessão*) is used in Brazilian neo-Pentecostal discourse to describe the *continuous* presence of malignant entities in the body, usually in the heart, the liver, or the belly. The Universal Church of the Kingdom of God (*Igreja Universal do Reino de Deus*, hereafter IURD)—one of the largest neo-Pentecostal organizations in contemporary Brazil (Kramer 2005)—defines possession in its website as: "Demonic manifestation that takes place when a demon occupies the spirit of a human being. The Bible teaches us that many demons can enter into a single person's body in order to control his/her thoughts and actions ... Through time the demons prefer hiding themselves so that they can exert control without opposition."[3]

As opposed to the Afro-Brazilian context—where possession episodes are effervescent, intense, and ephemeral (Hayes 2008)—entanglement with demonic entities within this neo-Pentecostal framework could last for years without the afflicted person's awareness of the demon's presence in his or her body. Moreover, whereas possession in Afro-Brazilian religious contexts is untainted by moral impropriety (Halloy 2012; Silva 2007), in neo-Pentecostal circles it is interpreted as the manifestation of "inherent" (or "hereditary") evil (*mal heradado*).

Possession in this context thus indicates long-term unselfconscious subjection to demonic activity, whose residence within the body is seen to cause a multiplicity of negative outcomes (Reinhardt 2007). These might include chronic diseases, problems in the family or the conjugal relationship, depression, poverty, addiction, and misfortune. To cure these afflictions, the entities must be revealed, confronted, and replaced by the Word (or the Spirit) of God. As it relates to the wider context of spiritual worship in Brazil, this neo-Pentecostal discourse of possession demarcates its own unique space for action, which differs from liturgical Catholic demonology because it uses the terms "liberation" (*libertação*) and "discharge" (*descarregar*) instead of exorcism (Chesnut 2007, 80–3).[4] To categorize evil entities, neo-Pentecostal discourse in Brazil borrows several terms form common Afro-Brazilian terminologies, including *encosto/encostado* (a spirit that leans-against or clings onto one's body), *invisível* (invisible), and *espirito do mal* (evil spirit). Brazilian neo-Pentecostals also sometimes use the Christian designations of *demónio* (demon, usually inside the body) and *inimigo* (enemy, affiliated with the devil). This overall terminology constitutes a vocabulary as well as a moral content to this battle between the forces of good and the forces of evil over a person's wellbeing and health (cf. Birman 2012).

Some people actively seek spiritual intervention because they suspect they may be suffering from satanic activity that originated in different forms of witchcraft, gossip, or expressive jealousy. Symptoms can include insomnia, stress, health problems, unexplained aggression, or depressive moods. But according to the common view, sometimes the demons hide so well within the body that the person in question does not even notice their presence there. In different IURD branches across Brazil, congregation members are asked to pass by the altar while church functionaries (*obreiros*) extend their hands and gently roll the congregants' heads on the bases of their necks. In some cases, these functionaries sense an unusual vibration, a tremor or a stiffening of the neck, which incites demons to manifest. When this happens in the space of the church, it demands the intervention of the Pastor. I have seen several people who were effectively coerced into liberation rites by church functionaries in this way. In both these cases—that of an active search for spiritual healing and that of spontaneous involvement—confronting and expelling demons is seen as actively combating the eternal spiritual Enemy. While both men and women equally become possessed, in all cases I have seen in person—and in much of the available material online—charismatic male pastors rather than women enact the ceremonies in which demons are confronted and expelled.[5]

In the contemporary Brazilian neo-Pentecostal social context it is ultimately possible to divide every such rite of liberation into three main consecutive stages: identification, expulsion, and testimony (see also Kapferer 1983).[6] First, the pastor must lure the demon out of its hiding place. When the demon finally reveals itself, this also shuts down or temporarily paralyzes the possessed person's consciousness, who often appears to be in a state of complete cognitive dissociation. Afflicted persons' face expressions in that stage often communicate rage, hate, or otherwise deeply embodied antagonism. Numerous clips available online showcase determined Pastors interviewing one or several entities, exposing their names and at times also foreclosing in great detail what types of "poison" they have injected into the afflicted person's life.[7] These demons commonly talk in low, intimidating, raucous, or devilish voices. Throughout this conversation the body of the possessed person is almost always enfolded into him/herself, either spontaneously due to the power of the demon or under the command of the pastor, who would at times order the demon to twist its hands backward, lower its head, curve its back, bow down, or submissively fall on his knees.[8] Pastors contrarily maintain a stiff, upright posture, one hand holding a microphone while the other typically extended toward the possessed person or pointing up toward the sky. Since demons usually declare that their final goal is to destroy their victim and his or her family, a confrontation must come next.

Following on from this mostly verbal interaction—which includes the identification of one or several demons and the reaffirmation that these demons have indeed been functioning as a chronic adversity in the victim's life—the second stage consists in expelling the intruding entities from the suffering body. At this stage the Pastor authoritatively commands the demon(s) to leave the victim's body, sometimes counting to three before shouting "leave!" (*sái!*). In many occasions congregation members join in and cry out with the Pastor, their hands stretched in the direction of the altar with a typical Pentecostal gesture aimed at both capturing the Holy Spirit of God as it descends on the faithful and project it forward to assist with the expulsion of the demon. It is common for pastors to touch the afflicted persons' forehead at this stage, transmitting their own authority (and maybe also a divine essence) into their bodies, which often curl and spin violently as the demons fight to remain within them. Persons at times literally roll on the ground in agony, shouting hysterically in pain or attempt to hit the pastor and his helpers.

In most cases, the demons do not give in immediately. In every expulsion event I have seen pastors command the demons to leave several times before the afflicted person is freed from their malignant influence. The battle can therefore go on for some time, ranging from just one minute in mild cases up to hours on end during the treatment of "difficult" cases, where thousands and sometimes even millions of demons are identified as possessing a single parson. The São Paulo-based Apostle (*Apostolo*) Agenor Duque, the charismatic leader of the Apostolic Church Plenitude of the Throne of God (Igreja Apostólica Plenitude do Trono de Deus), in fact specializes in liberating large numbers of demons from people's bodies. His church website and YouTube channel showcase dramatic clips in which he conducts elaborate spiritual warfare against these legions of demons, developing long conversations with them on stage, and ultimately expelling them using dramatic rhetorical speech, glossolalia, and evocative music. One clip documents Duque liberating a person who had no less than five million demons in his body.[9]

Crucially, displacing the demons at this stage is frequently accompanied by concrete acts that fill the body instead with the solemn purity of Jesus Christ, the Abrahamic God, the Holy Spirit, or all three. This is done through touch, as I indicated above, but also through evocative requests for Jesus to "enter" the afflicted person's heart and by attaching consecrated objects and substances to the afflicted person's body.[10] For example, during a field trip to Maranhão in August 2016 I participated in a rite in an IURD branch where the pastor sprayed congregation members with an unidentified green substance he called "the great discharger" (*o descarregão*). He used this substance both as a general repellent against demonic activity in church and to exorcise several young women in front of the altar. He later also offered bags of that substance for sale, promising that when it is sprinkled on the floor this substance would expel demonic entities from one's house or office and instead bathe that space with the Spirit of God. In the spectacular rites of liberation that high-profile IURD bishops conduct at the Temple of Solomon in São Paulo, the transmission of this divine essence into bodies may even occur on the pastor's direct request from God, which dramatically knocks possessed persons down on the floor as the Holy Spirit replaces the departing demons.

This act of liberation is also often seen as a concrete "closing" of the body. For example, in a clip published online, a member of the crowd is heard shouting at Apostle Agenor Duque that he will kill him. Duque in response declares that he is accompanied by an Angel of God, who will now pull the demonized person to the stage for confrontation. The man is pushed by unseen forces as Duque incites the entire congregation into ecstasy, occasionally speaking in tongues or asking people to cry out for God's "sword of fire." While the demonized person is wobbly, bent, and convoluted, barely able to walk, his hands behind his back; Duque himself, his helpers, and the crowd of congregants all stand firmly erect with their hands occasionally pointing upward toward the sky or toward the altar. When the person finally arrives on stage Duque embraces him and declares: "this man threatened to kill me. If the demon in him is stronger than the Holy Spirit that is in me, Lord, kill him and kill me too; but if the spirit of God that is in me is bigger (sic) than you ... manifest!" The demonized man then cries in agony and begins to jump uncontrollably. Duque in turn commands him to kneel next to a painting of a Star of David or anoints him by pouring red wine on his head, arms, nape, head, and bare feet. Duque declares: "you are now liberated forever ... you are armoured ... this is closing up [of the body] ... nothing will bother (*atingir*) you." He ultimately asks the person to lift his right hand, and repeat after Duque on the microphone: "Lord, you surround me, from behind and in front. Your hand is [laid] on me. Put you hand [over me]."[11] The sealing of the body, in this case as much as in others I have witnessed, eventually suggests that previously afflicted persons have achieved contact with God, and they can now live by His Word.

The moment of the expulsion of the demon, which is seen as a literal moment of "liberation", is often intense. Afflicted persons collapse, their eyes shut, their body weightless, muscles relaxed. Sometimes they also fall backward to the hands of family members or church functionaries. Several seconds later they nonetheless recover, stand up, and face the pastor, visibly moved, sometimes crying. While it remains unclear where exactly the demons go, in some of the available clips online pastors or narrators indicate they must be getting back to their natural place in the underground kingdom of Satan. I also saw in person at least two events in which demons begged pastors to allow them to return to the Kingdom of God and reunite with Jesus Christ. In most cases, however, it is simply understated that the demons leave earthly reality and travel to a different dimension where they can no longer harm humans. The cosmic battle here produces a moral transformation.[12]

The third and final part concerns the reaffirmation that a tangible transformation has indeed taken place. As I mentioned, at the moment of liberation people often seem shocked, and they sometimes burst into tears. Several minutes later they recover, sometimes announcing that they feel "lighter" or that they have been freed from a heavy burden. Pastors then embrace them or simply ask them to say "*Gloria a Deus*" and thus attest publicly to the mighty power of God. The long-term effects are transmitted and shared through public testimonies. All major neo-Pentecostal denominations in Brazil today regularly record, edit, and broadcast testimonies in their television channels and online social networks (Kramer 2002; Oosterbaan 2011), in which persons report the instantiation of miracles in their lives after the expulsion event. These may include the disappearance of chronic health problems, the unexpected gain of material prosperity, and the reconstruction of broken intimate ties (usually with estranged spouses or children). In these testimonies the once-convoluted, suffering bodies of those who were previously possessed are now straitened-up. They are well dressed, at times wearing expensive jewelry, and they ultimately become a living evidence to the kinds of excessive good and bliss that can be achieved if one allows Jesus Christ to step in and chase the devil out of town. The meaning of liberation here is the ability to act within and under the Word of God.[13]

A Theory of Mind or a Theory of Passage?

Tanya Luhrmann (2012) has recently suggested that the range of spiritual convictions reported to ethnographers may be understood as culture-specific "theories of mind." Luhrmann borrows the term from developmental psychologists Wellman, Cross, and Watson (2001), who coined it to describe how toddlers learn to differentiate their own knowledge of reality from that of meaningful others around them. Adding the element of cultural construction, Luhrmann suggests that "an anthropological theory of mind would ask about the specific features of mind modelled in different social worlds and the way those features shape inference and experience" (2012, 382). While correctly insisting that an anthropological analysis of ethnographic theories of mind cannot be reduced to universalizing psychological claims about how mechanisms of mind work (2012, 383; contra Boyer 2001; Cohen & Barret 2008), Luhrmann also indicates four experiential dimensions that she argues characterize the alterity of mind-theories cross-culturally: (1) boundedness (how porous or bounded the body is taken to be); (2) interiority (how important intentionality is in making claims about reciprocity with external agents);[14] (3) sensorium (how the senses are valued, what is their role in connecting with the divine, and which sense is the most important for such communication to take place); and (4) epistemic stance (what makes knowledge valid, how people classify experience).

Luhrmann focuses mainly on the fourth feature. She argues that a prevalent neo-Pentecostal theory of mind in the contemporary United States surprisingly complies with a secular late-modern epistemic stance, which emphasizes openness, pluralism, and doubt rather than narrow biblical literalism. She bases this proposal on her ethnography with the Vineyard Christian Fellowship in the United States, wherein churchgoers are encouraged to employ their imagination and their ability to play with observed reality on a regular basis. In such intervals, for example, God is "invited for a coffee" to converse about various mundane issues. Luhrmann argues that congregants thereby invoke an "as if" reality in which God is simultaneously present and absent, a spiritual source of authority that is very real, and then again, fictional. Due to that simultaneity, Luhrmann argues, God ultimately becomes more-than-real, or as she puts that, hyper-real. This is so because empirical experimentalism—which in Euro-American cultural contexts actually connotes with disbelief and the search for observable proof as the final validating mechanism for any hypothesis on the nature of reality—functions here as a medium for the actualization, naturalization, and objectification of His power. Building on a Batesonian approach to play-framing (2000 [1972], 172ff; cf. Handelman 1998, 68), Luhrmann argues that by employing imaginative play-scenarios her interlocutors endow their omnipotent God with an ontological quality, and in this way they prove his existence.[15] She concludes (2012, 383–4):

> The playfulness in the epistemic stance of this American evangelical model of mind makes belief more comfortable for those who live supremely conscious that others do not believe. It is a style of ontological commitment, a way of knowing, that gives the believer the freedom to infer that his or her account of God is in

part fictive (you thought God told you to wear the blue shirt, but maybe you were making that part up) and so gets the believer into belief by sidestepping his or her doubt …. The function of the imaginative play, I suggest, is to make the player's commitment to the serious truth claims embedded in the play more profound by enabling them to suspend disbelief explicitly and then to take the play stance as a real epistemological claim.

This analysis is compelling because it creatively and convincingly shows that as congregants deliberately play with the quintessential ethereality of their God, He is then capable of appearing at once as a constant or monolithic object of faith and as an elusive subjective force capable of dodging and eluding those who attempt to know Him. As such, God becomes both tangible and ephemeral, and this solves the problem of doubt that Luhrmann claims is at the center of believers' world.

It is possible to use Luhrmann's analytical tools—boundedness, interiority, sensorium, and epistemic stance—to compare Brazilian neo-Pentecostals' expulsion rituals to the Vineyard "play" scenarios in the United States. Within this framework, a porous body (boundaries) enables the infiltration of symbolic forces that secretly manipulate a person's autonomous self (interiority) through the numbing of their affective faculties (sensorium) in order to transform them into unselfconscious demonic agents while the person in question remains completely unsuspicious (epistemic stance). The rite of liberation from these demons can then be seen as fully compliant with this theory by way of reversing it: the forces of Good here exploit bodily porousness for the expulsion of evil from people's lives through excessive sensual arousal, which results in the reiteration of God's almightiness and trust in His Word. The final "closing" of the body would then indicate both a measure of emotional mitigation for personal minds suffering from psychological and physical distress (Chesnut 2003) and the formulation of an exemplary moral message directed at the entire community (Bilu 1985).

The problem with this comparison, I suggest, is that it initially assumes that employment of imaginative play in the American case—and by extension the Brazilian use of the idea of "liberation" in the expulsion rituals described above—is primarily directed toward the resolution of the tension between doubt and doubtlessness. Consequently, in both these ethnographic contexts, it is not necessarily God or other divine forces that are at the center of congregants' attention as much as it is their own psychic clarity.

I would like to challenge this conclusion and ask: what theoretical insights can be gained if we change our perspective and assume that Vineyard practitioners' theories of knowledge and intelligibility—much like Brazilian neo-Pentecostals' theory of "liberation under the Word of God"—are both focused on *cosmic passages* rather than on mindful suspension of disbelief? What if that which is at the center of congregants' attention in both these cases is not disillusionment with the possibility of divine salvation but rather God's myriad (and mysterious) channels of enchantment? Or, to put this another way, what if participants in both these social milieus do not in fact cast doubt in the actual *existence* of God, but rather question *when* and *where* He makes himself efficacious in the visible human/earthly world? I now turn to think how this alternative analytical focus on God's manifestation through particular cosmic passages—which replaces a focus on human minds—may inform the analysis of the Brazilian case study I described above.

Paradox and the Theory of Cosmic Passage

A mind-centered focus overlooks the fact that for many of the pastors and congregant involved in the intensive rites I described above, liberation from demonic influence is framed and expressed as the ultimate victory of God and his angels over total evil. Here, different entities are seen to *really* manifest in mundane reality regardless of second-level interpretation such as "doubt," on the one hand, or "belief," on the other (cf. Shapiro 2016a). The expulsion drama is very concrete and "earthly," but the logic that legitimizes it always relies on what participants consider an encompassing cosmological Order. In this Order, God and a variety of demons as well as angels are regularly infused with everyday realities, rather than regarded as reflexive properties of mind (Pina-Cabral 2007). These forces and entities regularly cross dimensions of time and space in the ultimate struggle over control of people's souls. When Brazilian pastors interview demons publicly to expose their evil deeds they consequently also assert cosmologically that these demons have managed to infiltrate into somebody's body and exploit it. The ensuing exorcism or "liberation" is then a manifestation of a *cosmic struggle* as much as it is a social or personal one, and it is aimed at proving that God and His message will eventually prevail (cf. Kramer 2005). I suggest that it is this theory of cosmic struggle, and especially the emphatic description of passages between spatiotemporal dimensions it entails, which should be at the center of our analysis.

The constitution of cosmic passages in the two ethnographic contexts I presented above is also essential for the solving of an inherent paradox, which entails far-reaching cosmological consequences. Think first of the Brazilian case: when demons hide for long periods of time inside people's bodies there is a direct continuity between them and the victim's earthly, everyday reality. This is problematic, and potentially paradoxical, simply because the official theology regards the demons as the "enemy," an anathema, something that is utterly opposed to the human essence, which is created in the image of God. There is an intolerable continuity here between cosmic domains, the human and the demonic, which should ideally remain distinct, antagonistic, and separated. The period during which a person is seen to have been possessed by demons thus reveals a breakdown in the ascribed cosmic order. In the context of the United States, on the other hand, the paradox is locally framed in terms of doubt or a clash between mutually exclusive cosmological explanations, one which is focused on disbelief and the impossibility of the existence of God, and the other which assumes that God is always watching us from a mysterious Beyond. The paradoxes are different, but in both cases they demand action—in Brazil something must be done in order to rearrange the correct cosmic setup so that demons become separated from humans, and in the

United States action is required to prove that God is really an active force in the lives of the faithful.

In both cases, then, a theory of passage is offered as a heuristic device with which church members can reimagine the correct structure of the cosmos, including how different entities move between its different sections. In the Brazilian case, as I have shown, it is the experience and imaginary of the body as divided into internal and external surfaces which supply the pragmatic grounds for this theory to manifest itself as truthful in the lives of the faithful. As the example of Apostolo Agenor Duque above implies, the "closing" of the body after a demon has been expelled cuts the connection between demons and humans. When the passageways are blocked, the moral superiority of the Word of God prevails. A spatial metaphor is employed here to create difference, which people later on recount in their public testimonies (viz. Birman 2012). In the Vineyard context it is the carving of a special dimension through ritualized play scenarios that opens a literal passage for God to manifest, thus strengthening belief in the truthfulness of a biblical cosmic order, which is sustained and celebrated in church. Rather than that construction being a mere psychological tricking of oneself into that belief, I suggest, these play scenarios literally carve out an experiential dimension from the naturally observed phenomenality of the world, a dimension that in this context makes it possible for God to move across cosmic boundaries. While church rituals such as preaching, singing, and praying authoritatively facilitate scripts for collective encounters with God, play here becomes a self-made script tailored individually by actors for the intimate experience of the cosmic order through their senses.

In both cases there is a consequent moral result. In the case of Brazilian neo-Pentecostalism, those who participate in expulsion spectacles come to imagine their own bodies as active elements in the eternal cosmic battle between good and evil. Expelling the demons from the sphere of mundane activity also entails a sense of victory for God in His total moral war against the demons. It is this victory that pastors repeatedly accentuate during these rituals, in addition to the psychological and physical well-being of the afflicted person in question. And in the case of the Vineyard Fellowship in the United States, as Luhrmann shows convincingly (2012, 383), it is the "ontological commitment" to Church theology which is strengthened through the explicit demand to "suspend disbelief." Vineyard magical realism, and Brazilian real magic, if I may put it this way, both assert different moral transformations quite powerfully through different local theories of cosmic passage. As opposed to the problem faced by Vineyard congregants in the United States—a lack of passage, or too little movement between visible and invisible dimensions of the cosmos—Brazilian neo-Pentecostals must restrict an excess of movement. While in the United States congregants must labor to craft or carve an opening for God to manifest, in the Brazilian context a theory of passage is employed in order to block the cracks through which demonic entities might leak into bodies and mundane reality more generally.

The ethnography from both Brazil and the United States, then, makes it possible to problematize the exclusive analytical role of the mind in our own analytic imagination, which locates all human action—including reciprocity with the divine—in the natural world. In this latter framework, all nonobservable agents in social reality are classified as either nonexistent altogether (sometimes as hallucinations) or as fabrications of the imagination (see Espírito-Santo 2016, 97–8). Within this prism a "spiritual" dimension of reality is just another aspect of a singular, all-encompassing Nature (cf. Holbraad 2012). Instead, as I have shown, a focus on local theories of cosmic passage and their intrinsic metaphors of connectivity or separation may allow us to look comparatively at different ethnographic configurations of moral transformations. I suggest that it is this tangible traversing between different cosmic territories, both in the United States and in Brazil, which produces certainty; certainty not in one's own relationship with God, which is regularly solidified through ongoing participation in congregational gatherings and other events (viz. Harding 2000), but in the image of a spatio-spiritual map of the cosmos as it is seen from a pragmatist neo-Pentecostal perspective. Transgression between different cosmic territories, heuristically articulated as a form of passage, here becomes essential for a holistic sense of living and praying and being a moral person in a universe that *evidently and experientially* includes invisible spaces filled with divine grace, where He dwells.

I have now come a full circle to my initial speculation, which holds that quite often ritualized engagements with cosmic passages are not supposed to answer a question about the object of belief, the "what" question. Evidently, that which crosses or manifests is often already described as a matter of fact; it is God or His angels in the context of the United States and it is the demons in the Brazilian case. *That which the passages allow to imagine, then, is when and where cosmic phenomena actually take place.* Here, an organic theory is devised to think of *how* things take place, rather than whether they actually exist at the ontological level. The paradoxical tension between belief and doubt in the Vineyard case, and that between demons and humans in the Brazilian case, thus both seem to be focused less on the a-temporal solidity of God and more on "when" and "where" He will make himself present, jumping across different domains of the cosmos, for His own reasons, occasionally manifesting in some spatiotemporal intervals more than in others.

Conclusion

In a spiritual context characterized by a multiplicity of entities—which means that various different entities and forces are seen to inhabit broad cosmic territories and interpenetrate each other's domain (Handelman 2004)—we almost expect to find a theory of passage. After all, in such cosmological contexts entities are expected to move across boundaries all the time (Handelman 2004; cf. Bastide 1978). Tanya Luhrmann's analysis is so fascinating precisely because it convincingly illustrates how even within a skeptical, positivist, proof-based late-modern Euro-American cultural milieu, the cosmos can be seen to spread across distinct plains of references, some of them invisible or occult, wherein divine grace constantly extends into and recedes back from the human surface of mundane activity. Even in the contemporary United States, these distinct plains of reference only make a conceptual whole when they are empirically verified as structurally interconnected (cf. Birman 2009, 2012). And in order to verify this connectivity, to really know that there are relational areas of both divine and mundane activities, people produce a theory of passage and transfiguration (cf. Butticci 2016). Rather than focusing on mind, in short, I suggest that we can gain much from a comparative analysis of such theories of passage.

I want to demonstrate the methodological scope of this suggestion with two short examples. I will begin with Don Handelman's (1992) analysis of the Indian myths about Lila (the quality of effortless expenditure, the essence of fun) and Maya ("the faculty by which [deities] weave changes into the continually shifting fabric of the phenomenal cosmos") (Handelman 1992, 11). Contemplating on how a cosmos is depicted in myths, Handelman claims that the ways different sociocultural collectives *play* is also directly related to the way they imagine and therefore practice the spatiality of the entire universe. In conversation with Bateson's (2000) idea of play as paradox (cf. Nachmanovitch 2009), Handelman argues that the transformation from "not play" to "play" can be imagined as a journey through a passage, and that by tracking this journey ethnographically we can understand how grand cosmological schemes are organized. The idea of a passage here is premised on Handelman's conviction that conceptual boundaries should not be seen as finite lines, but rather more like border-zones, which include elements of the two sides they separate (cf. Handelman 1998, 241). According to Handelman, then, those cosmological traditions that perceive "the passage to play" as a border zone would differ from those cosmological traditions that perceive that passage as an abrupt cognitive "switch" (viz. Bateson 2000) between different frameworks of interpretation or different grades of reality (cf. Handelman 2004). A "theory of passage" may complement Handelman's conceptualization of border-zones because it would enable us to think about passages that otherwise would have remained ethnographically blocked or disconnected (cf. Espírito Santo 2016, 88).

The second example concerns Claude Lévi-Strauss' famous analysis (1979 [1973]) of an incantation used by shamans among the Kuna in Panama to deal with near-fatal childbirth events. The song, Lévi-Strauss tells us, is used only at times of extreme danger, when the midwife has failed to deliver the baby and the prospects of death become real. The shaman arrives to the hut where the birth-giving woman struggles with pain. He calls upon his spirits, who aid him in the healing process, and then recounts the journey these spirits are taking through an enchanted dreamworld in search of the home of Muu, "the power responsible for the formation of the foetus" (Lévi-Strauss 1979, 319); who has abused her power when she refused to detach the placenta. The journey is dangerous and it includes several obstacles, struggles against wild beasts, and a competition between the shaman himself and the ethereal Muu. Crucially, when the shaman finally wins and a child is born, further measures are made to keep Muu in her enchanted domain, so that she does not attempt to flee and pursue her visitors back to the world of the living.

Lévi-Strauss uses this analysis to compare shamanic healing with Western psychoanalysis, and to proclaim the power of mythmaking as a significant universal device in human psychology, which is able to concretize processes in the social and physical world. But it also becomes possible to think about this process of concretization as one outcome of the enactment and diffusion of a spatial imagination. Quite literally, when the passage for the baby to come is blocked, a shaman is called to infiltrate into the womb, in metaphoric ways, thereby connecting internal and external surfaces as he recounts the perils of the journey. He then entangles these surfaces to achieve a safe birth-giving, and later detaches them from one another, sealing the passage again to restore a clear separation between the inside and the outside.

These two examples join the ethnographic material I presented above to indicate that cultural phenomena, tropes, or metaphors that reveal images of cosmic passages can be seen as the articulation of dynamic paradoxical processes premised on the possibility of continuity between surfaces that are otherwise locally thought to be antagonistic or segregated. A focus on local theories of cosmic passage and their intrinsic metaphors of connectivity or separation may then allow us to look comparatively at such manifestations of paradox, which include the crossing of impossible barriers or thresholds, and see how people "solve" them (or not, at times). It is my conviction that this focus on ethnographic theories of passage, including the moral or other types of transformations they locally entail, will then open a new hermeneutic passage for anthropological exploration.

The Threshold of the Cosmos: Priestly Scriptures and the Shamanic Wilderness in Southwest China

Katherine Swancutt

Thresholds are the *locus classicus* of anthropological theorizing on rites of passage, but in this chapter, I set out to conceptualize the threshold as a shapeshifting space in its own right. To this end, I draw upon my ethnography of the Nuosu, a Tibeto-Burman group of Southwest China, whose priestly and shamanic practices unfold through cosmological passages and within threshold spaces that simultaneously separate and encompass the world(s) around them (cf. Handelman 1992, 1998, 2006; Lash 2012). I do not mean to offer an alternative approach to the ritual process here. Instead, I propose that the threshold has a more elastic and expansive heuristic quality to it than anthropologists often realize. Beyond its celebrated role as the space of transition within a ritual passage, the threshold may alternately bring together and disperse diverse beings in the cosmos.

The Nuosu, who are the subjects of this chapter, reside in the temperate Liangshan (Cool Mountain) highlands of Yunnan and Sichuan provinces, where they are also known by their Chinese ethnonym of Yi, an umbrella term that encompasses multiple ethnic groups across the nation's southwest. My fieldwork among Nuosu has been conducted mostly in the Ninglang Yi Autonomous County of Yunnan, hereafter referred to in Nuosu as Niplat, where I spent much of my time in the company of local priests, shamans, ethnohistorians, and anthropologists. While Nuosu consider that their "traditional" life revolves around agriculture, animal husbandry, and forestry, their religion may be described as animist with some Daoist elements. Both their everyday life and rituals require navigating a multiplicity of thresholds.

Typically, Nuosu consider a threshold (*moptup* ꂿꄲ) to be the raised wooden board or stone sill positioned at the base of their household doorways. However, their notion

I would like to thank Diana Espírito Santo and Matan Shapiro for inviting me to contribute to this volume. This chapter is part of a project that has received funding from the European Research Council (ERC) under the European Union's Horizon 2020 research and innovation programme (grant agreement no. 856543).

of thresholds extends far beyond this to include doorways to the household and its livestock pens, entranceways to courtyards and prestigious vocations, gateways to various strata of the heavens, pathways to and within the wilderness that are crossed by wily ghosts or spirits, cosmological passages along which spirit helpers travel to religious specialists, and ritual passages to be traversed when training to become a priest (*bimox* 毕摩), male shaman (*sunyit* 苏尼), or female shaman (*mopnyit* 莫尼). The Nuosu world and wider cosmos is thus replete with thresholds, some of which are invisible, dangerous, or not meant to be crossed. Many Nuosu are familiar with the Chinese equivalent term for a threshold (*menkan* 门槛), which among the Han ethnic majority refers to a doorsill or step, but is also idiomatic for a "knack," "trick," and in particular a "bartering" threshold, where back-and-forth negotiations are undertaken to obtain something for a cheaper price. Ambiguous, hidden, and even trickster-like qualities therefore pervade both Nuosu and wider Chinese imaginaries of the threshold, which range from the prosaic doorsill to the abstract vision of a portal on a journey or the broker's transactions in a marketplace. Nowhere, though, are the hidden ambiguities of thresholds more apparent among Nuosu than in the crafts of their religious specialists, which harness the powers of priestly scriptures and the shamanic wilderness.

In this chapter, I set out to show ethnographically that thresholds take the form of shapeshifting spaces or cosmological passages within the Nuosu world. I start with a very brief discussion of the classic anthropological literature on thresholds, ritual passages, and liminality before turning to some contemporary studies of recursivity, their connections to my own findings, and related works on Inner Asia, the ethnographic region in which the Nuosu reside. From there, I move on to describe the thresholds that Nuosu priests and shamans cross when acquiring their spirit helpers and learning or practicing their crafts. Since it is the duty of priests and shamans to help ordinary persons navigate a world filled with ghosts, illnesses, and other troubles, I turn to a discussion of Nuosu exorcisms, which are highly common rituals that are often composed of multiple stages and thresholds. My argument throughout is that thresholds are shapeshifting spaces that respond to the pressures of what lie within and outside of them. To underscore this point, I provide one poignant case study featuring the Nuosu priest I call Fijy, who recounted to me his experience of responding to the pressures of spirit helpers and ghosts. Fijy's experience suggests that spirit possession among Nuosu is itself a threshold space that simultaneously separates, even as it encompasses, the priestly and shamanic disciplines. Finally, I conclude with remarks on the value of conceptualizing thresholds as shapeshifting spaces, some of which unfold as cosmological passages, rather than viewing them as static, linear, and hard boundaries that compartmentalize the world into discreet locations.

Anthropological Thresholds, the Liminal, and the Limivoid

It is common knowledge in anthropological circles that Victor Turner popularized Arnold van Gennep's (1960) *The Rites of Passage* through his lifelong study on the social processes, passages, and performances of rituals, art, pilgrimage, and even certain everyday experiences (Turner 1974, 1982, and 1986; see also Thomassen 2014,

78–88). Turner (1967, 97) built upon van Gennep to show that when persons cross the margin, limen, or threshold of a ritual, they have no specific mode of selfhood, but are "betwixt and between" their old selves and the social status and position that they have yet to acquire from their ritual passage. In the wake of Turner, anthropologists have often conceptualized the changes that persons (and many other beings) undergo when crossing a threshold as products of liminality, transition, instability, ambiguity, flow, and even recursivity (although see Bloch 1992, 1–23). Going a step further, some anthropologists have suggested (not always in direct dialogue with Turner) that entire cosmologies may unfold in recursive ways, too (Handelman and Shulman 1997; Espírito Santo 2009, 2013 and 2016; Holbraad 2012).

Revealingly, recursivity is a key theme within Nuosu myth-historical accounts of the world and wider cosmos. Nuosu hold that more than one creation moment gave rise to today's humans and animals, who having been the successors to an earlier population of proto-beings, were later almost wiped out by a flood sent by the sky god, Ngetit Guxnzy (Bender, Aku Wuwu, and Jjivot Zopqu 2019, xxiv, lxviii–lxxiii; Bender 2008, 29–32). Only by joining forces with animal friends did humans survive and ultimately propagate themselves into the future. Accordingly, Nuosu consider that, from ancient times to the present, humans have responded to the incidental, accidental, deliberate, hidden, and serendipitous vicissitudes of daily life, which are shaped not only by the whims of the sky god or forces of nature such as the sun, but also by the interactions of ancestral spirits, mountain spirits, guardian spirits, ghosts, spirit helpers, humans, animals, insects, and a multiplicity of other beings. These myriad beings make for a complex world that priests and shamans often manage by sending spirits, ghosts, and human souls along the paths that would be of greatest assistance to their clients. But to perform these feats, they must summon their spirit helpers from the heavens, wilderness, or some other location to the living environments of their clients, which serve as the threshold spaces for many rituals. The person's living environment is often referred to as "one's own position in the world" (*cyp njuo dde jjo dde* ꍤꆃꄉꐨꄉ), which, among other things, encompasses his or her household and guardian spirits (Swancutt 2021, 20). Priests and shamans must also summon the client's guardian spirits to join forces with their own spirit helpers. Thus, they conduct their work in threshold spaces and along cosmological passages that separate, and simultaneously encompass, the living environments of their clients and the environments of spirits, lost souls, and ghosts.

Notably, these threshold spaces respond not only to the pressures of the various beings that occupy them—including priests, shamans, clients, and sacrificial animals—but also to the pressures of the spirit helpers, ghosts, and human souls that enter and exit them during a ritual. When put under pressure, the Nuosu ritual purview shapeshifts in ways that may cause the living environments of human beings, the wilderness, and even the heavens to overlap. But this overlapping is not exclusive to rituals. Everyday Nuosu life is also filled with moments in which persons inadvertently enter threshold spaces that separate, even as they simultaneously encompass, human habitations and the wilderness. Errands undertaken in villages and the outskirts of cities, such as collecting firewood, shepherding livestock, hunting game, and traveling across a stretch of forested land to visit relatives and friends or reach one's fields, are all activities that can lead persons and their domesticated animals into threshold spaces or along cosmological passages where they may inadvertently cross paths with ghosts or spirits.

Certain newer theorizations of ritual passages and everyday journeys across the landscape suggest that, within Inner Asia, it is not uncommon for the wilderness to be conceptualized as a kind of threshold space or cosmological passage. Morten Axel Pedersen shows that Darhad Mongols (and Mongolians more broadly) distinguish between places of human habitation and the "void" of the wilderness that lies beyond it (2007, 315). He observes that the Mongolian cosmos is composed of "many *parallel worlds*" that persons routinely navigate for herding, hunting and other purposes (Pedersen 2007, 316, emphasis in the original). Crossing the void of the wilderness offers opportunities to harness the powers of renewal, as persons make offerings to safeguard against the latent dangers that it routinely presents "as an unmarked territory, at particular junctures, or rather along specific paths (*güidel*) or tracks (*zam*) of which the social life of humans and nonhumans occur" (Pedersen 2007, 316). Notably, when Mongols relocate to fresh pastures as part of their seasonal nomadic movement, they carry items of veneration and, upon arrival, quickly imbue their new places of habitation with the protection of local spirits that separate them from the surrounding wilderness, even as they harness and encompass its powers (Humphrey 1995, 142–9). New pastures and camps thus become the spiritual centers of the moment until it is time to move on again across a terrain that is often conceptualized as vast and, by human standards, empty. Building upon Deleuze and Guattari's (2004/1992) study of "nomadology," Pedersen further proposes that Mongols juxtapose the "deterritorialised" backdrop of the void to "a 'reterritorialised' grid across which the different nomadic units (persons, households) are moving, or rather jumping, from one point to the next" (Pedersen 2007, 317). Given this, he suggests that Mongolian nomadic movement unfolds "as a sort of intervalic leaping" between pastures in which the person is "abruptly 'jolted' from one singularity to another within the great nomadic void (as a trampolinist)" (ibid.).

There is a sense in which this crossing of the Mongolian wilderness resembles the crossing of a threshold in a rite of passage, *sensu* Turner (1967 and 1969). Just as the ritual passage ideally culminates with a new selfhood and reentrance into everyday society, so the nomadic journey concludes with a resumption of everyday life in more abundant pastures. But the fruits of crossing the void suggest that more is at stake here. Caroline Humphrey and Hürelbaatar Ujeed (2012, 164) point to the "freedom from limitation" that Mongols seek to obtain when beckoning good fortune after moving to a new encampment. Drawing upon Pedersen (2007), they describe these travels through the void as "acts of 'going beyond' social personhood [which] do not frighten the Mongols" because they are meant "to be attained by a subjectivity that temporarily forgets the socially bounded self" (Humphrey and Ujeed 2012, 164). Key to the analysis here is the act of remembering (and then finding) the socially bounded self at a later point in a space that is separated from, even as it encompasses, the energy of the void. In my observation, both Nuosu and Mongols hold in common their responsive approach to threshold spaces, from which they seek to harness the best of both their living environments and the surrounding wilderness (Swancutt 2007, 245–7 and 2012a, 268).

But what about cases in which no return to the everyday is in fact meant to happen? Bjørn Thomassen describes Euro-American extreme sports and thrill-seeking ventures, such as bungee-jumping, which entice persons to leap into the "limivoid" and escape everyday life through "the inciting of near-death experiences, a jump into nothingness, [and] a desperate search for experience in a world of ontological excess" (2014, 16, see also 169). In contrast to the intervalic leaping of Mongolian nomads (à la Pedersen 2007, 317) or the liminality and "liminoid" qualities of performance (*sensu* Turner 1982), those who leap into the limivoid explicitly seek "out-of-the-ordinary" lifestyles (Thomassen 2014, 169). Their leaps are not meant to effect any change or resume everyday life within the social order precisely because their "jump is into a void which is simply … a bottomless void with no other meaning" (Thomassen 2014, 188). No exact counterpart to this exists in the Nuosu world, although I show later in this chapter that Nuosu ghosts come close to experiencing the limivoid when wandering through the wilderness. Eventually, though, these ghosts seek out the food, warmth, and living environments of human homes. Let us, then, consider how persons, spirits, animals, and other beings respond to the pressures exerted upon the Nuosu world, and in particular, the threshold spaces that priests and shamans navigate.

Priestly and Shamanic Thresholds

Learning and practicing the priestly or shamanic crafts requires Nuosu to cross myriad more thresholds than they would do in the course of daily life. Particularly important to this work is the religious specialist's summoning of spirit helpers to the threshold space of a divination, ritual, or other healing session, where they can lend their support. The Nuosu anthropologist Jiarimuji pointed out to me that the term for spirit helpers (*wasa* ꆈꌠ) is composed of two words: *wa* (ꊂ), which means at the back of or behind a person, and *sa* (ꌠ), which refers to either a very happy, good, and comfortable feeling or a secret and typically unseen spirit. After summoning their spirit helpers along the cosmological passages that connect the heavens or wilderness to the threshold space of their craft, priests and shamans often feel their spirit helpers hovering near to their backs, shoulders, necks, and above their heads. There are, though, some notable differences between priests and shamans. Priests must be men, members of specific priestly lineages, and willing to learn scriptures, whereas shamans can be men or women from any lineage and do not read scriptures. This may give the impression that the priestly vocation is built upon a more set repertoire than the shamanic craft. But a closer look reveals that priests often intersperse their formulaic chants with creative and imaginative approaches to spirit possession, which enable them, like shamans, to see ghosts. Conversely, shamans rely upon the powers and inspiration brought to them by their spirit helpers, who inform their ritual exegeses that often resemble the chants of priests.

When Nuosu explain the differences between priests and shamans, they often start by saying that priests are more powerful because they hold an esteemed position or "seat" (*nyix dde* ꑌꅅ) in society and hone their craft over the course of a lifetime. Keeping track of priestly teaching lines is common. Thus, when Fijy was my fieldwork host in Niplat in 2007, he told me that he had traced his own mentorship back to the earliest priests, who in popular Nuosu understanding lived around 4,000 years ago. At the heart of the priest's vocation are the scriptures that they learn to read, write, and interpret from their mentors. While Nuosu often learn something of the priestly vocation from their fathers, they are expected to train under a mentor from outside of their immediate family, such as an uncle or a priest from a different lineage. During their training, priests cross three specific thresholds of learning that are marked by the gifts they give their mentors, starting with a new suit of clothes gifted at the start of their training, followed by a fine horse gifted upon its completion, and culminating with the slaughter of an ox at their mentor's funeral, which the students of a priest perform free of charge out of reverence for the mentorship they received. These gifts are enumerated in a saying that Jiarimuji and my other Nuosu research partners have shared with me: "The priest gifts a suit of clothes when entering [his apprenticeship], he gifts a horse when graduating [from it], and he gifts an ox at the death [of his mentor]" (*bi vur hlat cup, bi jjie mu ma, bi sy le jix*; ꀘꃷꇤꊂ, ꀘꐚꃅꂷ, ꀘꌦꇐꐛ). This emphasis on the lifelong learning of priests resonates with the expectation that they become increasingly powerful with the passing of time, as they expand and refine their knowledge of the scriptures. Still, priests who are quick to acquire their talents may become popular early in life. Especially talented priests grow their reputations by crossing thresholds of learning time and again, facilitated by mentors, self-taught study, and the holding of rituals in which they calmly chant scriptures and invoke their priestly spirit helpers (*bimox wasa* ꀘꂾꃰꌺ).

By contrast, the shaman's vocation is built upon the powers of spirit helpers that descend upon them suddenly from the wilderness, making them behave wildly while sometimes speaking non-intelligible language that resembles the speech of animals. When shamans are possessed by spirit helpers and imbued with the qualities of the wilderness for the first time, they often display powers that are so spectacularly raw and wild as to be overwhelming and even potentially dangerous to themselves. Many Nuosu relish witnessing these awe-inspiring displays of newfound shamanic powers, which bring them into proximity with the void of the wilderness—even if this means that they need to steer clear of a shaman who runs fast enough to literally climb the walls of the home.

To practice effectively, shamans must undergo the ritual for spirit helpers (*wasa hlo* ꃰꌺꉸ), which is a kind of initiation held by a priest. This ritual makes any dangerous spirit helpers, such as the shaman's ancestors who died in youth, into tamer beings. Both the spirit helpers of male shamans (*sunyit wasa* ꌠꆀꃰꌺ) and the spirit helpers of female shamans (*mopnyit wasa* ꂿꆀꃰꌺ) are often traced in some way to actual ancestors who may have died in adolescence, while still childless, which prevented them from entering the ancestral heavens (*Shypmu Ngehxat* ꎁꃅꈔꉙ). Adolescent ancestors reside in the wilderness as unfulfilled and dangerous spirit beings until they descend upon a shaman as spirit helpers. Shamans, however, may trace their spirit helpers to a wide variety of sources. Some shamanic spirit helpers were ancestors who lived a good and full life, during which they obtained outstanding skills and accomplishments. These more fortunate ancestors received the funeral and post-mortuary rites that enabled them to enter the ancestral heavens but chose to leave their skills behind in the wilderness for posterity. Once decoupled from an ancestor, skills take the form of spirit helpers that may suddenly descend upon a person, making him or her a shaman. Notably, the skills of a spirit helper are diverse and not necessarily iconic of the shaman's craft. They can range from expertise in religious practice to mastery of other techniques, such as women's embroidery or the cadre's facility for administration, politics, and bookkeeping. It is therefore not uncommon for Nuosu shamans to acknowledge Han Chinese cadres as their spirit helpers, who bring them leadership skills, political acumen, bureaucratic clout, and a penchant for literacy that is not only associated with Chinese officials but marks them out as persons with a presumed mixed heritage.

Tellingly, any Nuosu person who is known (or suspected) to have non-Nuosu ancestry, and particularly bloodlines traceable to the Han, is considered to be a member of the lower ranks of Nuosu society, which were composed of slaves and serfs until the Democratic Reforms of 1956–7 (Ch. *minzhu gaige* 民主改革). Former slaves with Han ancestry were also appointed as village cadres during the Chinese land reform and collectivization campaigns that unfolded in Nuosu areas, with some of these slaves becoming the shamanic spirit helpers of today. Many spirit helpers from the wilderness, then, evoke ethnic otherness, the slave-like characteristics of non-Nuosu persons, and the threshold spaces that former slaves and persons of slave descent still must routinely cross as members of Nuosu society who, as Ann Maxwell Hill and Eric Diehl observe, remain "somehow outside the system" (2001, 54). Beyond this, both shamans and priests refer to their ritual implements as spirit helpers, which are imbued with the might of their ancestors and typically made from materials gathered from the wilderness, such as wood, bamboo, and in the case of shamanic drums, the hides of animals. Finally, "guardian spirit spirit helpers" (*jjyp lup wasa* ꂷꆦꊈꄉ) that take the form of wild animals, or more commonly a pair of wild animals such as two white tigers or two boars, may assist shamans and occasionally priests or laypersons—albeit usually in less powerful ways than the spirit helper that is traced to an ancestor.

Nuosu consider the wild qualities of shamanic spirit helpers to be both an asset and a liability. This is because the shaman's powers are at their peak when spirit helpers first travel to them along a cosmological passage from the wilderness. In these early days, the threshold space between the shaman's own living environment and that of the wilderness overlaps significantly. However, both shamans and their spirit helpers start to lose their wildest and most potent qualities after the ritual for spirit helpers. I have often heard Nuosu say that shamans' powers diminish significantly within two to three years of practice. Although some shamans may receive new spirit helpers that spontaneously descend upon them from the wilderness, this usually does not enable them to fully regain their former powers. What makes shamans most potent, then, is their ability to become possessed by—even as they simultaneously control—the rawest powers of the wilderness. Nonetheless, Nuosu also admire renowned shamans who have practiced for many years and still manage to evoke something of their original strength.

Altogether, then, the priest's and shaman's crafts can be understood in terms of the cosmological passages from which they acquire their expertise and the threshold spaces in which they practice. Despite the varied prospects and possibilities that priests and shamans face, they routinely summon their spirit helpers from various locations, such as the heavens or wilderness, to the ritual purview. Once joined by their spirit helpers, they take a similar approach to rituals that unfold within a shapeshifting threshold space, which is the subject to which we now turn.

The Shapeshifting Threshold

One chief duty of priests and shamans is to help ordinary persons navigate a world replete with thresholds, which, I suggest, resemble the "Moebius surface" as discussed by Don Handelman in his study of ritual "framing" (2006, 578–81). Perhaps the simplest kind of Mobius surface is the strip of paper fastened into a loop, but with a single twist in it. Whenever put under pressure, a Mobius Strip changes shape, responding either to what has filled it from the inside or what has squeezed it from the outside. Scott Lash therefore calls the Mobius Strip a "topological figure" that will "deform" whenever it is made to encompass or exclude various activities within its bounds (2012, 264). My argument is that, like a Mobius Strip, each of the multiple threshold spaces and cosmological passages within the Nuosu world and wider cosmos shapeshift in response to the pressures exerted within and outside of them. These thresholds and passages are full, active, and hyper-mobile spaces, rather than linear doorways or hard boundaries that compartmentalize the world into discreet and static locations.

Exorcisms, which Nuosu routinely hold within the home, provide a clear example of how priests or shamans, their clients, spirit helpers, and ghosts all put pressure on the threshold space of a ritual. Many exorcisms are composed of a set of three or six rites, for which priests and shamans (often with the help of their clients) obtain plants from the nearby wilderness, which are used to mark out the roads that ghosts should follow when leaving the home. Some exorcisms also involve lining the doorsill of the home, or even the entire doorway, with lengths of thread that bring them sharply into focus. Spirit helpers are summoned at the start of an exorcism to travel along cosmological passages from the heavens, wilderness, or some other place to join the ritual. Having positioned themselves at the back of the priest or shaman, spirit helpers then facilitate the process of luring ghosts into the ritual purview with attractive offerings or effigies that typically are daubed with sacrificial meat and blood. The threshold space of the ritual becomes increasingly filled not only with the religious specialist, his or her spirit helpers, clients, sacrificial animals, effigies, chanting, and the often militant forms of weaponry used to expel ghosts (such as ploughshares heated until they become red-hot in the fire), but also the ghosts who set out to subvert their efforts by entering and exiting the ritual purview at whim, hiding in unexpected corners of the home, and generally seeking to destabilize (if not deform) the ritual purview to avoid being exorcized from it (see Swancutt 2015, 152–5). Long battles that last upward of 48 hours straight between priests or shamans and ghosts are not uncommon, in which they continually respond to the pressures they put on each other.

Now in theory, these battles may lead to fleeting moments of what Diana Espírito Santo and Matan Shapiro (this volume) call "no-alterity," which evokes the structural paradox of simultaneity. In this dramatic condensation of space-time, any sense of alterity—including the distinction between self and other that sets shamans apart from their spirit helpers—implodes so that nothing can be anticipated in advance. Among Nuosu, moments of no-alterity are not desired, but they are common among shamans before they have completed the ritual for spirit helpers. Similarly, these moments can also arise if priests or shamans fail to control their effigies, thus allowing ghosts to imbue the effigies with their presence and effectively transform them into platforms from which to stage a surprise counterattack (Swancutt 2015, 136–7). These dangerous scenarios are ones that priests and shamans, assisted by their spirit helpers, take care to avoid. By watching out for ghosts that clamber into, across, over, and through the ritual purview of an exorcism, priests and shamans seek to prevent them from sabotaging it.

Once ghosts are within reach of being exorcized, priests and shamans expel them across the thresholds of the client's household, courtyard, and livestock pens. This nesting of thresholds within the Nuosu exorcism reveals its fractal, or self-scaling qualities. After the ghosts have been expelled, the lost souls of each client who is present—and sometimes the souls of their livestock too—are called back across these same thresholds (see Swancutt 2012b, S105, see also S113 and Swancutt 2012c, 63). Yet despite the long and arduous labor of exorcisms, they only ever achieve temporary results because ghosts cannot be killed. Nuosu are often quick to point out that whenever ghosts leave a household, they wander in the nearby wilderness for a while before moving on to another household, which eventually will require its own exorcism. Any home that is freed of ghosts will inevitably be invaded by them again in the future.

Seen in this light, the Nuosu world unfolds as a threshold space unto itself, in response to the ghosts that have no stable position within it. Ghosts spend much of their existence as vagabonds in the wilderness, teaming up, disbanding, and joining one another again as erstwhile companions in their mostly limivoid existence, *sensu* Thomassen (2014, 16). Having said this, no one can force a ghost to leap permanently into a limivoid or disappear forever. Priests, shamans, and ordinary Nuosu alike concede that exorcized ghosts are doomed to wander into human homes, courtyards, and livestock pens in search of food, shelter, and clothing—bringing illness and other troubles in their wake. Conversely, ghosts may harm persons and domestic animals when they travel through the wilderness, often by trapping their souls beneath stones so that they cannot return to their owners without a soul-calling ritual. But it is not only ghosts that are a cause for concern; mountain spirits can cause illnesses including madness when angered, particularly when trees within their range of the wilderness are felled. Nuosu do not have much other choice than to keep alert to these dangers, which may put pressure on their living environments and the wilderness until they literally shapeshift (as happens, for example, when new prohibitions on felling trees are introduced due to a particularly aggressive mountain spirit).

The Most Difficult Threshold to Anthropologize

So far, I have shown that Nuosu priests and shamans set out to manage both the threshold spaces in which they practice their crafts and the cosmological passages that connect their clients' living environments to the wilderness. Each of these spaces shapeshift and overlap with one another. I now want to go further by suggesting that what anthropologists sometimes gloss as "spirit possession" also unfolds as a shapeshifting threshold among Nuosu, thereby adding an extra layer of complexity to the routine distinctions they draw between priests and shamans.

As Fijy explained, nearly every priestly spirit helper had in life been a priest himself, who properly received each of his death rites and now assists in the priestly vocation. When invoked, priestly spirit helpers travel along cosmological passages from one of three locations where they tend to reside: the household grounds of their own descendants where they enhance the fertility of the home, the ancestral heavens where the deceased are sent during funerals and post-mortuary rituals, and the spirit capsule (*maddu* ᎮᎲ) that contains an effigy of the deceased and is hidden in a secret cliffside crevice during the final post-mortuary ritual. Each of these locations—along with the scriptures and implements that certain spirit helpers inhabit—can be understood as the living environments of priestly spirit helpers. There is, though, ambiguity surrounding just how wild of a place the cliffside crevice happens to be. On the one hand, it is especially selected as a dry place that will protect the spirit capsule from damp, disturbance, and destruction by animals or the weather. Its secret location conceals the whereabouts of an entire lineage's spirit capsules, which, as Fijy glossed in Chinese, is a collective "graveyard" (*mudi* 墓地) for the dead that is in some sense analogous to the ancestral heavens. Yet on the other hand, the cliffside crevice is part of the wilderness. Priestly spirit helpers thus may bring with them the powers of the heavens, the fertile home, the lineage, and certain qualities of the wilderness that are closely aligned with the ancestors residing in the afterlife.

Two related approaches to spirit possession are thus facilitated by the qualities of the spirit helpers that priests and shamans invoke. Priests typically take a calm, controlled, and measured approach to their craft, in which they chant scriptures in an ideally sonorous, clear, aesthetically pleasing, and powerful voice. Notably, they do not lose their own human and priestly perspectives when practicing their craft. Nuosu views on the priestly vocation are also influenced by the field of "*bimo* studies" (Ch. *bimo xue* 毕摩学), which emerged during the early 1980s as a new form of scholarship on Nuosu priestly religion (Kraef 2014). Collaborative scholarship between Nuosu ethnohistorians and priests has since propounded the view that priests draw their powers predominantly from the scriptures and therefore cannot see ghosts during rituals, even if they are aware that they lurk in the recesses and doorways of the home.

Shamans, by contrast, are renowned for being able to see ghosts. They source their own abilities to their comparatively wild spirit helpers, some of which reside within their drums, bells with fabric tassels, and homemade wooden dowsing rods—all items that have become iconic of shamans across Siberia and Inner Asia (see Oppitz 1998). But while Nuosu shamans may adopt the perspectives of their spirit helpers, they simultaneously strive to retain their human perspectives. This is because the shamans who lose their human perspectives usually hold spectacular but ineffective rituals, in which they communicate through the wild animal language of their spirit helpers. Many Nuosu are quick to point out that shamans need to communicate in human language that can be understood not only by their human clients, but by the ghosts and other unwanted spirits that they seek to expel them from the home.

It is also desirable for shamans to have sonorous, clear, aesthetically pleasing, and powerful voices.

Let us now consider my case study on Fijy, which suggests that spirit possession among Nuosu is itself a threshold space that separates, even as it encompasses, the priestly and shamanic disciplines. On more than one occasion, Fijy told me that he freely draws upon his priestly expertise and the typically shamanic ability of seeing ghosts, which gives him a certain special control over the ways in which ritual events unfold. Fijy told me this even though he has never practiced as a shaman or received shamanic spirit helpers from the wilderness. He explained that it is possible for some persons to master both the priestly and shamanic crafts, in which case they become a "shaman-priest mix" (*nyit bi ssut* ꆅꀜꌠ). However, Fijy declared that this was not the case for him, while assuring me in a jovial and swaggering manner that he can see ghosts without being a shaman because he is an especially powerful priest. Describing how ghosts lurk in the shadows near to the household threshold, Fijy added that they look dishevelled, dirty, and pathetic. Often dressed in rags, ghosts hope not to be noticed or exorcized. A ghost's appearance, then, reflects its own efforts to access the food and warmth of the home without anyone noticing. With a theatrical flair, Fijy asked whether I might wonder how he can see ghosts enter the threshold space of a ritual using both the priestly and shamanic modes of vision.

Offering me his own solution to this puzzle, Fijy reminded me that every shaman must undergo the ritual for spirit helpers that is conducted by a priest. He added that he had once led this ritual, which illustrates the priest's ability to see ghosts and spirits, for a male shaman who was an important leader in his home village. The ritual requires that the priest launches an elaborate exercise for taming the shaman's new spirit helpers. To this end, the priest prepares three cups of distilled white liquor: one that is dirty, another that is clean, and a third that is part dirty, part clean. However, the priest conceals his preparation of the cups so that when he instructs the shaman to collect his "drink," the shaman is forced to rely upon his or her new spirit helpers to guide the way to the clean cup. After drinking from the clean cup, the shaman proceeds to the next phase of the ritual, which requires mustering all the verve and power of the wilderness to collect "food." Assisted by spirit helpers, the shaman must bite the neck of a sacrificed sheep that has been laid out on the floor—and then using only his or her teeth—must swing the whole sheep onto his or her back, without using his or her hands, feet, or anything else. Revealingly, just as the shaman requires the aid of spirit helpers to complete this feat of carrying off food with the strength and style of a wild animal, so the priest must be able to see the spirit helpers himself if he is to officiate at this ritual. A priest must see how the new spirit helpers interact with the shaman to judge whether they have been rendered tame enough to provide the proper assistance for the future. Accordingly, Fijy declared that priestly sight is superior to that of the shaman-in-training, who relies upon the priest to harness his or her shamanic spirit helpers for the first time. Triumphantly, Fijy added that no equivalent rite exists in which a shaman helps the priest to master his spirit helpers.

Having piqued my curiosity, I asked Fijy what it is like for him to hold rituals and if he could sense his spirit helpers working with him. Fijy assured me that he could, telling me that when summoning his spirit helpers, he can feel them arrive. They appear at Fijy's back and, as he gets further involved in chanting scriptures, they rise up to his shoulders where they hover for a moment before continuing up his neckline until they reach just above his head, at which point they arch ever so slightly forward and overhang him. As his spirit helpers move, they create frisson, making Fijy's hair at the back of his neck and on his head stand up slightly. By sensing the arrival and growing presence of his spirit helpers, Fijy knows not only when they have entered the threshold of his craft, but also when they are expanding it with their own presence and putting pressure on any unwanted beings, such as wily ghosts, that are competing for space within it.

Some years later, in summer 2011, I shared Fijy's reflections with his close friend and occasional colleague, the ethnohistorian I call Mitsu, who was trained (among other things) in Marxism Studies in China. As we chatted in his household courtyard in Niplat, Mitsu appeared surprised and told me in a serious tone that it was impossible for Fijy, as a priest, to see ghosts or spirits. Dismissing Fijy's reflections altogether, he assured me that priests must rely on their strength in chanting scriptures precisely because they cannot see or sense where spirits or ghosts happen to be during a ritual. He explained that the priest's strategy is to summon ghosts so powerfully that they cannot fail to enter the ritual purview, whereupon the priest, aided by his spirit helpers, flushes them across the household threshold and out into the wilderness. Not yet willing to give up on Fijy's account, I asked Mitsu whether it might be the case that for certain exceptionally powerful priests, such as Fijy, it is possible to sense the arrival of priestly spirits and see ghosts. In bookish Chinese, Mitsu joked that Fijy could imagine this kind of experience, as he is an extraordinary priest with a vivid "imagination" (*xiangxiang* 想象). But Mitsu grew thoughtful and sober when I pushed him with the follow-up question of whether talented priests use the imagination—much like they use their priestly scriptures or implements, which are spirit helpers in their own right—as a tool for sensing how a ritual unfolds. Quietly, Mitsu admitted that the imagination may be used to access the most noumenal properties of the cosmos. He then voiced aloud this question of wonder: "Who might know what Fijy experiences as a priest?" Spirit possession, Mitsu conceded, requires that priests master otherworldly experiences in imaginative ways that are perhaps never fully accessible to ethnohistorical, ethnological, or anthropological analysis. The priest's use of creativity and the imagination, then, is yet another tool in his arsenal for combatting ghosts and expelling them from the shapeshifting threshold of his own vocation.

Concluding Remarks on Threshold Spaces and Cosmological Passages

Throughout this chapter, I have suggested that the threshold is a shapeshifting space in its own right that simultaneously separates and encompasses the world(s) around it. I have proposed that, like the Mobius surface discussed by Handelman (2006), threshold spaces and cosmological passages may expand, contract, and even "deform" à la Lash (2012) in response to the pressures that humans, spirits, ghosts, and other beings put on them. Reconceptualizing the threshold in this way throws fresh light onto spirit possession, which, as Espírito Santo and Shapiro (this volume) propose, may occasionally become a zone of "no-alterity" that collapses all distinctions between the possessed, such as a novice Nuosu shaman, and his or her wild spirit helpers who do the possessing. However, Nuosu priests and shamans seek to avoid the condition of no-alterity, which prevents them from harnessing their spirit helpers, practicing effectively, and keeping unwanted ghosts or spirits at bay.

Thus, threshold spaces and cosmological passages are important for the recursive qualities they bring to priestly, shamanic, and everyday life. Every Nuosu person must at times engage with the living environments of other human beings, the wilderness, and even the heavens. It is within the threshold spaces that connect these living environments that Nuosu engage with their ancestors, battle with ghosts, access the energies of the wilderness, respond to the vicissitudes of daily life, and reflect upon the legacies of their myth-history. Threshold spaces, then, do not compartmentalize the Nuosu world and wider cosmos into discreet locations with hard boundaries; instead, they open up myriad ways of engaging with them.

Both welcome and dangerous prospects arise from this. Just as the fluidity of threshold spaces and cosmological passages enable Nuosu to harness their spirit helpers and guardian spirits, while benefiting from the support of their ancestors and other vital forces in the world such as the sun, so these same spaces and passages bring with them wily ghosts, spirits, illnesses, and everyday troubles. Nuosu must therefore keep alert to the subversive transgressions of ghosts that slip in and out of these threshold spaces, unsettling and occasionally even deforming the living environments of human beings. To protect themselves from these unwanted incursions, Nuosu invite a priest or shaman to hold an exorcism that will force ghosts to depart from the multiple threshold spaces of the home, exiting through its doorways, livestock pens, and the entrance gates to the courtyard. Once expelled from the home into the wilderness, ghosts are left to resume their wandering, which comes close to approximating a limivoid existence, *sensu* Thomassen (2014). Yet since ghosts cannot be killed and eventually reenter human homes, Nuosu must learn to live with them in the threshold space that connects their own living environments, those of their spirit helpers, and those of wily ghosts.

Perhaps, then, the most salient feature of threshold spaces among Nuosu is that they enable persons to draw creative connections between priestly scriptures and the shamanic wilderness. Assisted by their spirit helpers, creativity, and imagination, priests like Fijy may harness the somatic skills and vision that are closely associated with shamans, thereby gaining access to the often hidden, and unacknowledged, threshold space between the priest's and shaman's craft. By working within the shapeshifting thresholds and cosmological passages between priestly and shamanic expertise, priests like Fijy separate their client's living environments from void of the wilderness, while simultaneously ushering in the energies that it brings. As Mitsu suggests, the priest's penchant for drawing unexpectedly upon the powers of the scriptures and the wilderness is what makes analyzing them a uniquely challenging threshold for anthropologists to cross.

The Mormon Dead

Jon Bialecki

The authors of this edited volume make a vigorous case that, at least as a heuristic, possession is marked by three traits that work to quicken and transform the social: Paradox (in the possessed doubled status as being and not being the physical individual seized), movement (in the form of crossing over uncrossable barriers), and cosmological passages (i.e., "the importance of thresholds or passages as modes of enactment and revelation" capable of constriction and dilation).

As a catalyst to comparative thought, this appears to be a striking innovation. The difficulty, though, is that when the comparative field is only drawn from cases that meet these criteria, the full effects of the underlying phenomenon that the heuristic points to are obscured. Often, it is absence that can be the most telling—or even better, absence that points to other presences that can be laid alongside each other in a series, so that the work done by the underlying phenomenon can be seen clearly. This essay takes that very tack. Drawing on contemporary and nineteenth-century Mormonism, we investigate an instance of intimacy between the living and the dead that logically and experientially teeters on the edge of possession, without falling in. Instead of paradox, movement, and passages, though, the Church of Jesus Christ of Latter-day Saints works to present this intimacy as a knitting together across a stable cosmological divide, rather than as a paradoxical movement across open cosmological passages. There are many reasons why the Church could be taking such a stance, ranging from a protestant inheritance to aesthetic and affective dispositions. However, drawing upon what happened when a nineteenth-century Mormon dissident movement purposefully embraced paradox, movement, and passage instead of hypocognizing or foreclosing those effects, this paper argues that one of the reasons the institutional Church tamps down on these possession-related phenomena is political. Movement and paradox ended being corrosive not only of otherworldly hierarchies, but of this-worldly system of restrictions and controls set up by Brigham Young as he attempted to build up Zion in the Utah Territory. While it may not always do that work, paradox, movement, and cosmological passage can at least in some instances have destabilizing effects, which may explain a recurrent antipathy to possession in many forms of "institutional religion."

Indexing the Dead

Mormons[1] have a name for the particular genre of speech that we will start with: Testimonial. Testimonials are, on one hand, attestations as to the truth of the Bible, of the Book of Mormon, of Joseph Smith as a prophet, and also of the validity of the "prophets, seers, and relevators" who constitute the current leadership of the Church of Jesus Christ of Latter-day Saints. But testimonials are also a means of fashioning an identity and an ethic, and of crafting a self-narrative that one can inhabit. They can be a way to make sly editorial comments on the Church or on fellow believers, of expressing oneself aesthetically, and, when shared before gathered co-believers in a Sunday Sacrament meeting, of performing vulnerability and building community.[2]

But ultimately, for members of the Church Jesus Christ of Latter-day Saints, testimonials in the end are a means of proselytizing. That is certainly the case with this particular testimonial. Unlike most Mormon testimonials, which are usually short improvised talks given in regular Sunday Meetinghouse services, this was one that was practiced, filmed, and edited, so that it could be posted on the Church's lds.org website.[3] The video starts by showing a heavyset, white, Southern Californian man, wearing a generously sized Hawaiian shirt. He begins to talk, describing his childhood in a family that "was LDS, in a very good LDS ward."[4] As he talks, we cut to an image of a decades-old school photo of an awkward towheaded child, presumably our narrator. We cut back to him as he continues his testimonial. After High School, [jump to a grainy, oddly color-saturated picture of him as a smiling, confident young man dressed in high-school-prom white] he tells us that in order to raise money for his time as a missionary, he went off to work in an oil field.[5] But rather than being a step to greater faith, this expedition ends up occasioning a break with the Church. On his return, he tells us, he stops taking his LDS commitment "too seriously."

Excommunication from the Church follows, as does addiction: addictions to alcohol, to drugs, to pornography. He tells us that he got "wilder and wilder." While he recounts this narrative, the video cuts to more still photographs of him as a young man, to contemporary shots of him driving [his fingers tap the wheel nervously], shots of him walking beachside while the waves crash on the sand. In the background, inspirational music swells, and he recounts shaking some of these addictions through a combination of scripture reading and participation in twelve-step programs. He is better, but he is not yet *all* better. He tells us that there were still dependencies that he could not uproot: "coffee and cigs and pornography … and sex and blah, blah, blah." He tells us that despite all his progress, he was still "depressed and despondent." The background music turns slightly maudlin.

We already know, due to the genre we are dealing with, that this is a temporary condition; in time, our testifying narrator will be saved. He will lose his remaining addictions and returns to Church. How he returns, though, is unexpected, and of particular interest to us here. In the video, our narrator recounts a phone conversation with a brother of his. At this point we cut to the brother. He has close-cropped hair and rimless glasses; he is wearing what looks like a funeral directors' suit and a lavender tie. The brother tells us that our lost protagonist was literally "begging the lord" to help him "find a way back." The brother recalls that during this in retrospect pivotal phone call, he mentioned in an offhand way that he had been "indexing." As he says so, the brother leans forward ever so slightly in an almost subliminal moment of emphasis. There is a flicker of a smile on his face.

We cut back to our testimonial narrator and hero. He mentions "indexing" as well, and tells us that on that very same evening, inspired by his brother he "downloaded the program" and "got into it." At this point, we cut a shot of him typing, with the computer screen clearly visible. As the video continues to play, we cut away too quickly to track what is on that computer screen, but if it were to be stopped, what would we see? A gray interface, with various icons on top. Underneath the icons, in the primary space of the "window," we see the fields that he is in the process of filling out. It gives us "record type" that is being filled out as "deceased," "Deceased's Given Name" ("Gina T"), deceased surname (Gronseth), "Deceased's Gender" ("F"), Age (83), "Death Month" ("Apr"), "Death Day" (25), "Death Year" (1979), "Death Town or City" ("Dorvay"); "Death County" and "Death State or Country" are also listed fields. We cut back to our protagonist, now in profile as he enters this data, while in a voiceover he tells us that "almost from the beginning, I could *feel* the Spirit. I could feel a difference." We cut back again to the brother, who tells us that our protagonist called the next day to tell him that he had indexed his first hundred names, and was staring on his next hundred.

And there the transformation begins. Our protagonist realizes that he has gone the longest stretch he could recall not looking in pornography (an achievement that gets him "excited"). Although still excommunicated, he starts talking to people in his bishopric. All sorts of temptations drop away, including internet and TV; and when these dark urges do return, they can be beaten off in "1.2 seconds" by clicking on the "icon" that fires up the indexing program. At long last, he has found a way to conquer himself. He prays, he reads scriptures, he dreams of being re-baptized, and sooner than he imagined he finds himself accepted by his local bishop and once again a full member of the Church. There is a still shot of him in (re)baptismal white, arm wrapped around his brother, as he tells us that he now "just doesn't feel like doing anything wrong when I'm indexing … it brings the spirit almost at will. Redeeming the dead has redeemed me. And it can work for anybody—anybody."[6]

Feeling the Spirit during Missions-to-the-Dead

Indexing is just one part of a larger cosmological project that can be referred to as "missions-to-the-dead." To understand the scope and work of this singular mission, it is crucial not just to address this video testimony, but also the other projects, institutions, and practices that testifying and indexing are imbricated in. This testimonial is not some passing bit of autobiography that has somehow tumbled onto the internet: carefully edited and with impeccable design, it is obviously an idealized presentation. Specifically, it is an idealized picture of how at least some official elements of the Church of Jesus Christ of Latter-day Saints would like believers and potential believers to think about the genealogical work that is an important plank for many of its members. It certainly works to attach faithful genealogical work with faithfulness in itself, as can be seen by the video narrative's culmination in (re)baptism.[7]

But what works as the unstated background to this video is that baptisms of various forms, "indexing," and the dead are already joined in a nexus of multiple cross-cutting contemporary and historical ties. The link between baptism and "indexing" exceeds this single testimonial, much as the link between our testimonial's protagonist and indexing exceeds family ties. Let us start with that latter point and work back toward baptism. The indexing that both our prodigal son and his still-faithful brother were doing was not the creation of a genealogical database of their immediate family members (or at least their family members as narrowly conceived). While researching one's own ancestors was standard practice for part of the twentieth century, the Church now also asks members to do genealogical work classifying data it provides. Other than the hypothetical kinship that comes from a common descent from Adam (a common, but not universal, Mormon understanding), those names that came in batches of a hundred for voluntary data entry by the narrator of the testimony were almost certainly not the names of any relatives of the genealogist's own. Rather, they were names of deceased strangers, pulled from various digitized records that have been gathered by the Church; some of these records may have been pulled from sources that are centuries old. Nor are these names being tended to by him alone. Each name is "indexed" by two different people, in an attempt to ensure that they are being re-recorded correctly (instances of disagreement between two indexers are refereed by a third person).

The indexing here is in service of one what is thought by many as a peculiarly Mormon tradition, the baptizing of the dead. Baptizing the dead has roots in the Church of Jesus Christ of Latter-day Saints that go back to Joseph Smith, the self-proclaimed American prophet that founded the Church in New York, during the opening decades of the nineteenth century. Originally carried out in the rivers and stream surrounding the Mormon settlement of Nauvoo, Illinois, the first instances of this ritual (or "ordinance," as it is referred to by Mormons) featured individuals being baptized as proxies for family members who never had the chance in life hear the Mormon Church's particular variation of Christianity (for instance, Joseph Smith's brother, Hyrum stood as a proxy for Alvin, another Smith brother who had predeceased his siblings) (Baugh, Alexander 2002, 49).

Since those days at the Nauvoo side of the Mississippi river, things have changed. Currently baptizing the dead is a ritual that is now carried out worldwide within the closed confines of Mormon Temples, which are large edifices that are different from the open-to-the-public meetinghouses where Mormons hold their more typical Sunday services. Due to the Church's interest in ensuring the similarity of all temple ordinances, no matter where a temple might be located, the details of the practice are the same in all these locations. During the ritual, an individual dressed in white robes (the "proxy") will be submerged in a large baptismal font that is held up by twelve columns, with each column in the form of an ox. The submerged individual is not being baptized in his or her own name.[8] Rather, he or she is serving as a proxy for a known, dead individual, a person who is believed to have not been baptized (at least during life) in the Church of Jesus Christ of Latter-day Saints.[9]

One usually doesn't serve as a proxy for baptism just once in the course of a single Temple visit. Rather, one typically serves as a proxy on multiple times during any particular Temple outing. This ritual is often repeated with an almost Fordist dedication to mass production. On a single day someone may be baptized in the name of a great number of individuals; in some temples, the names are shown on a TelePrompTer so that the person performing the baptism can read them aloud without having to stop to refer to any documents. The proxies are commonly, but not solely or always, teenage LDS members, brought in as part of their junior high or high school LDS religious educational. There often is a line of young men or women, twelve years or older, with each proxy stepping into the font when another leaves to keep things moving at a pace. It is not completely unknown to be baptized in the name of an actual relative (the church does recommend that one has one's own deceased kin baptized, covering the four previous generations). But such a proxy baptism for a particular known baptism takes some planning, including bringing a church-approved slip naming a particular ancestor. Except for those rare times when the proxy goes out of the way to arrange to be standing in for their kin, one is usually being baptized for an unknown individual who has been pulled from the Church's vast genealogical database and then nominated for baptism by some Church member. This, parenthetically, is much like the rule that one rarely if ever indexes one's own family members; it is the wider project, and not individual ties, that is being attended to here. It is worth noting that at least in Mormon understanding, this act does not coerce the dead to become Mormon; the usual account is that in the afterlife the departed must still willingly accede in some way to the baptism for it to take. But, speaking hypothetically, if Mormon baptism of the dead is effective, and the Mormon cosmological vision is accurate, then it is hard to image under what circumstances the now-baptized dead individual would demur.

Despite the assembly-like, almost anonymous nature of both indexing and of baptism for the dead, for some proxies it can be a peak experience. Recall from our introductory video that when indexing, our testimonial-protagonist felt "the spirit." While other than being informed that it is somehow associated with a sense of peace, a common descriptor used by Saints[10] when speaking about proxy baptism, we are not told what this was like as a sensual experience. Considered that way, it is something akin to what is referred to in both Mormon scripture and speech as a "burning in the bosom," which has been described as a sort of affective surge and cognitive certainty that is used not only to signal the presence of some divine or supernatural force, but also as a mode of confirming some truth. It is an emotional wave of peace or joy that stands apart from other colors of the believers' affective palette; it is sometimes discussed as bordering on the ineffable. Something similar to this burning in the bosom is often reported by the proxies during baptism for the dead. While many people going through this ritual feel nothing, others undergoing the process report an experience of deep peace, a state that is also attributed to "the spirit." This spirit is of course the Holy Spirit.[11] It is also at times referred to as an ineffable "temple"-like experience, marking the particular set-asideness of the Temple as a sacred space.

But the presences sensed during baptism for the dead need not always be the anonymous or abstract Holy Spirit or temple. Sometimes when one is being baptized in the name of specific kin, Saints say that they feel the presence of the individual for whom they are undergoing the baptismal ritual. Many say that they feel "heart of the fathers [turning] to the children, and the heart of the children to their fathers," a phrase taken from Malachi 4:6 in the *Book of Mormon*. (This sense of intergenerational turning is sometimes referred to as the "Spirit of Elijah.") They report feeling connected to their ancestors, even that they are "standing in their place" in some way.

One Saint recounted to me even briefly thinking that he physically saw his grandfather during a proxy-baptism for this ancestor. But there are reports of feelings of palpable presences of the dead during anonymous baptizing as well, of the audible sounds of voices or of other "manifestations." I have heard reports of people becoming "obsessed" with some of these dead for whom they serve as baptismal proxies. Some report experiencing a bit of the personality or sensory impressions that marked the dead during their life on earth; it is as if they momentarily see through the dead's eyes. For a moment they will taste a bit of life as, say, a samurai, or as a civil war soldier, during the baptism.

In short, while not falling into a full paradoxical violation of the principle of identity, this is a moment where the baptized and their proxies can enjoy a degree of entanglement together, and at times can seem to blend into one another. And yet, proxy baptisms do not fall into possession proper, either as an anthropological or local category. This is because this practice is not part of an effort to have the dead cross the borders between the living and themselves. Instead, these ritual and archival works are done to knit the Mormon Dead and the Mormon living together into a kinship system of literally cosmological scale.

"Use a Little Craftiness & Seal All You Can"

Part of this effect of knitting together is due to the use of technologies to standardize and organize baptisms across the vast number of temples where the procedure occurs. In discussing the Mormon dead, different technologies repeatedly appear in different guises at different moments. It can be seen in the index-vetting procedures that help regiment genealogical information. But we can also see technology in the layout and operations of the ritual itself (that TelePrompTer is perhaps not just an incidental aspect of the ritual). And there is also a wider web of recording and archival technology, records management, and storage, in a process that is so audacious that it aspires to document the genealogical facts about every human being who ever lived. But we cannot resort to a kind of lazy technological determinism alone; as we will see, other technologies (such as the planchette) can serve as agents of disruption. Rather, it is the integrative drive that works to shut down possession, creating not an unstable hierarchy of traversing spirits and uncertain identities but instead a cosmic form of kinship.

Again, turning to a particular instance helps concretize this issue. It was 1877, and Wilford Woodruff, current President of the newly opened St. George Temple and apostle in the Church of Jesus Christ of Latter-day Saints, had a series of disquieting visions—or rather, had the same disquieting vision two days in a row.

The temple that Woodruff presided over was the third temple that had been built by the Church. But what was more important, it was the first temple to have been built in Utah, which meant that it was the only one that Utah Mormons had access to (the temple built in Kirkland, Ohio, was under the control of a different Moron group than the one led by Brigham Young, and the Church had lost control of the temple in Nauvoo, Illinois, when a group of anti-Mormon vigilantes had stormed the building in 1846). As such, it was the first post-Utah exodus site where the full run of Mormon endowments (the term used to describe religious rituals) could be carried out.[12] There had also been an "Endowment House" built in Salt Lake City in the interregnum between the abandonment of the Nauvoo Temple and the dedication of the Saint George Temple, but the endowment house only allowed for a limited set of ritual, and for the most part focused on rites for the living.

This would have been a particularly dear accomplishment for Woodruff, who not only was known for a long-running deep interest in what was called "temple work," but was also one of the individuals who had practiced open-air baptisms for the dead in Nauvoo, Illinois, in the period before the Nauvoo Temple had been constructed and dedicated (Baugh 2002; Bennett 2005). Despite this accomplishment, Woodruff was troubled. The scope of baptism for the dead was not enough. Before traveling down to St. George to oversee the temple, he reported that "the spirits of the dead gathered around me, wanting to know why we did not redeem them" (Bennett 2005, 65). In order to placate these spirits and expand the number of possible proxy baptisms, in the first year of the St. George Temple's operation, Woodruff was moved by a vision he had during prayer and broke with the till then standard practice and allowed for people to serve as baptismal proxies for people that they were not related to (Ibid., 65). As we saw in the discussion of contemporary baptism for the dead, allowing for unrelated proxies facilitated the ease with which baptisms could be carried out.

But the reach of post-mortal baptismal font would be extended even further after Woodruff had another vision. On two successive nights in August of 1877, the collected spirits of the signers of the declaration of the Constitution of the United States appeared before his to issue a complaint. As Woodruff reported it, they stated that

> you have had the use of the Endowment House for a number of years, and yet nothing has ever been done for us. We laid the foundation of the government you now enjoy, and we never apostatized from it, but we remained true to it and were faith (Woodruff 1886, 229, in Stuy 2000, 65).

It seems that the body of the posthumous Church should thus be expanded to include not just individual ancestors of living members, but the founding fathers as well. It turns out that Woodruff need not worry; though he was not aware of it at the time, all the signers of the Declaration of Independence, as well as George Washington, had actually already been given posthumous baptisms in the Salt Lake Endowment House (Stuy 2000, 76). But that oversight on his part is not the point. Rather, his vision marked a shift and an expansion of the Mormon dead, a ratification by a highly placed authority.

This was a new turn. As indicated by Smith's anxieties about his pre-deceased brother Alvin, the salvaging of immediate family ties in the face of dead was one of the driving concerns for baptism of the dead; it is not enough to be saved oneself, but for all of one's family to be saved as well, and thus be co-present in the hereafter. The salvation of the family unity was not the sole reason—baptism for the dead was a response to concerns about theodicy (what of all those who died without hearing the truth?), as well as a response to some of the interpretation of a particularly puzzling line of New Testament scripture.[13] But when it comes not to intellectual or interpretive puzzles, but to actual ritual action, it appears that concern for close family was the chief driver for people to arraign and serve as proxies for such baptisms.

This understanding of baptism for the dead places was practiced alongside other nineteenth-century Mormon religious innovations, such as sealings and polygamy. And it turns out that despite their differences these practices actually strongly resonated with one another. Sealings were a ritual form used to create what were understood to be eternal bonds; these could be both martial bonds, parent-children bonds, and also same-sex ties between males that were understood as friendship or adoption. Absent something monstrous like apostasy, those sealed together could not be broken apart. Through the creation of networks of sealed individuals, kin groups could be created that could not be shattered by either the vagaries of the world or even by the divine fiat of God himself. As put by Smith himself during, fittingly enough, a funeral oration:

> If you have power to seal on earth & in heaven then we should be crafty ... go & seal on earth your sons & daughters unto yourself & yourself unto your fathers in eternal glory ... use a little Craftiness & seal all you can & when you get to heaven tell your father that what you seal on earth should be sealed in heaven. I will walk through the gate of heaven and Claim what I seal & those that follow me & my Council (Smith, as quoted in Brown 2011, 145).

In short, while still done as part of the divine plan, in a way these sealings were done as much to limit God's agency as to carry out His will.

Even the contentious practice of polygamy, or "celestial marriage" as it was referred to, could be seen as a form of extending and eternalizing kin and affinal networks. Polygamous practice before the move to Utah was a complicated, cross-cutting affair, where Smith would often marry the wives of his friends or fellow Church leaders, creating polyandrous nodes in a larger polygamous network. And while the record seems clear that some of the "celestial marriages" that occurred before Smith's death were consummated, some were not, and seemed to have been committed solely in furtherance of growing relations that could extend into eternity.

It was that expansive net that allowed for Woodroof's even wider-ranging visions. It is not inaccurate to see the proxy baptisms of the signers of the Declaration of Independence as an exercise of a nationalist leaning theo-political imagination. But this is to ignore how much this move indicates not so much a shift in the uses of baptism for the dead, but a growth. The extension from actual fathers to the metaphorical fathers of the nation is thus an expansion that results from an intensification of efforts. Conversion, intermarriage, and new genealogical discoveries will always ensure that there will be more immediate ancestors to baptize via proxy. But just as an expanding circle has an expanding circumference, as the sense of the breadth of who are sealed together grows, the perceived horizon or border that lies between the baptized and the unbaptized grows as well. As the network of those sealed together both on earth and in the hereafter grows, so does the number of imaginable individuals who can be incorporated through baptism and sealing.

This expansion of the horizon of those who can potentially be sealed is at once a crisis and an opportunity for the Church of Jesus Christ of Latter-day Saints. In order to facilitate easier access to Temple Work, since the late twentieth and early twenty-first century, the Church has radically expanded the number of temples, with over 164 currently operating, 8 under construction, and 36 publicly announced as planned.[14] It has presented genealogical research as religious obligation, a duty that at least ideally falls to every church member; it has also worked to make a culture of record keeping among living members, recommended the creation of life histories, books of remembrance, and other similar documents to serve as informational touchstones for later generations of Mormon genealogical researchers (Otterstrom 2008). The Church has not only worked to make baptism of the dead more sensible, but also more systematic. The Church has purposefully acted as a catalyst for this process in several different ways. Starting with Woodruff's ascension to the Presidency of the Church, there has been a persistent effort to systematize genealogical data, and to prevent any duplication of efforts in either research or baptism. And this information was (and is) being gathered in the hope that the Church will be able to collect genealogical data about every human being whose life has ever been recorded in any way. The Church built a network of Family History Centers to support genealogical research, with a Family History Library (the headquarters of which is located just one block away from the Salt Lake Temple) serving as the central node. In the mid-twentieth century, the Church set up a notecard-based system for members to use to track, disseminate, and correct genealogical information; this system was the precursor of the online indexing system discussed earlier. Drawing from the census, marriage, and birth records of various governments, the baptismal records of different parishes and churches, public death announcements, and other necrologies, it has amassed information regarding well over two billion individuals, in what is almost undoubtedly the largest collection of genealogical data in the world (Akenson 2007). In addition to being digitalized, this information has been recorded on microfilm (a medium chosen for its supposed long-term stability) and placed within a 700-foot deep vault stored in Granite Mountain Utah; the hope is that the material placed in the vault will not only not deteriorate over time (due to technologies such as controlling temperature and humidity), but will protect this information from natural disasters and human destruction. (Parenthetically, it is striking to note that members of the Long Now Foundation, a futurist organization working on building a "10,000-year clock," a monumental timepiece whose chimes would only sound once every 10,000 years, have not only looked to the Granite Mountain Utah Archeological Archive as a model, but have even been granted a tour of the usually inaccessible facility by the Church).[15]

This expansion of temple work and genealogical labor has in turn given the Church a certain power to shape access to the privileges of Church membership. As temple work has grown in importance, this made right of access to temples increasingly important as well. To enter a temple, an individual does not merely have to be a member of the Church of Jesus Christ of Latter-day Saints, but has to have what is called a "temple recommend," which entails a member being interviewed by a Bishop regarding his or her faith in Joseph Smith, the Book of Mormon, and current Church leadership, as well as to whether they are abstaining from premarital sex and following Mormon food taboos involving alcohol and some forms of caffeine. There are other reasons for a Church member to desire a temple recommend beyond an ability to participate in some way in Baptism for the Dead; to name perhaps the most prominent reason apart from temple work that a temple recommend is desirable, there is the fact that effectively all Mormon marriages are conducted behind temple walls. This means that those without a temple recommend cannot attend these marriages, regardless of whether that status is the result of not being a member in good standing, or simply not being a member of the Church at all (this is often particularly hard on the family and friends of converts to the Church). But still, access to temple work is one of the goods that come with having a temple recommend, which makes the Church's control of access to this mode of acting for the dead notable. (After this essay was drafted, the Church has changed its position and now allows for an additional ceremony roughly contemporaneous with the Temple marriage to celebrate the civil marriage to be held outside the Temple.)

But control is sometimes driven not by a capacity to shape and value different forms of Church membership, but in order to head off the crises that the action of members can cause. The extended freedom to baptize the dead may theoretically expand the universe of human beings who can be sealed to one another. But it brings dangers as well. There is the possibility of baptismally sanctified fictitious genealogical chains, which may do little direct damage to the religion, but which over time can wear on the credibility of both believers and outside observers. While most Mormon genealogists are relatively sober, there are those who create seemingly improbably long genealogical chains that tie them back to figures as distant as Old Testament patriarchs, and at times all the way back to "Father Adam." Part of this tendency is a function of the logic of Mormon genealogy itself, which takes all of the myriad forms of kinship found through the world's cultural and historical breadth, and forces it through the sieve of Anglo-American inflected bilateral descent and nuclear family models that are ready-at-hand concepts for the majority of American Mormons (Akenson 2007). And part of this is a function of the fact that after a certain point in history, genealogical information was intended to serve mostly legitimizing work, whether that legitimacy involved something as august as a claim to rulership or as simple as landholding. Lay that over the inevitable false entries, and confusion about namesakes and shared names, and these features along with shift in form and indifference to intended purpose allow for the unconscious or conscious gaming of genealogy. Then there are the problems that come from baptizing the dead who belong to populations who are quite sensitive around this issue, often due to past religious motivated persecution or genocide; the baptizing of Jews, and particularly of Jews who perished in the Holocaust, has caused the greatest outcry, in part because the Jewish names being pulled were being taken from Nazi records gathered during the Holocaust (Oppenheimer 2012). To control these problems, the Church has encouraged members to focus their attention on only nominating likely or possible ancestors for baptism. Other baptisms are discouraged, especially when drawn from lists of dead celebrities or Jewish Holocaust victims; the Church has even instituted as part of their genealogical software an automated process that triggers an alert whenever Holocaust-associated names are put up for proxy baptism.

Planchettes and Possessions

The preceding discussion focused on proxy baptisms. But we should keep in mind that, via similar ritual substitutionary methods, a deceased individual can go through additional rituals: confirmation, priesthood endowment (if male),[16] and earthly marriages rechristened as sealings which unite the married couple for all time. And between these other ordinances and our prior discussion of genealogy and baptism, we have enough to speculate as to why proxy baptism, despite encouraging an intimacy and at times even a conflation of the living and the dead, does not read to either Mormons or anthropologists as a form of possession.

First, proxy baptism does not court the kind of paradox identified as a recurrent part of possession phenomena. This is because, in proxy ritual, the living and dead stand in a structured, genealogical relationship. And given the highly gendered and often patriarchal nature of Utah Mormon families, these genealogical relations, now transformed into cosmological ties as well, ultimately work to position and fix individuals in a larger structure, rather than encourage the sorts of strange overlaps and doublings that seems to be at the heart of possession. This fixity is also why there is none of the movement and dilations and constrictions seen in this volume's presentation of possession. Rather than open the way for a shuttling between worlds, what proxy ordinances do is create a lattice-like, almost crystalline structure with all the cleanness and order of a genealogical chart. Here, no matter how strong the connection feels, spirits do not move between worlds. Instead, baptisms and other proxy ordinances join the Mormon dead and the Mormon living through the cosmic commemoration and recreation of kin relations that cannot be broken by death because they are indifferent to death. This also allows us to clearly understand the role of the various technical and social mechanics associated with proxy baptism. Thus, we can see the various technologies and bureaucracies surrounding proxy baptism not as forcing the regimentation of the Mormon imaginary. Instead, they are summoned into existence by the regimentation inherent in a cosmicization of contemporary American genealogical charts.

What happens when cosmological movement and paradox are introduced into this crystalline structure? We can see this in the Godbeites, a set of individuals who, after a mix of breaking with, and being expelled from, the Utah Church headed by Brigham Young, in 1870 set up their own rival organization: the "Church of Zion." The Godbeites were many things. They were prominent, converted English Mormons, who, before they came to Brigham Young's Zion in the desert, had enjoyed a relatively less hierarchical British form of the religion, which also had a greater tolerance for free thought and debate. Many of them were also businessmen who had felt hemmed by Young's restriction on trading with "gentiles" (i.e., non-Mormons) in the area, and also by Young's tendency to order them to engage in specific, and sometimes spectacularly unsuccessful, business endeavors, while also prohibiting other opportunities (Brigham Young was notoriously against any mining in the Utah territory). Other Godbeites were authors or publishers (publishing being a surprisingly lively enterprise in Utah), which gave them venues for arguing against what they felt to be Young's heavy hand over both the Church and the territory (see generally Walker 1998).

But the Godbeites were also something else: spiritualists. Both Spiritualism and Mormonism sprung at roughly the same time (the starting decades of the nineteenth century) and from roughly the same place (upper New York state). They were also both understood to be dangerous religious novelties, and both claimed to have definitive evidence of forms of life-after-death that stood in sharp relief to those usually imagined by Anglo-American Protestantism. As such, defenders of the prominent Protestant denominations often spoke of the two movements as if they were related evils (with Mormonism itself occasionally subsumed as a sub-species of Spiritualism) (Homer 1994, 172–3).

Given these shared aspects, it should be little surprise that there were instances of spiritualist experimentation at Mormonism's edges. One such experimentation occurred during an 1868 business trip to New York, where the merchant and publisher William Godbe (the individual who would eventually give the movement's name) and author, publisher, and architect Elias Harrison attended a series of seances led by noted medium Charles Foster. During these sessions, via Foster, Godbe and Harrison communicated with a recently deceased friend and mentor, the Mormon Apostle Heber C. Kimble. For three weeks, Kimball lectured Godbe and Harrison on "higher" doctrines. It was during these discussions that "[t]he whole superstructure of a grand system of theology was unfolded to our minds," as Harrison put it (Walker 1998, 124). No doubt that this new system of theology was filled out a bit by encounters with a raft of other spirits, including Joseph Smith, Jesus Christ, three Apostles, King Solomon, and the German naturalist Alexander Humboldt (Ibid., 119). Harrison and Godbe's "theological superstructure" was given an opportunity to thrive after their excommunication a year later. Through both the Church they founded, the lecture series they sponsored, and the publications they put out, they argued for a "liberal" Mormonism where individuals were unimpeded by religiously directed economic mandates, and where novel ideas could be entertained, particularly novel Spiritualist ideas.

Spiritualism here could be thought of as just another plank in the Godbeite's campaign for a more liberal form of Mormon religion. After all, spiritualism was a then cutting-edge movement that had a whiff of the modern while not also smelling of disenchantment or atheism; such a reading would lean into a materialist, and specifically economic, account of causation. It is alternately possible to read Godbe's and Harrison's Spiritualist adventures as the accelerant that took normal contestation about economic activity and authority in the Utah basin and brought it to the level of religion. It could even be seen as an unintended effect of the opening up of the Utah territory (the Utah Central Railroad was completed in 1870, connecting Salt Lake City to the also just established First Transcontinental Railroad). The best understanding is that it was a confluence of these disparate forces, an instance of structural causation, or alternately that these religious and economic motivators were different faces of a wider deterritorializing arc that shifted the direction of institutional powers towards the individual. But this was not a stable system. The combination of spiritualism and Mormonism proved to be a poor admixture. Even when painted as "liberal," Mormonism's insistence on there being *some* Church went against the decentered, individualist, and entrepreneurial nature of most dedicated spiritualists. And spiritualism's draw was diminished by the established Utah Church's continual campaign against it as a trick of the devil. As both a religious and political project, neither the Godbeites nor their Church of Zion would last long enough to see the beginning of the twentieth century.

How much importance can be given to the Godbeite movement? It is possible to see the resistance to and ultimate demise of the Church of Zion as the result of realpolitik. Going to war with Brigham Young's communalist but hierarchical blend of church and state would invite not just financial and political attack but also attempts to impeach the religious doctrines that served as planks in the Godbeite platform. Under this understanding, the Godbeites were not attacked because they were spiritualists, but rather that spiritualism was attacked because it was associated with the Godbeite movement. But such an analysis is placed into question by the fact that well before the Gobeites took on Young's Utah theocracy, the Utah branch of Mormonism expressed a great deal of anxiety about Spiritualism in general, and about the modes of spiritualism that did the most to facilitate paradox and usher in the movement of spirits.

Only a few years after spiritualist knockings were first heard in Upper New York State, various Mormon leaders and Mormon-associated print journalism began to inveigh against spiritualism. In these attacks, one repeated theme was the uncertain—and hence, possibly nefarious—identity of the Spirits being contacted. In 1852, the *Deseret News* attempted to warn Mormons off of spiritualism, stating that "it is no uncommon thing for a spirit to assume a more plausible appearance to a casual observer, than a true spirit would on the same subject" (as quoted in Bitton 1974, 40–1). Similarly, in 1853 Apostle Parley P. Pratt compared spiritual mediumship to "telegraphic wire as a medium of communication between New York and Boston. Through this medium .... Could be communicated words of truth in relation to news, business, transactions, the sciences, &c.; and alow every species of lie, error, imposition, fraud, &c" (Watt 1851, 43). Not much later, another Church apostle would read the advent of spiritualism as a desperate rearguard action by supernatural foes who knew that they were on the losing side of divine history. (This particular line of Mormon attack on Spiritualism would continue, well after spiritualism itself seems to have been spent as a social or cultural voice. In Apostle Bruce R. McConkie's pugilistic yet encyclopedic book *Mormon Doctrine*, published mid-twentieth century, McConkie would rehearse these prior accusations; he closed his dissuasion with a reminder of the Book of Leviticus's admonition that "[a] man also or a woman that hath a familiar spirit, or is a wizard, shall surely be put to death.") (McConkie 1958, 686–7).

But beyond problems of spiritual provenance, what also stood out to Mormon critics was that unlike the genealogically organized Mormon Dead and the hierarchically stratified Mormon Church, spiritualism seemed to be corrosive of order. In an 1870 attack that was directed not toward the Gobeites in particular, but toward the new religious movement as a whole, after again stoking anxieties about the nature of otherworldly agents that might be encountered during a seance, Brigham Young took time during the Annual Church Conference to contrast Mormonism structure with spiritualist chaos:

One [Mormonism] forms a perfect chain, the links of which cannot be separated; one has perfect order, laws, rules, regulations, organization; it forms, fashions, makes, creates, produces, protects and holds in existence the inhabitants of the earth in a pure and holy form of government, preparatory to their entering the kingdom of Heaven. The other is a rope of sand; it is disjointed, jargon, confusion, discord, everybody receiving revelation to suit himself (Evans and Grimshaw, eds, 1871, 281).

The comparison between this earthly ecclesiological order and the post-mortal sanctified genealogical order is not accidental, nor should the resonances between these orders be lost on us.

Of course, Latter-day Saints *were* forced to acknowledge that there was a likeness between Spiritualism and Mormonism, and particularly between spiritualist mediums and Joseph Smith. The ways that they acknowledged resemblance while still maintaining a distinction are insightful, though. First, they stated that it was improper to access the spirit world in any physical locales other than with a Mormon temple. The objection to the proliferation of potential points of cosmological passage is not clearly explained, but it appears to be a problem of policing; we are told that

> [t]he Lord has ordained that all the most holy things pertaining to the salvation of the dead, and all the most holy conversations and correspondence with God, angels, and spirits, shall be had only in the sanctuary of His holy Temple on the earth, when prepared for that purpose by His Saints; and shall be received and administered by those who are ordained and sealed unto this power, to hold the keys of the sacred oracles of God (Watt 1855, 46).

The parallels between, on the one hand, Mormonism in general, and Smith in particular, and on the other hand spiritualism, were harder to refute. From its beginning Mormonism had space for guidance from beyond the grave; the angel Moroni, who informed Joseph Smith about the Gold Tablets on which the *Book of Mormon* had been inscribed, was after all the post-mortal form of the prophet-warrior Moroni, who had died in New York after burying the same plates that he would later tell Joseph about. (And for that matter, later in his career Smith would be visited by John the Baptist, as well as by the Apostles Peter, James, and John; at another point, Smith was also visited by Elijah, but this probably doesn't count since according to the Jewish Bible, Elijah never actually died but instead ascended to heaven). The difference between a medium and Smith, though, was based not on the location of contact, as with concerns about the temple, but instead in the manner that contact affected the contactee. As set out in an 1870 issue of Desert News, the difference is "that the Prophet Joseph received visitations but did not lose his identity in the process" (Bitton 1974, 48). Framing Smith's distinctive as his continuation of identity is telling, and it suggests that while Mormons were unnerved by the inability to confirm the identity of spiritual interlocutors, and by a seeming lack of order in both the spiritualist picture of the afterlife and the spiritualist movement on earth, the doubling of identities was a factor too. In short, it was not the planchette that they disapproved of, but the way that mediumship complicated personhood. Similar anxieties can be seen in a jibe at Spiritualism in a Utah Territories humorous gazette, though this time it points more toward fraud than the uncanny. In the narrative, an "enthusiastic believer" in Spiritualism tells a skeptic that

> [O]n a certain occasion the spirit of his wife, who had been dead several years, returned to him, and seated herself upon his knee, put her arms around him, and kissed him as much to his gratification as she used to when living.
>
> "You do not mean to say," remarked the skeptic, "that the spirit of your wife really embraced and kissed you?"
>
> No, not exactly that,' replied the believer, "but her spirit took possession of the body of a female medium, and through her embraced and kissed me (Ibid. 1974, 46).

Given this Mormon interest in confusion between body, voice, and identity, it's also notable that Foster, the medium introduced Godbe and Harrison to the spirit world in New York, was known for communicating with the spirit world through numerous means, including having spirits using Foster's own blood to write their name on his body. But despite various means of contact and verification, the only means of communication that Godbe and Harrison appeared to be interested in was in "direct" spoken conversations with the spirit world, through the apparent mechanism of Foster's trance-modulated voice (Walker 1998, 109–27).

It is immaterial whether Mormon anxieties were firmly grounded in spiritualism as an actual practice, or whether spiritualism can properly be classified as a form of possession as used in this edited volume. Whether or not spiritualism is possession, many of the dangers that Mormons associated with it could be seen as effects of questions about doubled identity and paradox, and about a proliferation in place and number of spirits erupting into the world of the living—in short, about how spiritualism allowed for cosmological passage. And in turn, these twin phenomena that are so closely associated with possession ushered in something more unnerving—a democratization of the nature of the Mormon dead. Traditionally, it was possible to contact the dead. But these were peak events generally limited to a certain echelon of Church leadership. Even then, the experiences were understood not to be under the control of the person receiving the visitation. So, for most, temple work was the only real alternative. But with the Godbeites, and with spiritualism more generally, we have a democratizing of the experience, as well as a shift to the ephemerally experiential and the openly discursive. There is also a change in the nature of the dead. Before, they were ignorant, and in need of assistance from the living by way of the ordinance of baptism, which was controlled by Church leadership who held a monopoly not just on who could do this, but also on the knowledge of how this was done. In the Godbeites and spiritualism, the departed's residence in the Spirit World is a boon for religious knowledge, allowing the dead (at least potentially) to guide, rather than be the ones in need of the guidance. And they guide the living in a form unmediated by any ecclesiastical structure.

Generalizing from the history of this set of "peculiar" people, as Mormons sometimes refer to themselves, can be dangerous. Religion is a slippery category, and it may be expressed in different ways when it is a part of different constellations of secularism, and even more so in "non-secular" environments. And Mormonism's post-Copernican theology stands apart regardless. But the Mormon allergic reaction to possession, expressed both negatively in the regimentation of their intimacy with the dead, and positively in their campaign against spiritualism, suggests that the core elements of possession as identified in this volume are not innocent. For better or worse, together paradox, movement, and cosmological passage can be corrosive of hierarchies and buck attempts at systematic regimentation. And as such, attending to situations where they are either merely absent, or are actively foreclosed, may be as enlightening as attending to their presence.

On the Existence of Witches
(Or How Anthropology Works[1])

Marcio Goldman

In 2006, I was in the town of Ilhéus, in the South of the State of Bahia, in the Northeast of Brazil, for one of the beautiful sacred feasts at the Terreiro de Matamba Tombenci Neto, a Candomblé (one of the so-called Afro-Brazilian religions) *terreiro* (temple) where I have conducted intermittent fieldwork since 1983 (see Goldman 1984, 2007, 2009, 2016). The members of the Tombenci tell that the temple was founded in 1885 by the grandmother of the current mãe de santo, the "saint-mother," Dona Hilsa Rodrigues, the priestess of the temple since 1973. Mother to fourteen children, with dozens of grandchildren and great-grandchildren, Dona Hilsa turned eighty-six in March 2020, having been initiated into candomblé at twelve, in 1946. She was initiated to an orisha, a divinity, known as Matamba in the Angola Bantu nation, and as Iansan or Oyá in the Ketu Yoruba nation. This is why the *terreiro*'s main festivity is devoted to Matamba, and held every January since at least 1974.

For reasons that I cannot get into here, the 2006 feast was marked by a series of tensions and conflicts, which led to a meeting being called, so I was told, by the "owner of the house"—which did not mean Dona Hilsa, as I first understood it, but her orisha, the divinity for whom the feast was held—for the morning following the night of the celebration.

Though it was meant to begin at eleven in the morning after the feast, the meeting began inside the *temple* well after noon. The heat was so intense that the palm oil usually kept on a pot standing on a beam under the ceiling began to boil. The saint-mother, twelve of her sons and daughters (those who lived in Ilhéus at the time), one of her sons-in-law, and four people from outside the family, including myself, were

Part of this text was initially presented at the Federal University of São Carlos in 2014, and later published, in 2015, in R@U. Revista de Antropologia da UFSCar 6 (1): 7–24. Another part was presented at the panel "What Spirit Possession 'Does': The Production of Cosmology and Change in Afro-Latin Religions", at the XXXIV International Congress of the Latin American Studies Association, in 2016 — and later published at the Cuadernos de Antropología Social 44: 27–35, in 2016, and at Working Papers Series #23: 1–6. Open Anthropology Cooperative (OAC) Press, in 2017. I would like to thank Phillip Villani for the translation of the text, Julia Sauma and Luisa Elvira Belaunde for its review. To Geraldo Andrello, Stephan Palmié, Justin Shaffner and Huon Wardle I would like to thank for the many comments that have helped to improve this text.

present. All of us had a long-standing connection to the *terreiro*—in my case, for twenty-three years at that point.

The meeting started with aggressive exchanges of recriminations. Very unexpectedly, at a certain point someone asked **me** what I thought. I tried to minimize the conflict, saying that fights happen in every Candomblé *terreiro* all the time, and I strongly insisted that it was not worth dwelling on what had happened, as it would only lead to more conflict. Looking back, I think I just hoped to shorten a meeting in which the human and meteorological atmosphere was becoming unbearable to me.

When I naively believed, or hoped, that the meeting was coming to an end, one of the main protagonists of the dispute—who was the second-in-command at the temple—announced that he was "giving up his position" in the *terreiro*. One of his sisters immediately became possessed by her divinity and was taken into a separate room. On her return, we saw that she was no longer possessed by her main divinity but by an *erê*, a spirit that is much like a supernatural child, and who usually acts as a divinity's messenger. It was therefore a child divinity that gave the following message to us: "if things go on this way, something really bad is going to happen." Upon listening to these words, someone began to cry and said: "don't you people see what it is?" Others also began to cry and I realized that they were fearing the saint-mother would die. She remained serene, unlike everyone else. The mood worsened and more people began to weep.

Soon after, the child spirit said that it was not what everyone was thinking and that they should make peace. Silence fell until, for some unknown reason, I asked to speak. I said that we had witnessed something very powerful, that it was a moment for reflection, and that we could come back later to talk about it all. After a few minutes of silence, someone suggested a prayer to end the meeting. When, I thought, the meeting was finally coming to an end, the saint-mother's divinity possessed her in the most gentle way I had ever seen. She sang in a low voice until her son, the one who had just given up his position at the Terreiro, also became possessed by his own divinity. So, we all praised them and asked for their blessing.

The son's divinity turned to his mother's divinity in order to praise her. I don't know how, but he was holding a ferule he had placed above the drums before the feast. It was meant to be a "symbol of discipline in candomblé," he had explained. Upon exchanging greetings, the son's divinity handed the ferule to his mother's divinity, but she promptly refused it; he thus knelt down, placing one hand on the floor and began to violently hit with the ferule held by his other hand. Some people ran and struggled against him until they took away the ferule from him. Before standing up however, he still very violently slapped both his hands on the floor.

At this point his mother, who was still possessed by her divinity, became possessed by her *cabocla*—an Amerindian spirit very common in Angola nation Candomblé. At the same time, her son also became possessed by one of his other spirits, who is always very playful and he announced: "no more sadness, it's time for a feast." I noticed that the cabocla was saying something to somebody and immediately chairs and electric fans were removed from the room, the drums were uncovered, and a caboclos' feast began, lasting the rest of the day.

Looking back, what strikes me is my difficulty to deal with what went on. Why did I think I could bring the meeting to an end just because I could not stand it? Why did I imagine it was about to end at various points? And finally, what was the source of my unease and my inability to really understand what was happening?

There is no doubt there were psychological and even physical reasons at play. The heat was unbearable but, more important, for an anthropologist who hopes to get on well with all his "natives," it is never pleasant to notice they are just like everyone else: at once similar and different, and ready to engage in the most violent disputes about issues trivial to others, including the anthropologist.

However, I believe that my unease and, above all, my incomprehension really came from what I would call the *political* nature of my own position. And I say "political" in the classical sense of the term, that is, one that presumes that situations like the one I witnessed are limited to disputes between human beings, and therefore, disagreements may be solved through dialogue and mutual understanding. That is why, at the time I believed that what was laying behind it all was actually a quarrel between the president of the *terreiro*'s civil association and the president of the Cultural Group linked to the *terreiro*, as someone had suggested. That is also why I had thought that things could calm down if I called upon every one's common sense.

However, as the unfolding of events reminded me in the most direct way, a Candomblé *terreiro is not* a political space in the Ancient Greek—our—sense of the term. That is, it is not an exclusively human space where supposedly rational human beings face each other. A *terreiro* is filled with other beings and other forces, and all of them come into play, even when the anthropologist does not wish it. And as we all know, when the Ancient Greeks defined the *polis*, they excluded women, children, slaves, and aliens, as well as natural and supernatural forces and beings.

* * *

I'll come back to this point but now I would like to remember that in a very similar way, when anthropology defines the scope of its investigations or explanations it often tends to exclude a significant part of what constitutes the world for the greater part of the people whom we study. Let's take a great example.

At the start of the fourth and central chapter of his magnificent book about witchcraft amongst the Azande (entitled "The Notion of Witchcraft explains Misfortunes"), Evans Pritchard wrote:

> I have described some of the prominent characteristics of witchcraft in Zande thought. Others will be developed in this and the following chapters. It is an inevitable conclusion from Zande descriptions of witchcraft that it is not an objective reality. The physiological condition which is said to be the seat of witchcraft, and which I believe to be nothing more than food passing through the small intestine, is an objective condition, but the qualities they attribute to

it and the rest of their beliefs about it are mystical. Witches, as Azande conceive them, cannot exist. The concept of witchcraft nevertheless provides them with a natural philosophy by which the relations between men and unfortunate events are explained and a ready and stereotyped means of reacting to such events. Witchcraft beliefs also embrace a system of values which regulate human conduct. (Evans-Pritchard 1937, 63)

In the "abridged" edition of the book (elaborated by Eva Gillies), the excerpt, summarized in what was to become the second chapter, is still more direct: "In the way that the Azande conceive them, witches evidently could not exist" (Evans-Pritchard 1976, 18). I cannot say why or how the adverb "evidently" was introduced into what was to become the first sentence of the chapter. However, this does not really change the many things there is to say about this passage.

Firstly, that it was not written by just anybody, but by maybe the greatest ethnographer of all time, who was capable of providing empirically rich and analytically lucid descriptions of a set of highly complex phenomena. The excerpt cited opens a chapter that follows three others, where Azande witchcraft is minutely described, chapters that follow in their turn an introduction that presents the Azande and the book to its readers.

Rarely suspected of a lack of empathy with his natives, Evans-Pritchard even wrote that "I have only once seen witchcraft on its path" (Evans-Pritchard 1937, 34)—the Azande arguing that, under certain conditions, witchcraft can be seen by humans in the form of a moving light. Believing that it was someone's lantern, Evans-Pritchard discovers the impossibility of this hypothesis the following morning, while some Azande guarantee that it was indeed witchcraft and that the death of two people that same night only confirmed this diagnosis. Still not convinced, Evans-Pritchard concludes that

I never discovered its real origin, which was possibly a handful of grass lit by someone on his way to defecate, but the coincidence of the direction along which the light moved and the subsequent death accorded well with Zande ideas. (ibid)

The second thing to observe is that what most calls attention in Evans-Pritchard's phrase isn't so much the simple decree of the nonexistence of Azande witchcraft as an objective phenomena (few anthropologists in the 1930s or even today would say different), but the introduction of a curious clause: "witches, *as the Azande conceive of them*, could not exist." This means, on one hand, that to the objective inexistence of the witches the author feels the need to add the empirical inadequacy of native knowledge. However, it also seems to mean that according to *other conceptions*, witches could, who knows, exist. What these other conceptions are is exactly what the book as a whole develops and which the excerpt already quoted allows us to perceive. Finally, says Evans-Pritchard, there is a "physiological condition" (objective) "said to be the seat of witchcraft"—but this is "nothing more than food passing through the small intestine"; there is a lack of knowledge (empirical) of this situation, and there are ("mystical") "qualities" attributed to this objective condition on the part of equivocal and equally mystical beliefs.

None of this, however, prevents witchcraft from existing in a certain manner, which evidently is not that of the natives however. In the absence of empirical knowledge, witchcraft, which Evans-Pritchard tellingly designates as a "concept," on one hand, provides the Azande with "a natural philosophy by way of which the relations between men and misfortune are explained, and ways, ready and formulated, to react to these misfortunes," and, on the other hand "a values system that regulates human conduct."

The true mode of existence of witches can only be, therefore, epistemological (in the form of empirically false knowledge, but which satisfies the need to explain the world) and/or sociological (in the form of an equivocal system of accusations and punishments, but that fills the need to "regulate human conduct"). Here, we perceive the two approaches that since Evans-Pritchard have sustained the anthropological investigation of witchcraft and analogous phenomena, studied on one hand as modes (erroneous) of explanation, on the other as modes (equivocal) of accusation. From this, it results that witchcraft could only exist to the extent that it is something other than what natives think it is; in other words, witches can only exist as anthropologists know them to.

What would this anthropological way of conceiving witches be? Here, I believe, an important bifurcation emerges and the type of anthropology that is conducted will in a sense be decided by the path taken. The first, and most common, consists of simply assuming the nonexistence of witches as the natives understand them as a type of ontological equivocation, that is, they think that something exists that effectively does not—and it is this that in general is nominated belief. This operation is based on the introduction of an extra-anthropological premise, in other words, a premise that does not consider the impossibility of, as Wagner (1981, 12) writes, the anthropologist not having "any preconceptions, and, therefore, no culture," or in the words of Strathern commenting on Boon (Strathern 1987, 256, note 13), "the fact that there is no outside of culture "except in other cultures or in their fragments and potentialities" (see also Viveiros de Castro 2013).

Of course everyone would probably agree that this extra-anthropological premise can only emerge from a specific culture, our own. However, maybe it is no longer so probable that everyone will be in agreement that this culture presents characteristics that distinguish it from all the others. That is, the fact that at least in some of its areas, it imagines itself to be less cultural, in other words, less arbitrary than the others, or in Latourian terms, that it imagines itself as coinciding with objective reality (Latour 1993). Of all the common senses of the universe, ours is the only one that is also "good sense," given that it can appeal to the definitions of the real provided by "Science" (which, however, is never anthropology itself) and proclaims its privileged access to universal nature to which the other cultures are submitted but do not know.

This seems so obvious to us, I would say culturally obvious, that we do not even experience the need to entirely explain the question. Evans-Pritchard, for example, did not need to spend much time on this because he knew that the appeal, explicit or implicit, to our good sense would produce the desired effect and that, to use Deleuze's definition regarding the "dogmatic image of thought," "everyone knows it, nobody can deny it," (Deleuze 1968, 170) that "witches do not exist"—or whatever you may wish to think of as not existing: divinities, spirits, and mysterious forces, certainly, but also races, invented traditions, impossible genealogies, etc.

This does not mean, in any way, that the alternative to this type of perspective would be a pure decree on the part of the anthropologist that indeed witches exist and that from there, we can present and explain what we learn in the field. Firstly, because this would continue to express the arrogant and metaphysical Western pretension of being able to decide what does and doesn't exist. Secondly, and most importantly, because as Clifford Geertz (1983, 57) writes, "an anthropological interpretation of witchcraft should not even be written by a witch or by a geometer." However, this is not because we are seeking to, as Geertz seems to believe, encounter the just, median point between proximity and excessive distance with lived experience. Rather, it is because explaining whatever it maybe through the actions of witches, spirits, or mysterious forces means falling into the same error of explaining something through the action of genes, the climate, individual impulses, cultural values, social necessities, etc. Therefore, it is not a question of existence or nonexistence, but that in anthropology we deal with relations, not with substances or even actions. Our problem, consequently, is how to include witches (or whatever it maybe) in the set of relations that we describe and analyze.

It is here, I believe, that what we could consider the possibility of a specifically anthropological form of symmetrization. As it is well known, Bruno Latour (1993, 92–6), following Michael Callon, established a distinction between what he calls "the first principle of symmetry" and a "generalized principle of symmetry." While the first only refuses to accept the selection between what the sciences consider, in a determined epoch to be the true and the false, and attempts to explain them "in the same terms," the second equally refuses the possibility that the terms that they use can come from the "sciences of society."

The Latourian distinction is part of the project to establish a "symmetrical anthropology," capable of studying the "moderns" in the same terms in which traditional anthropology, so to speak, would study the "others." Latour's project seems however conditioned by two important variables. Firstly, by a certain image of the anthropology "of the Others." As Latour (2003, 7) said to François Ewald, "the concepts developed by anthropology seduced me less than its methods." It is this, which explains the other strange change of position of the author in relation to anthropology. Because, if *We Have Never Been Modern*, from 1991, announced a "symmetrical anthropology," and nominated anthropology generally as a model to describe an anthropology of ourselves, the sequence of Latour's work seems to have led it rather toward a new sociology. Therefore, in 2005, he would write that for "sociology to finally become as good as anthropology," it is necessary "to concede to members of contemporary society as much flexibility to define themselves as that offered by ethnographers."

This final and apparent homage, however, soon becomes an open criticism, because everything indicates that sociology is not only "as good" as anthropology, but better than it, to the extent that it is not prisoner to the "culturalism" or "exoticism" which makes anthropology unable to move beyond the "metaphysics" of the diversity of worlds, to an "ontology" of the common world. This incapacity ends up reducing these metaphysics to simple representations that feed a cultural relativism that at the end of the day ends up presupposing a unity of the world explainable through science.

The other variable that conditions the project of a symmetrical anthropology that Latour is progressively abandoning is the fact that it does not consider the asymmetry between the research situation of an anthropology of ourselves and that of "the others"—and this of course does not mean any asymmetry between the others and ourselves, whose recognition and attempt at overcoming is at the foundation of Latour's thought. Therefore, the anthropology of the moderns, starting from an anthropology of science, must avoid our tendency to confer to science the right to define our reality, endowing scientists with the power of imposing privileged points of view, forms of selection and categories that we are precisely attempting to research as anthropologists.

The problem is that, generally, other forms of anthropology—the anthropology of the "others"—start from a very different situation. The discourses of those who are studied, to the contrary of the scientific discourse, are generally considered false or, in any case, as presenting a truth that is not ours and that we tend to imagine as less true. This means that the symmetry between the analyses of scientific and other practices can only be obtained via the introduction of a sort of compensatory asymmetry, destined to correct an initial asymmetrical situation—more, or less, than "symmetrical anthropology" the point is how to elaborate anthropological symmetrizations. Only in this way we'll be able to investigate and reveal the destabilizing potential that other thoughts and the thought of the others possess in relation to our own ways of thinking and defining the real.

Almost twenty years after the statement about witches in 1937, Evans-Pritchard concluded his third book about the Nuer from Southern Sudan, the one regarding their religion, saying that the sacrifices practiced by this people are "a dramatic representation of a spiritual experience," concluding with the final words of the book:

> What this experience is the anthropologist cannot for certain say. Experiences of this kind are not easily communicated even when people are ready to communicate them and have a sophisticated vocabulary in which to do so. Though prayer and sacrifice are exterior actions, Nuer religion is ultimately an interior state. This state is externalized in rites which we can observe, but their meaning depends finally on an awareness of God and that men are dependent on him and must be resigned to his will. At this point the theologian takes over from the anthropologist. (Evans-Pritchard 1956, 322)

The juxtaposition of this affirmation with that about Azande witches certainly looks paradoxical. However, maybe it is necessary to recognize that the only thing somewhat strange is that they were written by the same author who, by the way, shifted from considering anthropology a branch of the natural sciences to seeing it as a historical discipline and even a form of art. Because this apparent paradox seems, rather, inscribed in the very constitution of anthropology. In the absence of a final objective reality that would serve as a reference for the indigenous proposition ("In the way that the Azande conceive them, witches evidently could not exist"), there is only the option of this "interior state," actually as real as any concrete referent but to which the anthropologist would not have access but the theologist would. The question is whether anthropology necessarily works between the objectivist notion of a reality to which only we have access, and in relation to which others have only beliefs, and the only apparently idealistic hypothesis of this interior state where whatever can be considered belief.

I think, to the contrary, that the elaboration of a properly anthropological symmetrical principle, of "symmetrization," can overcome this apparently singular choice. This symmetrical principle requires, in its turn, a modification of content and of emphasis in Evans-Pritchard's saying regarding the Azande witches. Instead of saying "witches, as the Azande understand them, *could not exist*," it would be necessary to argue that "witches can only exist *as the Azande understand them*," or as somebody understands them. However, it also requires not believing in any theology to determine "what this experience (that the anthropologist cannot know with certainty) *is*."

The general formulas of belief ("what they think that exists I know doesn't," or "what they do not know exists I know does"), or of skepticism ("I do not know what they know exists" or "neither of us knows what exists") should give way to a systematic investigation of "what I think that they think that exists" and "of what they think that I think that exists" (with all their refractions: "what they think that I think that they think that exists," etc.). This is the fundamental bifurcation in anthropology that determines the kind of anthropological practice that will be adopted: the pretension to discover the truth of the others or the much more modest task of mapping other truths.

This bifurcation is connected to an always reopened question in the history of anthropology: the degree of truth we are capable of accepting in the native discourses or practices. It is obvious that no anthropologist will deny some degree of truth to these discourses and practices, but the problem is the point up to which we are capable of going; up to what point are we capable of hearing and "bearing" the native word. Further, the degree of truth does not mean, evidently, trying to know if the natives are correctly describing or not some objective reality "out there," given that this would require supposing the exteriority of an observer who already knows beforehand what the truth is and that based on this privileged access to the real they can judge the others.

However, the acceptance of the native word cannot signify limiting oneself to repeating it, given that this would only serve to duplicate all the difficulties it poses for us. The problem, therefore, is not only up to what point *can we* follow the native word, but also that of the point where we *should* separate ourselves from it. My hypothesis is that this separation has to happen to the extent that we intend (it is our choice) to place more things into relation than the natives intend to. As I wrote elsewhere, "our knowledge is different from 'local knowledge' not because it is more objective, totalizing or true, but simply because we decide *a priori* to attribute the same value to all of the stories we hear" (Goldman 2013, 15). The capacity to accept the native word, effectively taking it seriously and allowing the anthropological reflection to go to its limit, seems to me to be the variable that makes the difference in the quality of anthropological texts.

In short, it is not a question of criticizing the native word, revealing what is behind it, what it really means to say or at the limit, instructing the natives themselves, nor of believing in it or simply repeating it or glossing it. It is its *acceptance*, in the sense in which it is necessary to draw near to it as much as possible and with the greatest respect possible to seek to explore the effects, that it produces on our thought and in ourselves more generally.

When Tylor (1871, vol. II, 453) wrote the last phrase of *Primitive Culture*—"thus, active at once in aiding progress and in removing hindrance, the science of culture is essentially a reformer's science"—he not only founded a discipline but established a certain "image of anthropology," in the sense in which Deleuze and Guattari (1994, 37) define "image of thought": "the image thought gives itself of what it means to think, to make use of thought, to find one's bearings in thought." From colonial administration to salvage programs, through public security policies and inclusion programs, this image of anthropology seems to be particularly durable. Further, it seems to be an image from which we never entirely manage to free ourselves: anthropology as a science destined to extirpate superstitions and contribute to the enlightenment of the ignorant. Furthermore, to the extent that the human spirit is one, the ignorant are not only the "primitives" of the other societies, and the world, even the civilized one, is still full of people who believe in witches, ghosts, and other things that "couldn't exist." Anthropology's task would therefore be not only to detect these illusions, but to perform a type of therapy capable of curing people of their own ignorance. In the paradigm shift that we are currently undergoing, witches are not so important anymore, but things such as race and tradition are, and there are plenty of people who intend to teach the ignorant that these things do not exist (or that they exist), independent of what they think of this. The idea that people are deceiving themselves regarding reality and themselves (but the anthropologist is not) appears to be situated at the heart of anthropology.

But let's return to Evans-Pritchard's phrase about witches. After arguing that that which the Azande consider witchcraft "is an objective condition" ("food passing through the small intestine"), the author concludes: "but the qualities they attribute to it and the rest of their beliefs about it are mystical." It is not difficult to guess what the theoretical reference of this reasoning or at least of this vocabulary is. In 1934, Evans-Pritchard had already published an article regarding "Lévy-Bruhl's theory of primitive mentality" (Evans-Pritchard 1934) where, in addition to recognizing the importance of his thought, he intended to undoubtedly make it more palatable for British anthropologists. To this end, however, Evans-Pritchard saw himself obliged to simplify Lévy-Bruhl on an essential point—that of the sense of the term "mystic," so important in this author's first works.

Roughly speaking, Evans-Pritchard argues that, in certain situations, mystical properties are added, in some way, to the objective properties that all humans undeniably recognize in the world. This means obviously that the "primitives" are not so different from us, but this betrays Lévy-Bruhl's thought on a fundamental point. It is not that we deal, for him as was so frequently affirmed, with deepening the trench between "us" and "them." The problem is more in the order of modes of thought.

In 1910, Lévy-Bruhl wrote that he had decided to use the term "mystical" for want of a better one. He then tried to demonstrate that what he named "primitive mysticism" consists in a perception of "forces," "influences," and "actions," which are felt as being real, though are not captured by sensibility, properly speaking. All of this, associated with the sensations, feeling, and representations, is felt as an indissociable block, which means, according to the author, that "the reality in which the primitives move is itself mystical" (Lévy-Bruhl 1910, 30). Therefore, not only everything that exists is gifted with "mystical properties," but these are understood as being as objective as they are sensible. This means, and this is a fundamental point, that the very distinction between sensible and mystical would not have value for the "primitive mentality."

That's why Lévy-Bruhl goes on, that the mysticism that can be found in Western society (that of the "superstitious man, frequently also of the religious man of our society"—Lévy-Bruhl 1910, 67) does not serve to understand primitive mysticism but, to the contrary, tends to hamper this understanding. This is because "our mysticism" is dualistic, supposing "two orders of reality, one visible and tangible, submitted to the necessary laws of movement, the other invisible, impalpable, 'spiritual', forming a type of mystical sphere that involves the first" (Lévy-Bruhl 1910, 67). Primitive mysticism, however, is monistic because it does not suppose the existence of two worlds, but only of one: "all reality is mystical, as is all action, and, therefore, also all perception" (Lévy-Bruhl 1910, 67).

As it happens so frequently, by trying to reduce the distance between us and the others, what Evans-Pritchard ends up doing is making those others slightly worse versions of ourselves. The effort of Lévy-Bruhl, to the contrary, had always been in the opposite direction, that of characterizing an otherness that cannot be judged in our own terms. It is obvious, however, that the destiny of Lévy-Bruhl's thought—initially well accepted but for bad reasons and subsequently interpreted with the worst of bad will, and finally placed in widespread ostracism—should serve as a warning. His refusal to accept the founding condition of anthropology (how to say in terms that can only be ours what is always said in terms that are not ours) partially explains this destiny and suggests that this refusal can only lead to incomprehension, incommunicability, and at the limit, silence. Therefore, how would it be possible to think the categories that are not ours without them immediately becoming like ours? Further, if it was possible, how can we communicate this thought? Would it be the same as refusing to use one's own language and evidently, not being able to use another because one could not be understood?

I believe that anthropology foresaw two "solutions" to this problem. One would be to speak a tongue that is nobody's and that, paradoxically, can be understood by everyone, or at least by those of goodwill. It is a universalist solution, which expresses itself in a substantialist manner, seeking to encounter "what there is in common between all cultures," be it in a more formal manner, with the determination of the structures or common processes, subjacent to everything that is human and which permits a mutual understanding.

The second "solution" is not as one may imagine that of classical relativism. This does not go beyond a variation of universalism, where instead of emphasizing the universal, variation is underlined. As Roland Barthes wrote, still in 1961: "in a classical world, relativity is never vertiginous because it is not infinite; it soon stops in the unalterable heart of things: it is a security, not a disturbance" (Barthes 1961, 139–40).

As we can see, both in universalism and relativism, the dualism from which one apparently starts is nothing more than a poorly disguised triad, with one of the terms in apparent dual opposition simultaneously occupying a hierarchically superior position from which we can judge the others. "They" are part of a culture and "we" are part of a culture; but additionally, we also have science, which allows us to decide in what ways the cultures are similar and different. *We* appears twice, as the defense and as prosecution; *they* only appears as the defense.

The only solution, or better, the only way out was suggested some time ago by Pierre Clastres (1968): to place oneself in the in-between space itself so that from the outset dualism can lead to more interesting forms of pluralism. Now, situating oneself in the in-between space means translating a system into another without going through any third transcendent or transcendental instance.

How to translate, however, other forms of thought and practice? By supposing that they are of the same nature as ours? A negative response would with difficulty hide the arrogance with which, as with all Western knowledge, anthropology has behaved itself. It is obvious that it would not be difficult to imagine an equally hierarchized way out, but inverted. It is enough to have a greater complacency with the richness of the lived world and a greater nostalgia owing to a supposed loss of direct contact with it, for our thought to be converted into a more or less spurious form, or at least impotent, of a human thought more connected with the real, more spontaneous, etc.

On the other hand, I am not certain that the "democratizing" solution will free us from all our problems. At the end of the day, who said that to think, it is necessary to think like us? Who guarantees that the small Greek philosophical accident or the birth of the modern sciences possesses such dignity that only they could guarantee rights of citizenship and other forms of thought? Would we not be going back to a type of meta-ethnocentrism that only refuses the more immediate ethnocentrism (we are better than they are) with the condition that they are equal to us? Or, with one of these forms of tolerance that, as Isabelle Stengers (2011) showed, constitutes only the other face of universalist arrogance? Tolerance ready to accept everything on the proviso that it looks like what we ourselves do. Now, without hierarchizing, and without democracy, what remains for us if not the transversal relations that Félix Guattari speaks of?

The singularity of anthropology can only be affirmed, then, when it is conceived, according to the words of Tim Ingold (1992, 695–6), as "philosophy with the people in," or, as science with the people, or peoples in, because, at the end of the day, for us everything starts from a very concrete meeting based on which our problems are presented. However, a philosophy or science with the people or peoples in leads us to the already mentioned intrinsically paradoxical character of anthropology. However, and to the contrary of other human sciences, the fact of dealing with dominated knowledge and alternative worlds means that anthropology, as grounded as it may be in Western reason, has never managed to rid itself of an impulse that leads it to dialogue with what Clastres named the "strange languages" that the West did not like to recognize.

As Pignarre and Stengers (2011) observed, the problem of an inheritance is not receiving it, but knowing what to do with it. Anyway, the double inheritance of anthropology does not come, as we tend to repeat too often, from its connections with supposedly opposing tendencies of Western thought: enlightenment and romanticism, individualism and holism, rationalism and emotionalism ... All of this, obviously, is on the same side, ours. The originality of anthropology comes, as Clastres (1968, 37) also suggested, from its bonds with the two sides of "the great divide between Western civilization and primitive civilizations."

Well, I think these two bonds should be understood in the threatening and at the same time creative sense of a *double bind* as proposed by Gregory Bateson (1956, 206–7). That is, the kind of situation where "a primary negative injunction" is accompanied by "a secondary injunction conflicting with the first at a more abstract level." In our case, we anthropologists repeatedly receive a "primary negative injunction" more or less like this: "one can not understand other societies from our own point of view"; and a "secondary injunction conflicting with the first" like this: "anthropology is, after all, part of the Western tradition and can not get out of it." In short, a situation in which, as Bateson (1956, 201) wrote, "no matter what a person does, he 'can't win.'" If anthropology accepts these terms, it has already lost!

On the other hand, Bateson also taught that the double bind leads to schizophrenia or death only when one is not able to jump from the level where contradiction is insurmountable to another where it can not only be overcome as it becomes productive: "The only way the child can really escape from the situation is to comment on the contradictory position his mother has put him in" (Bateson 1956, 215). In other words, I think that by double bind we should also understand a kind of "double fold," in the Leibnizian-Deleuzian sense of the term: a folding we have to apply at the point where different forces of thought meet or connect in order to escape the schizophrenic situation and reach the creative pole (Deleuze 1993).

The anthropological encounter always ends up in a problem of translation (see Asad 1986). However, the anthropological translation does not have anything to do with representation, explanation, or understanding; it has to do with agencies. Doing anthropology means constructing a free indirect discourse where the native and anthropological words intertwine. In this process, what is translated are discursive and non-discursive minoritarian practices that "were buried, masked in functional coherences or in formal systematizations" and "disqualified as not competent or insufficiently elaborated" (Foucault 1976, 163–4). We translate using notions and concepts from our own tradition created or chosen from elements that present some resonance with what needs to be translated. This translation makes more intelligible and magnifies what is translated and, at the same time, disturbs and destabilizes what we use to translate.

* * *

I am not really sure whether I could or should conclude this text by proposing an *explanation* of the events I witnessed at the *Tombenci* in Ilhéus I reported in the beginning. Anyway, I believe that trance and spiritual possession constitute an exemplary case to examine this anthropological compulsion to sort out what "exists" (i.e., *our* reality) from the inexistent or illusory beings and forces that, nevertheless, are part of other people's reality. And I believe that this exemplary character of possession is due to some factors.

Firstly, to the West's long and problematic relationship with ecstatic phenomena. As Weber (1967) showed, Judaism constituted itself as a religion through a process of centralization that involved combating clairvoyants, prophets, and all others who dared to make direct contact with divine forces, that is, without the mediation of sacred institutions. More or less at the same time, still in the Mediterranean region, in Ancient Greece, the control of truth was passing from the hands of mystics, poets, and clairvoyants to that of philosophers: sober men who had complete control over their volition, as Marcel Detienne (1999) argued in his famous analysis.

I suggest that this problematic historical relationship reveals the reasons underlying the exclusion of those who seek a direct experience of the sacred using only their own bodies as a vehicle. The Jewish case seems to demonstrate that the possibility of a relationship with sacred forces taking place outside an institutional setting threatened the development of Western religious institutions, and their monopoly of the relationships with these forces. The danger was to see the divine word directly *presented* when its legitimacy should depend on its *representation* by an institutionalized and hierarchical clerical corpus. Revelations that only occur once in a while should not be threatened by those brought through constant, repeated, variable possessions whose bearers could be virtually anyone.

The Greek case illustrates another basic antagonism between the West and ecstatic experience. Given that the possessed person is paradoxically more than one, what to do with this unity of the self so dear to Western thought? How is it possible to accept that a subject can leave his own consciousness, without perceiving it as a savage state, a malignant nature, or even the irruption of a pathological process?

Christianity brings together Jewish and Greek traditions. Clairvoyance, the splitting of the self, and possession, were all recodified as demoniacal and came to constitute a challenge and, at the same time, an instrument for the powers of the Church. And, as we all know, it is against this background that anthropological knowledge constituted itself and its work. Because the objects of our analysis are never what "actually" exists out there, but the result of an explicit or implicit dialogue between what we think and what the people who we live with propose. Whether this inevitable diffraction is deforming or creative is always an open question.

Among the so-called "apparently irrational beliefs" with which anthropology has fed itself, trance and possession have a special place. Partly because, as Roger Bastide already warned in 1958, these are very special phenomena, in a way more complicated than other beliefs and even rituals. For possession, as Bastide wrote, "is not a ritual-imitation but rather a lived ritual-experience [*rituel-expérience vécue*] that allows us to penetrate into the world of the gods more easily." He goes on to write that trance is a "*lived* reality," not just a representation or imitation of myth, and that the dance, which appears to simply imitate the divinities, is a "fabulous opera," so that "what we designate as the phenomenon of possession can be better defined as a phenomenon of personality metamorphosis." Bastide concludes then that, in the end, "trance is actually real" (Bastide 1958, 200).

When I first studied possession, thirty-five years ago, I identified no more than two anthropological explanatory models. One reduced possession to illness, by treating it either directly as a disease (generally mental illness) or giving it the status of a "pre-medical" treatment for psychophysiological disturbances. The other aimed, instead, to deal with trance by trying to see it as a direct or inverted reflection of the "broad social structure."

Today, I believe, the situation hasn't changed much. After all, whether we deal with possession as a performance or as a commentary, our explicit or implicit assumption that these things are not *actually* happening does not change—for we are certain that the beings who have the power to possess humans and take them into trance do not *actually* exist.

The problem is how to give up these premises and try to develop what I would call—using an old Malinowskian (Malinowski 1935) concept I rediscovered in my study of politics—an ethnographic theory of trance and possession. A theory that can only be elaborated when firmly based on "native" theories with their specific ontologies and epistemologies, as well as very particular notions of personhood, ritual, and agency.

It is worth saying that an ethnographic theory does not mean simply to repeat what we have already heard from our friends in a, perhaps, more sophisticated way. It does not mean we should just say "yes, the spirits possessing people are as real as the people they possess and this explains possession." Firstly, because such a statement would still express our metaphysical and arrogant pretention of being able to sort out what exists from what does not exist. Secondly, because by trying to explain things through the actions of spirits we would make the same mistake as when we try to explain things through the influence of genes, the environment, individual impulses, cultural values, social needs, and so on. The issue is not about existence or nonexistence but about the fact that we deal with relationships, and not with substances or even with actions. Consequently, our problem is how to include the reality defined by the people with whom we live within the relationships we describe and analyze, without sneakily negating the reality of that reality.

It therefore seems to me that here we are dealing with what has been called *cosmopolitics*. But not exactly in the sense anthropologists seem to interpret Isabelle Stengers' notion, just adding politics to cosmos or vice versa, as if it were simply enough to add some spirits to human actions to solve all our problems. I believe that the question is cosmopolitical in the most profound sense, as Stengers phrased it when she speaks about "the unknown"—a *fundamental* unknown, in the technical sense of the term (see Stengers 2005, 2011). In other and maybe enigmatic words, it seems to me that the question is whether we are able to practice anthropology through a type of transcendental *we don't know*.

* * *

I would therefore like to finish with another story and a slightly pretentious conclusion. The ethnographer and photographer Pierre Verger—who lived alongside African religions and religions of African matrix for sixty years, and who was initiated into some of them—regretted his inability to become possessed by the divinities, and attributed it to him being too Cartesian. I could probably say the same to explain my unease and difficulty in dealing with the events in Ilhéus, but I believe that there is something more than national or personal idiosyncrasies at work here.

As I have suggested above, it is a long-standing fact that even without knowing it we are all Cartesians and, more than that, Kantians. But this does not mean that all humans, not even ourselves all the time, have to be so. As Lévy-Bruhl wrote a long time ago:

> In our eyes that which is not possible can not be real. To his [the primitive], what his experience presents to him as real is accepted as such, unconditionally. If they reflected about this, they would undoubtedly say that it must be possible, since it is. (Lévy-Bruhl 1938, 101)

Perhaps, we are talking here about this now famous turning from epistemology to ontology; but perhaps, and less pretentiously, it could be only something they say in Cape Verde, "everything that has a name exists."

Afterword

Michael Lambek

Introduction

Generations of anthropologists have found spirit possession both good to think with and challenging to think about. The lively chapters of this volume continue to explore both the richness of possession and the challenges attending to it, adding another round to our ever-expanding conversation.[1] Indeed, I am tempted to say that this conversation itself has something of the quality of a Mobius Strip that the editors attribute to possession. It inevitably circles back on itself, and it has come to realize that possession is not one of those things it is possible to get to the bottom of or have the final word about.

Two main themes evidently run through this collection. First is a concern to acknowledge the dynamic quality of possession, its thrust, movement, and power. Second is the identification of paradox. Paradox is taken quite broadly, and many kinds of relations fall under it. One could argue that paradox negates the stability we typically associate with the concept of relation and hence is a source of the dynamism that possession manifests.

Before examining these matters more closely, a first question is whether there is an object (or subject) common to these essays and, if so, under what description to place it. Recently, the term "spirit possession" has come under scrutiny and a number of contributors problematize one or the other of its components. Thus Brent Crosson proposes the term "manifestation" to replace "possession" and other contributors suggest "powers."

I like these suggestions, but out of lazy habit and for the convenience of readers, I'll stick here to the older usage.[2] Even so, "spirit possession" is quite elastic and is used to cover quite a range of phenomena. This is as it should be; no single specific characterization of "spirit possession" qua object in the world or qua subject of anthropology is going to be sufficient. Generalizations are, therefore, on the order of what, in their engaging Introduction, Diana Espírito Santo and Matan Shapiro call thought experiments.

The majority of ethnographic examples are taken from the Americas, with a few from Asia, and often from Christian or highly syncretic contexts. This produces shades of emphasis that differ from the ethnographic corpus of work on African or Afro-Islamic contexts. In particular, there are differences according to how diverse and how personified spirits are (or Spirit is) and how sharply in a given tradition or set of practices, spirit, or spirits, is or are set off from the self. Within Christianity, as the chapters by Malara, Reinhardt, and Shapiro make clear, there are differing emphases on the expulsion of demons and of living with a non-personalized, even atmospheric, Holy Spirit or intimately with Jesus or one of the Saints. Where spirits are personified, they may be deceased humans, in which case matters of historicity are immediately raised, most complexly here in the cases described for Cuba (Espírito Santo and Panagiotopoulos), but also intriguingly in the counterexample of Mormonism (Bialecki).

In some instances, it may be appropriate to speak of shamanism, as at the onset of the rituals described by Espírito Santo where several experts collectively construct a complex mutual vision, albeit what follows is better described as possession. And it is a term that is appropriately used for the Nuosu as described by Swancutt. Jon Bialecki offers the example of Mormon baptism of the dead, which he specifically says is not spirit possession, and yet even to say that and include the essay in the volume suggests a family resemblance. Such family resemblance would be even clearer had a third ethnographic subject been included, namely reincarnation (and perhaps also masking). What these all have in common is the sharing of properties or partial identifications between different kinds of persons and the temporary displacements of one by the other. The cases challenge the notion of the primary, bounded, internally homogenous self (exemplified in the possessive individual); even the Mormons who, while concerned with accounting precisely for every single bounded individual, still allow others to stand in for baptism.

In sum, all of these chapters address the degree to which persons are part of one another. In that respect, the subject is as intimately connected to the domain anthropologists have called "kinship" as it is to what we have called "religion."[3] For some reason, the rationality debate has been placed virtually exclusively under the latter domain, whereas it could equally be discussed under kinship. Kinship is full of the paradoxes to which the editors allude: people being related to one another simultaneously in multiple ways—as spouse and cross-cousin, etc., or, to take a more complex example, as among the Inuit, who are simultaneously located in a kinship position in their birth families and in a different location with respect to the recently deceased person of whom they are a reincarnation. Many societies, especially small-scale ones, make much play over these ambiguities or thick and multiple qualities of persons and relationships. No one has only a single name or identity, and we apply multiple terms without a sense of contradiction. When and how this becomes paradoxical is not a matter of the application of principles of logic in the abstract but of how things arise or are presented to us in practice.

I will return to the subject of paradox below. In any case, we see possession intertwined with kinship in several of these essays, nowhere perhaps more explicitly and movingly than in Diego Malara's essay. "Demons," says Malara, "here, are not external to relationships, but inherent to kinship networks." This essay is exemplary because it works out its theoretical arguments by means of a case history, which, I think, is one of the most effective ways to depict the subject. For one thing, it moves between more or less intimate and more or less public contexts and idioms instead of focusing exclusively on the most public and dramatic moments of ceremony.

Motion, Force, and Passage

Paradigms in the anthropological study of spirit possession have shifted from the pathological to the functionalist and social epidemiological, and then to the interpretive. In this new phase, as I understand it, the editors want to take spirit possession "in its own right," to borrow a phrase from Don Handelman, the presiding intellectual spirit of this volume.[4] Spirit possession is no longer something to be exorcised, treated, dismissed, explained, or even interpreted (?), but something to be grasped, in itself, as itself, and for itself.[5] Yet at the same time, inspired by Deleuzian philosophy and more directly by the work of Handelman (and indirectly, Gregory Bateson), as well as by local intellectuals in Cuba and elsewhere who engage directly with the phenomena, spirit possession is to be understood not as a stable entity but as a force in motion.[6] Contributors share an interest in what possession is (as a mode of existence, not an essence), its happening, the kinds of experience that generate, characterize, and flow through it, and the happenings that it provokes or generates. Possession—whether the irruption of a new spirit, the settling of Spirit, or the exorcism of a demon—is frequently seen and experienced as a kind of *breakthrough*. This can be conceived in psychological, social, existential, or cosmological terms, or all of these simultaneously.

A significant point here is to clarify whether what is under consideration in a given textual passage is the immediate moment or movement transforming consciousness (the spirit rising, the demon leaving, etc.), the larger trajectory of becoming a spirit medium or a sufferer, or the yet broader picture of living with spirits. Also, whether the emphasis is on seeing all this as a product of learning or cultivation; *pathisch* reception (as Miho Ishii well puts it); submission; or rather as a more objective process or set of processes. Writers on spirit possession often talk past each other when they do not clarify which of these matters is what concerns them at any given point in their argument.

How to grasp force in motion is central to Diana Espírito Santo's descriptions of Afro-Cuban religion. Drawing on an idiom from Kardecism, she writes of spiritual flows and describes the buildup of intensity and pulses of energy moving through and between bodies. To generate energy you need synergy, whether this is between musicians, dancers, mediums, spirits, and here also in the collective calling out of visions. There are echoes of Durkheim's effervescence, which is a bubbling up and over. To this picture Espírito Santo adds Handelman's concept of ritual curvature that, according to its degree, marks out and generates something internal to itself and not a mere reflection of its environment. This builds to the onset of active possession and is followed by the transposition of the inward look into an outward gaze and spread.

Anastasios Panagiotopoulos complements and elaborates on this in showing the ways in which Cuban practices energize the present by means of the past, presenting a historical consciousness that is constituted not only as representation but as presence (ontology in his terms), creating folds in time and enabling spirits to break through them. Practitioners are not thinking abstractly, but imagistically and practically; much of the thought is embodied, like the excess sweat of his key interlocutor. This is science (or history) of the concrete. Panagiotopoulos argues that Cuban possession moves between representation and ontology, but these would be artificially abstracted concepts for practitioners. In their presence and their effects, spirits simultaneously represent and exist. And like any human being, they represent themselves.

Flow is also a central idiom in Bruno Reinhardt's essay, as it is with the Ghanaian Pentecostals with whom he studied. Working with possession and spirit in very different senses from the Cuban, Reinhardt depicts flow on two registers, on the one hand, atmospheric and, on the other, experiential. In the former, rather than considering the Holy Spirit as being either present or absent, its manifestation is a matter of modality or intensity and is further distinguished between descriptions of spirit acting "within," "upon," or "across." Here, "divine presence in (en)Spirited naturalism saturates the atmospheric medium while borrowing its capacity to be simultaneously visceral and evanescent, ubiquitous and modular, embodied and environmental." In the latter register, Reinhardt draws on Saba Mahmood's concept of "rehearsed spontaneity" and psychologist Mihalyi Csikszentmihalyi's (1990) concept of flow, a condition of being so caught up in an activity (rock climbing, playing music, etc.) that one loses self-consciousness. This is critical for describing shifts in consciousness (daydreaming, abstraction, focus ...) more generally. Finally, then, Reinhardt describes Christianity for Ghanaian Pentecostals as "more *a state of activity* amidst ongoing adversities than a stable religious identity" (my emphasis). This is a brilliant essay, exemplary of "ethnographic theory" at its best.[7]

Drawing, like Espírito Santo, from Handelman, Matan Shapiro sees neo-Pentecostal exorcism in Brazil as a passage, one concerning not only the possessed or exorcized individual, but a cosmic passage in which God is victorious over demons at large. Exorcism here is a masterful performance (well-illustrated in the linked video clips) between the pastor and his subject, happening on a very broad stage in front of hundreds of worshippers. Shapiro describes both the passage (removal) of the demons, imagined on a broad cosmological scale, and the passage (healing) of the individual, imagined on a moral scale. In some respects these appear to be analogues of one another. They are journeys and passages insofar as they confront border zones to be traversed rather than fenced borders that can be rapidly crossed. Despite the formal staging, this complicates the idea of possession or exorcism as a ritual simply framed within or beyond everyday life; instead the interconnections look more like a continuous Möbius Strip.

Passage is also a long-standing idiom in Central Asia, with respect to both nomadic economies and shamanic journeys. Writing on both Mongols and Nuosu, Katherine Swancutt draws on surprising metaphors of the trampoline and the springboard and writes of leaping across a cosmic void. She depicts thresholds as spaces that can collapse the distinctions they separate, thus between shamans and their spirit helpers. Moreover, the passage is simultaneously bidirectional as "priests and shamans work to enable their ritual hosts to simultaneously harness and oppose the powerful forces of the wilderness." Swancutt attends as well to passage in terms of the life course or careers of shamans and priests. Unlike most of the other ethnographic examples, Nuosu shamans face a shrinking threshold of their powers, which inevitably wane as they become overly familiarized with the wilderness and their spirit-helpers become increasingly domesticated. However, this is counterpoised to passages of increasing knowledge for priests, who draw on written texts. Her case illustrates the fact that in any given society practitioners of different kinds may be in some competition with each other, subject to a politics of knowledge and authority. This is evidently true in Brazil as well, where the Christian denominations debate the policies of exorcism among themselves, while deploring the Afro-Brazilian practices of spirit possession.

Both Swancutt and Shapiro seem to argue that a language of thresholds and journeys is superior to one of places. However, these authors realize that to speak of thresholds or journeys rather than stable places is to shift figure and ground; these are complementary rather than mutually exclusive ways of perceiving things and may be more salient in some ethnographic contexts than in others. Thus, in the Ethiopian case described by Malara, the site of pilgrimage is itself the source of power and the journeys to and from are important relative to the sanctity of place. This appears true as well for Mormon temples, described by Bialecki, where restricted access controls movement and centers institutionalized power. With the exception of the Mormons, all the cases appreciate *permeability*, which might be an appropriate term when weight is placed on persons or objects complementary to that of movement.

What all these chapters do, then, is to turn away from questions about the existence or reality of spirits per se, or of static "belief" in them, toward attention to their movement in and out of our lives or through the cosmos. Entities are not simply "there," or rather, "here," but forces ("power/s" in the words of practitioners in Trinidad and Karnataka) in motion. And to the degree that we do consider persons, spirits, or places as stable entities, the focus is on their permeability, an adjective that complements the adverbs and prepositions applied to verbs of movement.

Paradox I

Spirit possession invites responses from both participants and observers; indeed, one could say possession does not merely invite response but incites, demands, or begs it, whether to the disconcerting presence and provocative utterances of the spirits themselves, to their virtuoso feats and performances, or simply to the very existence of possession, whether understood as the disjunctive and temporary displacement of ordinary humans by other entities or as the co-presence, commingling or even unification of self and other, me and not-me, human and meta-human being. For the editors, if I understand them, it is the simultaneous distinction and indistinction of self and other that compel some kind of acknowledgment. They call this a paradox, and it is fruitful in the way that paradoxes are fruitful.

What is at issue for Espírito Santo and Shapiro is akin to what James Fernandez (1980) memorably called "edification by puzzlement." Metaphor brings together things that were originally contiguous but separate. Fernandez reminds us that "though part of the pleasure in metaphor rests in its suggestion of a relation between things thought to be separate if not opposite, at the same time the metaphor or the riddle-metaphor builds a bridge across the abyss of separated, discriminated experience" (1980: 178). Fernandez continues that, "out of the sense of similarities is produced a transcendent overarching sense of contiguity. This transformation of contiguities into similarities and similarities into contiguities is fundamentally edifying. And it is what Lévi-Strauss (1966) means when he speaks with (mysterious) edifying puzzlement about the transformation of metaphors into metonyms and vice versa." Fernandez identifies this process as also the work of African riddles, riddles that "constitute an ambiguous stimulus for creative and constructive responses." He suggests that "this kind of reasoning by the puzzle of analogy is a [congenial] mode of thought" insofar as it returns people to a sense of the whole, hence, "cosmogony by puzzlement" (1980: 179). He adds that riddling is iconic, "primarily producing and working with images more or less visual and concrete in effect ... It is the nature of iconic thought [in contrast to abstract or symbolic thought] to have much more of a personal component and also to excite contextualization" (1980: 185).

To excite contextualization. This is a fine phrase and one that speaks simultaneously to the volume at hand and to what its contributors say about their objects of study. But with possession, the work of puzzlement happens not simply through the discursive display of images but by means of embodied transformations (iconic and indexical). In a sense, possession might be seen as the inverse of metaphor, not conjoining the originally separate so much as separating and bringing into metonymic relation parts of what was once a single whole. But as suggested by the editors, this is a continuous and reversible dynamic process, one that might be captured (metaphorically) in the image of the Möbius Strip.

The source of the heightened puzzlement and excitation—we could call it an excitation of being[8]—can be described, as the editors do, as paradox.

The term paradox is used quite specifically in logic and more loosely in ordinary talk and language. The prototype in logic is the Cretan who tells us that all Cretans are liars, a statement that is false if it is true and true if it is false. Logicians tried to address this by means of a theory of types, the ostensible impasse being resolved at a higher order logical type. In ordinary talk (in English) the term paradox is often used to indicate the confluence of two things that were not expected to go together and that may have contrary inclinations or consequences. To return to the structuralist language deployed by Fernandez, one could speak of paradoxes of unexpected contiguity or unexpected similarity. Paradoxes are not strictly irrational. The point about the liar's paradox is not one of irrationality—of faulty reasoning—but rather of something that is inherently self-contradictory. If the thought or argument were merely irrational we could fix it. But insofar as it is a paradox, we cannot. The speaker, the Cretan liar (or truth teller), is actually very clever.

For Espírito Santo and Shapiro, paradox appears to indicate or conjoin one thing simultaneously with its contrary. They draw here for inspiration on Gregory

Bateson's understanding of play as action that is contextualized by the meta-message "this is not what it appears to be, not seriously what it says it is." For Bateson, play is distinguished by a frame that says, "what happens within this space is play." A clear illustration is the theater; the play is contained within the period of the curtain going up and being lowered and it is contained on the stage, albeit some theatrical performances experiment with these frames in a kind of meta-play. Actors act their part on stage and return to themselves off it. But in practice, the framing is often much more porous than the model suggests. Audiences are moved by the events on stage and may have to be reminded that this was "only" a play, and they may be expected to be "improved" by the exposure to classical drama. Moreover, as Espírito Santo and Shapiro note, following Handelman, the meta-message "this is play" becomes inherently ambiguous once one is within the frame, threatening to dissolve so that what is enacted or conducted becomes real, serious, and consequential. Players can forget themselves.

Jim Carrey becomes the person he is impersonating; he becomes the character offstage as well as on and he is not "merely playing" but living his life. While Carrey's engagement is an extreme form of identification or merger in the context of Western theater or filmmaking, this speaks to possession. Possession is theatrical, as several observers from Michel Leiris onward have noted; it is *like* theater and the performances of the spirits are often theatrical, but it is not theater. The hosts or mediums (each problematic terms) are not "merely" acting, they are not acting only "as," or "as if": they *are* the characters they perform, as they are also themselves, and their acts have consequences outside the frame. Spirit possession is characterized by the dynamic interpenetration of the playful and the serious, each opening out into the other.

While various genres of possession have their own means of framing, as spirits are formally invited into hosts and as hosts give way to spirits, the relations between hosts and spirits are more porous than framing suggests: spirits are somehow always (already and thereafter) a part of their hosts (though it is far less clear that the hosts are somehow always a part of the spirits). In other words, the difference or separation between humans and spirits is simultaneously established and transcended. The spirit speaking and acting through my body is simultaneously me and not me or, recursively, simultaneously not-me and not-not-me.[9] And contrary to how it might first appear, the separation that is maintained inside the frame is transcended outside it. That is to say, if the presence of the spirit is manifest during the performance of possession and thus marked in distinction to the human host, then outside of the performance frame, when the host has returned to herself, the spirit remains latent and not fully distinguishable from the host. It is always possible that the agent behind my acts or condition is not me but the spirit. Such inversion, reversion, or recursion is an aspect of the paradoxical quality of spirit possession.

The not-me can be more or less personalized depending on the genre. Most Malagasy *trumba* are understood as individuated persons, whereas Sudanese *zar* appear more as figures (in the sense of character types) (Boddy 1989). The interruption can be conceived as a personalized or impersonal force (as illustrated in several chapters of this book), and in the singular or the plural. Hence, specificity of person or intensity of force may be the salient factor. Again, these are not always strict alternatives. We might think of the multiple manifestations of the Hindu gods and their simultaneous articulation as singular godhead (Doniger 2014), or the paradox or riddle—the *mystery*, in theological language—of the Christian Trinity (cf. Mulhall 2015). With respect to meta-humans (Sahlins 2017), there is always a tension, evident both in practical religion and in theological debate, between their manifestation as persons and as concepts (Lambek 2021).

Returning to Bateson, when the meta-message and the message interrupt or confuse each other, when the two are in tension, or when the meta-message is both present and absent, the result can be received as paradox. Play and paradox can be edifying or pleasurable, as are frequently the paradoxes manifest in or as spirit possession. Yet, the most famous example of paradox in Bateson's oeuvre is actually an extremely negative and destructive one, namely the double bind, in which the message is directly contradicted by the meta-message. It manifests as "damned if you do and damned if you don't." The paradox here is certainly not playful. Yet it can become the subject of play. A playful illustration comes in the joke about the (Jewish) mother who buys her son two ties for his birthday. In order to please her, he immediately puts one on. And she responds: "So what's the matter, you don't like the other one?" Of course, if you try this joke on your own mother she may not find it funny; she might think your message—the contents of the joke—is conveyed along with an aggressive meta-message about her never being satisfied with you. The joke here (the meta-meta-message) is about inducing guilt and responding to that inducement. It also contributes to an unfair stereotyping of (Jewish) mothers, thereby illustrating a Möbius looping effect between the funny and the unfunny. Bateson saw repeated double-binding as generative of something much more severe than guilt, namely schizophrenia, an incorrect etiology that had very harmful consequences for the parents, especially the mothers, of schizophrenics.

Thus, if the paradox is a kind of binding of contraries, and if, pace Handelman, it cannot escape its self-contradiction and self-negation (insofar as it is constituted by them), then the perpetual movement that is said to characterize paradox is reiterative and constrictive, like a kind of pacing back and forth in a small space. Like the Möbius Strip, or like the liar's dilemma, the sequence is in perpetual motion, but it never ends up anywhere. If the paradox is a harmful one, the question is how to get out of it. The movement that is needed is eventually one of escape, whether by breaking the chain or transcending it in moving to a higher order.

Hence, the observation that spirit possession is not only engaged in paradox but also, to the contrary, unbinds or liberates, as Matan Shapiro proposes. Possession can disconnect the message from its contrary meta-message and let them stand equally and separately, enabling participants to move beyond their simultaneity or perpetual oscillation. Moreover, and somewhat like the privacy of the psychoanalytic consulting room, spirit possession may enable messages to be uttered in the absence of their ordinary meta-messages.[10] The uncoupling of the ordinary, habitual, conventional, or normative links between message and meta-message is one of the primary positive forces of possession, an aspect of its dynamism. The positive work that is done within the frame may then come to permeate ordinary life outside it.

In such a case, the oscillation is not only that internal to the paradox itself but between a paradoxical and non-paradoxical condition, much as, in the original illustration from Bateson, that one can move into and out of a clearly defined play frame.

In sum, there may be a certain productive tension between Bateson's concept of the frame or meta-message (as well as his cybernetic model) and Handelman's concept of passage. The theoretical project is how to articulate the relation; the ethnographic project is to follow how possession (in a specific local genre or genres) happens in practice, what it does and undoes for people and circumstances, how it pulls people in and out of frames, and how it generates fruitful paradoxes, displaces and breaks through unfruitful and destructive ones, and how it simply is itself.

Of course, whether a paradox is fruitful or not can be a matter of perspective. Even when a given paradox like the Cretan liar appears insoluble, it can be taken either as a place of frustrating aporia (as it was for some logicians) or a starting point for insight (as it may be for some religious thinkers, and even logicians). Reflecting on the liar's paradox will not lead to resolution, but it can be pleasurable and edifying in and of itself.

When someone is in an active state of possession they are simultaneously one person and another, or one person and not that person, and that it intrinsically interesting. Depending on circumstances it may be startling, disconcerting, illuminating, mysterious, frightening, or welcoming and comforting. It may be amusing or instructive, not least when the spirit acknowledges or plays on the difference between himself or herself and the medium—as a Creole sailor spirit said to me in French of his Malagasy-speaking medium's youthful attempts at painting, "*il n'avait pas de talent peut-être mais il s'amusait*" or when the child spirit in possession of a matron in Mayotte did all the things the host was always scolding her children for doing. I have taken these as meta-commentaries on the meta-message that is possession (respectively, Lambek 1981, 2002); in other words, framing can have multiple levels, each stimulating further thought and response.

In sum, where Espírito Santo and Shapiro state that "at the centre of spirit possession is a paradoxical play with alterity" and one that enables "the enactment of peculiar, adventurous passages" I can only agree and applaud the energy with which they think through what this means and thank them for having provoked us to think further on the subject.[11]

Paradox II

One disagreement I have is with the editors' depiction of possession as "one of the most baffling and self-contradictory social phenomena in social anthropology." First of all, I would not like to equate paradox with self-contradiction. Second, for societies in which it is practiced, and especially for its practitioners, possession is neither entirely baffling nor self-contradictory but simply part of the world as people find it. It is a mode of poiesis that draws on a neurological and cognitive affordance and the cultural capacity for structured genres of action or language games, much as the brain and human sociality enable distinct genres of art, music, and literature. For me, it is no more (or less) baffling or self-contradictory—and equally fruitful for thought and enjoyment—than the art of the novel (where the author both is and is not her characters …). Ethnographic studies of possession reveal underlying grammars. The participants I know in Mayotte and Madagascar consider possession neither baffling nor self-contradictory, though it is incommensurable with what they know about Islam, astrology, and science, and they do acknowledge the unpredictability of spirits, are sometimes amazed by what happens, and understand their practice with a leavening of irony.[12] Possession can be good to think, and for some, good to live with.

More needs to be said on the matter of perspective with respect to paradox. A logical paradox is supposed to be such from any perspective, truly intractable. But the paradoxes encountered ethnographically may be paradoxical only when viewed from certain perspectives and not from others. For example, paradox may result from mistaking deictic for denotative language.[13] When the pragmatics of specific utterances is taken into account, ostensible semantic contradictions disappear. The situation is particularly complex in multilingual settings where there is considerable borrowing and code-switching among several languages.

More generally, what are paradoxes from the perspective of one dimension or aspect of reality or within one language game may not be paradoxical from or within another. What appears paradoxical to science may not to religion, and conversely. If we alternate between seeing the world now from a scientific perspective, now from a religious or commonsensical one, along a passage that is not directly linear but Möbius Strip-like, what is a paradox from one place disappears from the other.[14]

Certain things appear as paradoxes only from a perspective of dualistic thinking. Dualistic thought (indeed any classificatory scheme) creates mediating figures, inversions, and dangerous, powerful, polluting, and paradoxical substances that transgress the mutually exclusive categories that it posits. The arguments and illustrations of Mary Douglas (1966) are particularly salient here. As Lorraine Daston has recently shown (2019), three different Western models of nature (as bounded, essentialized species, as local ecosystems, and as universal laws) give rise to three different kinds of anomalies—monsters, imbalances, and miracles, respectively, with concomitant "cognitive passions," among them horror, terror, and wonder. Forms of order distinct from those of Western/modern concepts of "nature," and particularly nondualist orders, would give rise to their own kinds of anomalies and cognitive passions.

If spirit possession is paradoxical from the naturalist perspective (or ontology) of anthropology, it remains unclear whether it is also paradoxical for its practitioners. Moreover, it may be anthropology that is mired in paradox. The question is implicitly raised by Marcio Goldman and others whether we can break through our own paradoxes.

In Goldman's provocative account of anthropology's dilemmas, it is anthropology, not witchcraft or spirit possession, that becomes the exotic object subjected to skeptical interrogation. His subtitle "how anthropology works" might have been "why anthropology doesn't (or cannot) work." As Goldman puts it, "The problem … is not only up to what point *can we* follow the native word, but also that of the point where we *should* separate ourselves from it. My hypothesis is that this separation has to happen to the extent that we intend (it is our choice) to place more things into relation than the natives intend to." If I understand the argument, it suggests that the anthropological position of both following "the native word" and separating ourselves from it is itself paradoxical, and the anthropologist caught in a double bind between romanticism and ethnocentrism.

Although in general agreement with Goldman, I find that he puts things too dualistically. He speaks of a "fundamental bifurcation" in anthropology between "the pretension to discover the truth of the others or the much more modest task of mapping other truths," when in fact what he shows is the way these remain in tension. He also makes quite a sharp distinction between natives and anthropologists, whereas natives often try to discover the "truths" of the world that produces anthropologists and use that to reflect back on themselves. Often this appears by means of spirit possession itself.[15]

A third dualism that appears to haunt several of the chapters is between the [modern] West and the [primitive] Rest. We all know the problems here.[16] This dualism, whether in terms inherited from Lévy-Bruhl rather than Tyler or Evans-Pritchard, reproduces the arrogance that Goldman rightly tries to undermine. It reappears here in responses to the important work of Paul Christopher Johnson (2011, 2014). Johnson argued that the modern liberal subject was constituted in opposition to the non-Western subject. Whereas the former came to be characterized as free (a free man), self-possessed, and a potential possessor of other men and women (slaves), the latter was seen as subject to slavery and enslaved already by his own mystifications. If the liberal subject possessed things, people, and ideas, the primitive was possessed by them. Hence, the etiology of the term "spirit possession" and the metaphor of the host as "possessed by"—enslaved to—the spirit becoming common parlance not only among anthropologists, but among slaves and their descendants as well.

The essays here are ambivalent in their responses to Johnson. Panagiotopoulos begins with the interesting observation that so many of the spirits who possess Cubans are black. Yet he undermines our immediate assumptions about this fact, showing that even where slavery, race, or the absence of voice are part of the historical picture, possession transcends rather than reproduces them. In describing the initial difficulty new mediums often have in their first attempts to manifest spirits, Panagiotopoulos draws an analogy to Cuban history at large; he makes the lovely point that "what is voiced is not so much a wide range of clear utterances but the previous inability to express them, and an insinuating and overarching call for this impediment to be overcome."

Slavery, of course, extends much further back in history than the Atlantic trade. Malara draws on historian Peter Brown's account of possession in early Christianity, and this suggests that the slavery mode of thinking about demonic possession is a Christian idiom of long standing. Conversely, not all Christian idioms see possession in this light and, in fact, experiences and idioms of possession are much more complex than can be encompassed by the slavery idiom. Thus, Reinhardt argues that self-cultivation and being acted upon by forces external to the body need not be seen as mutually exclusive. In charismatic Christianity people welcome the spirit. It is a matter, he says, of "yielding" to God and a "fusion between disciplinary submission and spiritual attunement."

Brent Crosson gives fullest consideration to Johnson's analogy between possession as property, and therefore slavery, and passion as being taken over by a spirit. As Crosson insightfully notes, Johnson's point that "the making of the willful, self-possessed Enlightenment individual needs (a reductive idea of) slavery as a constitutive foil" says more about Europeans than it does about what Crosson calls "spirit manifestation religions." Crosson also clarifies that this is why the idiom of "spirit possession" has been taken up by anthropologists, why, so to speak, the term and concept have taken possession of *us*. Hence, in exploring the origins and development of the Western concept of spirit possession we should not confuse this with the concepts and practices of our research subjects.

In fact, spirit possession is rarely understood as full subordination or ownership in the literal or legal sense by an external being (and in such a case, specifically a demon). The term "possession" may be influenced by its economic or legal sense, but anthropologists defer to local concepts and understandings.[17] Moreover, there is always the ambiguity as to who "possesses" whom. In Mayotte it is the human host (the term I have long deployed) who could be said to "have" or possess (*misy*) a spirit, not the reverse. Moreover, it is necessary to distinguish between conceptions of the immediate onset of a spirit—the displacement in the body of one person by another—a seizure that one of my teachers memorably described, switching to French while abruptly giving my arm a hard squeeze, as a "*coup d'état*"—from ensuing negotiations with the spirit to render it reasonable and companionate, and sometimes even coaxing it to enter. The idiom is a political one.

Drawing on a Trinidadian idiom, Crosson suggests that possession is "the 'catching' and embodying of a power."[18] "Catching power" is a catchy and powerful way to put things, but submission (however that is described) is also a salient aspect of becoming possessed. The "paradox" in possession is precisely that it is both of these at once. To catch a power is simultaneously to be subordinated to it (as in catching a disease). Moreover, this entails coming to terms with what one has caught. In Trinidad it is to contain or "work" (work with?) the spirit. Put in other terms, the paradox, as Crosson rightly observes, is one of action *and* passion simultaneously.

Paradox III

If Western Enlightenment thinkers were mistaken in their depiction of non-Europeans, were those anthropologists who in reaction emphasized rationality equally mistaken? Should we rather have been more attentive to Lévy-Bruhl's formulations of participation? Does Lévy-Bruhl's concept of participation depict a world that "we" cannot comprehend by means of our dualistic thought, such that what appears a paradox to *us* does not appear so to the inhabitants of such a world? Is it radically other? Or do the same rules of logic apply everywhere, and a paradox will always be a paradox?

I'll restrict myself to suggesting that posing things in this fashion is itself another example of dualist thinking. One way around the problem is by thinking more deeply and rigorously about language. In an extremely interesting essay, Miho Ishii addresses the problem by attending to grammatical voice. Since in one respect possession is precisely concerned with adding new voices to conversations, voice in the grammatical sense may be highly salient.

Ishii begins with Victor von Weizsäcker's concept of Pathisches, life simply "actualized within itself" as events occur of their own accord.[19] Pathisches is being that is receptive to its environment and constitutes itself by means of reception. Such reception could occur as a mode of suffering, but it is not meant as negative or strictly passive. This relationship to the world might be compared to Csikszentmihalyi's concept of flow discussed above but has the benefit, in the formulation of Takeshi Matsushima, on whom Ishii draws, of examining the relationships of people in synchrony with one other rather than directly to an activity in which they are immersed as individuals.

The pathisch mode is captured linguistically by a middle voice, which corresponds to neither the grammatical active nor passive voice. Following Matsushima, Ishii "defines the function of the middle voice as the expression of natural momentum without a subject-agent. The opposition between the active voice and middle voice is thus the opposition between the action of a subject-agent and the event that occurs of its own accord." The middle voice describes events rather than attending to agents of action or their will. Things happen and unfold; perhaps one could add they flow. Spirits, we could say, emerge.[20]

Diego Malara's case study exemplifies Pathisches. Here, the illness of the protagonist and its diagnosis as possession and subsequent exorcism are things that happen. Even the agency of the shrine and of the angel Michael are not directly manifest; the exorcism takes place behind the scenes as it were. And most telling is the way the mother falls under the very same spirit, exemplifying the mutuality of being pointed to with respect to very close kin, as in the formulation by Marshall Sahlins of kinship as mutuality of being (2013).

The more the middle voice is highlighted, it would seem, the more depersonalized the spirit, who may be conceived as a force or power rather than anthropomorphically. However, it is certainly the case that spirits often *do* speak decisively and in an active voice. Here, I suggest, the question of agency could be described (and distributed) by means of Erving Goffman's concept of footing and his distinctions among the animator, author, and principal of any utterance. Embedded within the "I" of any utterance is the I who voices it (the animator), the I who has selected the words and sentiments expressed (the author), and the I whose position is established thereby or is committed to the utterance (the principal) (Goffman 1981, 144). In ordinary conversation, these are generally one and the same, but possession uncouples them and renders their relations ambiguous. This is evident in Goldman's interaction at the *terreiro* with which his essay begins.

What spirits cannot do is speak directly, face-to face, to or with the people they are possessing at that moment. Here Ishii rightly notes the significance of the witness, the trusted person who observes and acknowledges the transition and through whom "the performer can realise his/her altered mode of being reflexively." This corresponds to my formulation of the basic communication triad (host, spirit, and third party) in which the third serves as the interlocutor of the spirit and can later report back to the host what transpired (Lambek 1981). The intermediary is of course a "middle voice" of a different, nongrammatical kind.

There is a tension between emphasizing, on the one hand, as Bialecki nicely puts it, paradox as violation of the principle of identity, and on the other, polyphony, displacement, mediation, and expansion to a third party. The displacement of voice is not only that of a given human by a spirit, but sometimes of spirits by one another. Malara writes, "The presence of the angel is dramatically evinced through his interactions with demons that suffer under his force, confess their misdeeds, scream, and beg him to stop inflicting pain on them. To echo [Peter] Brown again, 'nothing [gives] more palpable face to the unseen *presentia* of the saint than the heavy cries of the possessed'" (1981, 108). And again, "In this aesthetic of presence, demons become mediators of the messages of an angel that humans cannot hear or see." This expression of one force by means of its opposite is paradoxical in its own right.

Finally, I am in complete agreement with Ishii that spirit possession "shows some essential traits forming the basis of our experience of *life itself*, which may be acutely sensed in terms of affect, passion, and care." This is, in fact, an insight of the hermeneutic approach to possession, one that is neither reductive like functionalism nor reifying of difference like ontologism and hence could further help us avoid making all too definitive discriminations between so-called modern and primitive worlds (whatever values we place on them respectively).

One last point about language. Johnson assists us in returning to life and consciousness what had become a dead metaphor. But it may be that we cannot speak about these matters other than by metaphor, which in turn undoubtedly shapes the experience. In the powerful West African metaphor of horse and rider, it is not only the horse who needs to be broken to the will of the rider, but the rider to the will of the horse. Alternative metaphors include those of a chair, vessel, slave, host, medium, possessed, or simply, as Ishii would put it, a *recipient*. In Malagasy the words for being in a state of possession (*menziky*) or for a spirit in the act of possessing (*mianzaka*) (both, I think, in the middle voice) are related to words for ruler and (political) rule (*manzaka*).[21] Indeed, many of the most powerful Malagasy spirits are former monarchs. Mediums therefore could be said to be ruled by spirits. They are not their slaves, but their subjects. Here then, a caveat to Bialecki's point that possession may not correspond well with hierarchy. In fact, royal oracles have been associated with states like the Inca and precolonial Madagascar (before possession becomes democratized there) and it is common also in South Asia with its kingdoms and its temple and caste hierarchies. It is true, however, that possession is often a way to subvert hierarchy, not only injecting otherwise disempowered or dissonant voices or opinions into conversation but inverting values in carnivalesque performance (cf. Bakhtin 1984, Stallybrass & White 1986).

* * *

It has been impossible to do justice to the rich ideas flowing through each of these chapters or to channel them into a single picture. They are "thought experiments" insofar as they apply new concepts to possession and insofar as they accept the challenge possession provides to think through some of our own fundamental concepts and theoretical preoccupations.[22]

Possession is both an expression of paradox (the simultaneity of self and other, past and present, action and passion, etc.) and its resolution (in the emergence of the cure, insight, historical consciousness, etc.). The simultaneity of expression and resolution may itself be seen as paradox. Perhaps reflection on possession will help anthropologists resolve our own paradoxes. But, to follow a lesson of possession, resolution of paradox will not thereby terminate its expression, which will surely continue to pervade our "impossible profession."[23]

An important concept raised in Espírito Santo's essay, citing an earlier one for which Ishii was co-author, is that of tact. In my ethnographic experience, spirits often make what in other contexts would be considered tactless remarks; that is an aspect of their power and voice. And yet conversely, studying possession requires considerable tact on the part of the ethnographer; one cannot push spirits on matters beyond their knowledge or that might otherwise embarrass or anger them. And one should not draw attention to any infelicities of performance or slippage between what are purportedly distinct identities.

If tact is critical for ethnography, it can be a hindrance to theory. Theoretical disputation resembles much of the public talk enacted by spirits. It often runs tactlessly roughshod over subtleties to make its point and it is sometimes marked by an enthusiastic excess of signification, as if excess were a means of persuasion, the theorist's expression of power.

Possession is not theory per se; it exemplifies, displays, or manifests philosophical and critical thought rather than expressing it explicitly in abstract language. Such performance affords the possibility for theorizing, one that attentive ethnographers, attuned as well to the politics of their own situation and the latest developments in their own intellectual milieu, are able to take up. But care needs to be taken to keep clear the distinction between "our" preoccupations (qua anthropologists or concerned citizens …) and the means through which we articulate them, and the concerns and means of articulation of our interlocutors. Spirit possession is good to think with for anthropologists no less than for communities of practice—but that doesn't mean we think in identical ways or to identical ends. Spirit possession isn't a theoretical discussion of race or power, being or representation, rationality or paradox; it is simply … spirit possession (or rather, espiritismo, Santería, buta worship, etc.). Sometimes paradox is marked (highlighted, celebrated, queried …) and sometimes not.

As always, we have to be extremely cautious that our own heightened theory talk does not actually disguise the way we project our concerns onto others. There is a tension between the work that "spirit possession" does for anthropologists and the work it performs for insiders. That tension is found throughout this volume. Are we authors talking with each other and with our predecessors about the best way to think about, with, or though possession—or are we attempting to exemplify what possession says and does for the possessed and their local audiences and clients? Is it a paradox to attempt both simultaneously?

I wonder whether the paradox of anthropology might overdetermine how we see things elsewhere. I conclude therefore with three questions. First, if the *form* of spirit possession is inherently paradoxical (me and not-me, what the editors call the "momentary collapse of alterity"), does this mean the substance of what is learned or accomplished through possession must be paradoxical (or put within a frame of "paradox") as well? Second, what of the "collapse of alterity" between the anthropologist and her subjects? How should we distinguish interpretations of possession phenomena that are significant for "us" from those that are significant for members of the communities of practice themselves? And third, how do we know whether we have encountered a genuine paradox and not simply failed to fully understand what is being said or meant or done?

Notes

Introduction

1 Taken from director Chris Smith's recent documentary *Jim & Andy: The Great Beyond (2017)*, which depicts the making of Milos Forman's feature film *Man on the Moon* (1999).
2 This is a different thesis to the more recent Extended Mind theory proposed by Clark and Chalmers (1998; cf. also Hutchins 1995), in which "cognition"—and thus mind—can be seen to operate outside the borders of the skull and incorporate a multitude of social and material elements. Bateson's concept is more dynamical, mind defined by processes and transgression of boundaries, and further, unconfined to the realms of the purely social—or rather, proposing a kind of extended definition of sociality.

Chapter 1

1 A stimulant plant used in Ethiopia.
2 A spirit transmitted through bilateral descent lines (see Aspen 2001). While zar are considered amoral spirits and propitiated within the zar cult, in the context of the shrine, every spirit except the Holy Spirit is perceived as demonic and is accordingly exorcized. Thus, in this chapter, I use the terms spirit and demon interchangeably.
3 The possession of multiple kin is a consequence of the type of spirit involved: a zar. However, cases where generic demons engendered similar relational problems are not uncommon.

Chapter 3

1 "Recent studies (Ong 1987, Taussig 1993, Kramer 1993, Comaroff J. 1985) … suggest that spirit possession rests on epistemic premises quite different from the infinitely differentiating, rationalizing, and reifying thrust of global materialism and its attendant scholarly traditions" (Boddy 407).
2 Scholars who have treated possession as part performance (Leiris 1958), suggesting the loose analogy that actor is to role, as medium is to possessing deity, have helped to decenter the authenticity of the medium (see Stoller 1995 for qualifications of the theatrical metaphor).
3 The relationship between possession deity and possessed connotes a sense of "mounting" in Yoruba, implying the riding of a horse or of a sexual partner. Possession priests were also called the "brides" of possessing deities who mounted and penetrated their mediums (both gods and goddesses are penetrators in this human-divine intimacy).

4 "Possession," perhaps because of its connotations of domination or instrumentalization, refers to malevolent or negative experiences of spirits as afflictions, rather than therapeutic or empowering experiences of spirit manifestation in Trinidadian usage.

5 See also McNeal (2003) and Vertovec (1998) for more on the dynamics of Kali Mai shakti play.

6 That the head of this Kali temple was a woman is an exception to the rule of male leadership. Various authors have sought to address the apparent paradox of male control of goddess centered South Asian practices. Most notably, Sarah Caldwell's (1999) <u>Oh Terrifying Mother</u>, reads this dynamic as the male control of potentially uncontrollable, fierce female forces. The possession or enactment of female divinity by male dancers in Kerala again involves control rather than loss of self-control. By manifesting such fierce, female forms of Kali, Caldwell suggests, male players may contain anxiety-producing representations of female sexuality and power.

7 Stoller avows sympathy with the theatrical approach to spirit possession but asserts that he has moved on from this paradigm to emphasize a framework of embodiment.

8 Of course, it is possible to argue that the genealogy of possessive individualism that Johnson traces ends up producing a self that is determined by its possessions or possessed by them. After all, Marx's critique of "commodity fetishism" draws on (European ideas of) African religion to satirize the way that humans become objectified and material possessions assume life in industrial capitalism. At the very beginning of the genealogy that Johnson traces, Enlightenment writings on contract and rights constantly raise the specter of Man's possession by external powers. To take another example, the modern discourse of addiction represents another case in which the willful individual seems overcome by its material possessions creating what Eve Sedgwick (1994) has called epidemics of the will. Again, the specter of slavery lurks not far behind anxieties over addiction. The word "addiction" itself derives from a Roman legal term for the transfer of rights from a slave to its master, and the idea of humans enslaved to substances is a popular contemporary way of narrating the state of addiction. These examples underscore Paul C. Johnson's point—that the making of the willful, self-possessed Enlightenment individual needs (a reductive idea of) slavery as a constitutive foil. Rather than instantiating the compound agency of many spirit manifestation religions, however, these specters of slavery, commodity fetishism, or addiction again represent the inversion of proper subjectivity and the negation of the proper locus of agency in the human will.

9 In the context of Hayes' (2011) written and documentary film work (*Slaves of the Saints*) on "Afro-Brazilian religion," it should be noted that her racially diverse set of practicing interlocutors overwhelmingly cast their relationships with the "saints" as ones of aid, assistance, help, and protection. In this context, the occasional references to being a slave indicate not a recapitulation of a relationship of chattel slavery, but the notion of human obligation and sacrifice that the spirits' protection demands (2011, 12)—in other words, the same "difficult relationality" that I have presented in this essay.

Chapter 4

1 See, for instance, Taussig (1980), Geschiere (1997), and Comaroff and Comaroff (1999). See also Boddy (1994) for a review of anthropological theory on spirit possession.

2   According to Andersen (1989), who examined the term *páthos* in Dionysius Thrax's grammar, *páthos* in Classical Greek means that which happens to a person or thing, what one has experienced; experience, suffering, and affection. This term is translated into Latin as *passivum* (from *pati* "to suffer") and as *passive* in modern linguistics. Andersen argues, however, that the term *páthos* corresponds to the modern term "middle" rather than "passive." He writes: "the wide range of specific meanings expressed by the 'middle' have a prototypical component of 'affectedness' which is nothing more than the actual meaning of the term *páthos* in the Greek language" (Andersen 1989, 15).

3   Benveniste (1966) states that, in the case of the middle voice, the verb indicates a process in which the subject becomes the *site* of the process; in the case of the active voice, the verb indicates a process originated from the subject and conducted outside the subject. In the latter case, the subject controls the process as the actor from outside. Based on Benveniste, Jean-Pierre Vernant defines the contrast between the active voice and middle voice as follows: in the case of the active voice, the action is ascribed to the agent like an attribute to a subject, while in the case of the middle voice, the action envelopes the agent and the agent remains immersed in the action. Vernant points out that the disappearance of the middle voice and the predominance of the contrast between active voice and passive voice suggest the creation of a vocabulary of the *will* as well as the idea of the human subject as agent, the source of actions (Macksey and Donato (eds) 1972, 152).

4   The fieldwork on which this section is based was conducted from June 1999 to March 2000 and from June 2000 to March 2001. On suman worship in Southern Ghana, see also Ishii (2005).

5   Although a detailed linguistic analysis of Twi is beyond the scope of this chapter, it can be pointed out that phrases such as "*akɔm no faa me*" have a similar structure to phrases that express an affect or passion of the affected entity ("*me*"), such as, "*ɔkɔm de me* (hunger takes me)." On the linguistic analysis of the morpheme *de* and *fa* in Twi, see Lord (1993, 70–1). See also Kemmer (1993) for the middle system in Twi.

6   Lienhardt (1961) points out similar features in Dinka expressions for the manifestation of Powers (*jok*) on a person: "we often find a reversal of European expressions which assume the human self, or mind, as subject in relation to what happens to it; [...] in Dinka the disease, or Power, always 'seizes the man'" (150). Lienhardt considers these expressions in terms of *passiones*, which has the same etymology as pathos (151). While Lienhardt does not deepen his semantic inquiry, his descriptions indicate a key feature of events in the middle voice: the Power manifests itself and affects the person as the site. On the issue of self and *passiones*, see also Kramer (1993, 58–64), Lambek (1993, 312; 2010), and Okazaki (2003).

7   The fieldwork on which this section is based was undertaken for a total of about seventeen months during several periods between May 2008 and March 2015. See also Ishii (2013, 2014, 2015, 2019) on būta worship in South Kanara.

8   Among these terms, *darṣana* clearly designates the feature of the event in the middle voice, in the sense that it designates an involuntary motion of the affected entity (see Kemmer 1993, 145).

9   While most būtas have androgynous characteristics, they are often regarded as females (though Arasu is regarded as male in Perar). Here, I use a personal pronoun for female to refer to a būta incarnated in a medium in general.

10 The position in suman worship corresponding to the gaḍipatināṛu is called *aduruagya*, who is the host of suman as well as patron of a particular suman shrine. In this paper, I focus on the roles of ɔkyeame and gaḍipatināṛu for their close relationship with spirits/deities.

11 As described in Case 2, deities like Arasu are embodied by mediums in the realm of jōga and transact with others, while they are regarded as formless śakti in the realm of māya. Additionally, būtas have the power to make others vanish (*māya maḷpuni*). See Upadhyaya (1988–1997, 1339, 2566, 2567), Claus (1978, 9–10), and Brükner (2009, 44, 77, 133).

Chapter 6

1 At this level, possession evokes overarching moral economies and metaphysics of the social, resembling and rivaling other secular-religious categories incorporated by anthropology, such as totemism, fetishism, the gift or grace (see Debaise 2008). See also Crapanzano (1982) and Collu (2019) for alternative experiments with this analytical scale.

2 The problem of presence is defined by Engelke in explicitly anthropocentric terms, as "how a religious subject defines and claims to construct a relationship to the divine through the investment of meaning and authority in certain words, actions and objects" (9). As shown by Beliso De-Jésus (2015, 71–8), one of the side effects of cultural constructivism is the homogenization of "presence" itself across the religious spectrum, which becomes a passive, spatialized, and residual category without capacity to differ, hence also without ethnographic input into theory.

3 I highlight that this property pertains only to the Holy Spirit, which is the immanent manifestation of God's transcendent will. Demons have names that singularize them according to origins: "the spirit of poverty," "Internet demons," or "ancestral spirits." They will as Satan does, but they relate to him usually in terms of hierarchical organizations, such as the army, Satan being "the commander." These rhetorical operations indicate that demons are not transcendent, and Pentecostals indeed believe that the world actually belongs to Satan, and will be destroyed with him. I was often reminded that Jesus himself called Satan "the ruler of this world" (John 12:31).

4 "Background metaphorics" are discursive repertoires that trace "stylistic differences of a way of life back to a layer of elementary ideas that always shows itself most clearly where the 'supply of images' has been tapped" (Blumenberg 2010, 63).

5 Another similar technique is "loosening" one's tongue by uttering "Hallelujah" or "Jesus" rapidly and repetitively until the Spirit animates it.

Chapter 7

1 Neo-Pentecostal pastors often invoke in church such spiritual entities as caboclos, orixás, and *vodums*, which otherwise only manifest in Afro-Brazilian worship houses (*terreiros*). These spiritual entities are presented as diabolical within the confines of Christian binary (good-evil) cosmology (Silva 2007).

2   I used parts of this ethnography in an article published in Social Analysis (Shapiro 2019). The interpretation and the rationale of argumentation here go in a different direction.

3   See http://www.universal.org/noticias/2015/06/30/demonios-e-possessoes-33489.html (accessed February 15, 2017).

4   Catholic exorcism follows the Roman Rite Cannon, which, since its publication in 1614 prescribes specific liturgical instructions (Sluhovsky 2007). While unauthorized exorcism sessions do occur in contemporary Catholic contexts in Brazil, they are officially condemned (Chesnut 2003).

5   I attribute this gender bias to a resurging conservative turn in Brazil, which induces female pastors to take "educational" roles in the congregation while male pastors engage in direct combat with these entities (cf. Shapiro 2019). Further research into this bias is required.

6   Rather than analyzing a particular or even a composite case study I will supply a general overview of typical rites as they are conducted in a wide variety of neo-Pentecostal churches. This is because my aim is to point out their common features as these relate to a particular Brazilian neo-Pentecostal theory of passage, which goes beyond the idiosyncratic symbolic and performative aspects of each ceremony.

7   IUED leader Bispo Edir Macedo always asks the possessing demons which of them is "in charge." By naming the demon, Macedo achieves a measure of control over it (cf. Stewart 1991, 213ff). He then directs the spiritual battle toward this entity alone. When the entity is finally tamed and subdued—and ultimately exorcised from the body—a long chain of demons is destroyed with it. This logic is in fact identical to that informing basic notions of motion and connectedness in Afro-Brazilian doctrines, which assume that once a single entity has possessed a person, her entire family has the right to use the medium's body whenever they wish to do so. Bispo Macedo preserves the features by which a particular kind of passage between worlds takes place while altering its moral content.

8   See this clip of Bispo Macedo exorcising a demon after commanding him to twist his hands backwards and fall on his knees: https://www.youtube.com/watch?v=ghdMByLaYJ4 (accessed October 4, 2018).

9   Church website: http://www.iaptd.com.br/index.php; the expulsion of five million demons: https://www.youtube.com/watch?v=ceKoN4d7If0 (both sites accessed October 5, 2018).

10   Different churches use olive oil, consecrated pieces of cloth, or Jewish religious materiality (e.g., prayer shawls, head-caps, or *mezuzah* scrolls) to displace evil and replace it with a divine substance. Some denominations even call for the public to walk barefoot on consecrated salt, which they buy in Israeli supermarkets during pilgrimage journeys to the Holy Land. See Shapiro (2020).

11   See: https://www.youtube.com/watch?v=TFT96wJOo6c (accessed August 8, 2020).

12   Charles Stewart (1991, 76) similarly argues that in the Greek island of Naxos, where he studied local conceptions of demons, "the human struggle for moral perfection … takes place on the overtones of a cosmic struggle." This may extend the comparative scope of the analysis presented herein.

13   Often pastors use these public spectacles to ask congregant for donations and offering to the church. I have personally witnessed such occasion in July 2016 at the IURD Temple of Solomon in São Paulo. Eric Kramer (2005, 101) argues that this act is strongly related to Prosperity Theology. Since I would like to focus on passages and cosmology I cannot elaborate more on this issue here.

14 For example, how important it is to "really mean it" during prayer as opposed to the role of technical ordination and the sustenance of "proper" procedure for the successful realization of rituals.

15 Luhrmann contrasts this form of playful relationship with the divine to Christian doctrines that reject a multiplicity of frameworks of belief as an ontological possibility, thereby insisting on a single frame of reference through which spiritual phenomena can be experienced and interpreted. For example, Joel Robbins (2004) argues that the Urapmin are totally and fully engrossed with Christian ritual practice through everyday activities to the extent that any other spiritual practice is not only condemned but also excluded as a cultural impossibility. Following Robbins, Luhrmann calls this form of Christianity "never-secular Christianities." (cf. Meyer 2010)

Chapter 9

1 In the August 2018 recent General Conference (a bi-annual series of speeches from Church leaders that all members of the Church of Jesus Christ of Latter-day Saints are encouraged to listen to, either in person, or more likely via broadcast or internet live-stream), President Russel M. Nelson stated that members should only use the Church's full name, and rejected the use of "Mormon" to refer to the institution, its members, or the associated culture. The Church's official statement to this effect can be found, ironically enough, online at the Mormon Newsroom internet portal. I refrain from following his admonition here for two reasons. The first is that almost the entirety of the research on this project was done before the announcement, and hence my engaging in such a change in nomenclature would be ahistorical at best, revisionary at worse. The second reason is that the Mormon Transhumanist Association itself, which is the particular Mormon group I focused on and did the most work with, have declined to change their name. Part of the reason for this is institutional: as a non-profit corporation, this change would require amending its constitution. Another reason is that the term Mormon, though originally derogatory, was embraced by Joseph Smith, the founder of the Church of Jesus Christ of Latter-day Saints; further, a large part of the nineteenth-century religious speculative movement that the MTA draws some of its inspiration from having understood itself to be engaged in "Mormonism" as well. The MTA also notes that there are several religious movements that also trace back their origins to Joseph Smith, and include the Book of Mormon in their cannon.

2 For a review of some of the social uses of the language of evangelization, see Handman 2018.

3 The official website of the Church has since been changed to "https://www. churchofjesuschrist.org," as part of a concerted effort to reject both the term "Mormon" and the title of "Latter Day Saints."

4 A ward is the basic unit of local congregations, membership of which is determined territorially, depending on where a person or family lives.

5 Missionary service in the Church is open to men, women, and married couples, but the sort of missions referenced here are the voluntary two-year missions commonly served by young men, and which are generally understood as a rite of passage and a sign of good character.

6 http://media2.ldscdn.org/assets/family-history/stephen-jezek-indexing/2014-06-01-redeeming-the-dead-redeemed-me-720p-eng.mp4?download=true; (accessed September 5, 2018).

7   As we will see, the concept of genealogy is quite complicated, and far exceeds what will be discussed in this paper, as does discussions of ritual. For a more complete discussion on these issues, see Cannell 2007, 2013; for a discussion regarding the place of The Church of Jesus Christ of Latter-day Saints in the wider anthropological imagination, see Cannell 2005.

8   Though the name of the submerged individual, along with the dead person who the individual is serving as a proxy for, is a part of the formula recited during this ritual, or "ordinance" as it is referred to by the Church.

9   Since, as will be pointed out, one not only had to be a Mormon to enter a Mormon Temple, but has to be a Mormon in good standing, the reader may wonder how the author has access to this information. This is also the case because many aspects of Mormon Temple practice are secret (see Kramer 2014). This is based on available print depictions of Temple ritual, as well as on numerous formal interviews and informal conversations with current and former members of the Church of Jesus Christ of Latter-day Saints. This essay does not discuss the most sacred, and the most secret, parts of Mormon Temple ritual, the keywords, signs, and tokens; those are material that, even if the author hypothetically had access to (which he does not), he would not divulge.

10   Saints being a term that many Mormons historically have used to describe themselves.

11   In other instances, this "burning in the bosom" is experienced as atypical thoughts or hunches, often urging the recipient to action (compare with Bialecki 2017).

12   On the establishment of the St. George Temple, and on how it was opened up to new forms of endowments, see Bennett 2005.

13   In the often-debated passage, that is, 1 Corinthians 15:29, Paul seems to allude to baptism for the dead when he asks "Else what shall they do which are baptized for the dead, if the dead rise not at all? why are they then baptized for the dead?"

14   https://www.mormonwiki.com/Chronological_List_of_Temples; accessed June 30, 2019.

15   See Rose, Alexander. 2007. "The Mormon Vaults." *The Long Now Foundation*. https://blog.longnow.org/02007/04/09/the-granite-vaults-of-geneology/ accessed July 1, 2019.

16   In the Church of Jesus Christ of Latter-day Saints, all males in good standing usually hold priesthood status.

Chapter 10

1   It was only after I submitted this text for publication that I discovered that, in 1978, Sophie Oluwole published an article that has the same title as mine. And even though the spirit of our work is very different, I would like to acknowledge this coincidence: Oluwole, Sophie. 1978. "On the Existence of Witches." Second Order 2 (182): 3–20.

Afterword

1   I am grateful to Diana Espírito Santo and Matan Shapiro for their provocation and their patience, as well as to the anonymous reviewers.

2   Elsewhere I borrow from Marshall Sahlins (2017) the terms metapersons and metahumans.

3   For the Mormon case on this point, see Cannell 2013.

4   See Handelman and Lindquist 2005; Handelman, Shapiro and Feldman, 2021.

5   I see a closer connection between the interpretive approach (e.g., Boddy 1989; Masquelier 2001; Ram 2013; Stoller 1989, or my work) and the focus of this book than many of the authors appear to. See also psychoanalytical approaches, e.g., Crapanzano 1980, Obeyesekere 1981, and Pandolfo 2018.

6   The legacy is primarily one from the Manchester school, following from Victor Turner's discussion not of ritual per se but of what he famously termed "the ritual process" and the creative ways in which Bruce Kapferer and Don Handelman subsequently elaborated the phenomenology and aesthetics of passage (Turner 1969; Kapferer 1991, 1997).

7   I take the term "ethnographic theory" from *Hau: Journal of Ethnographic Theory*, as first enunciated by Giovanni da Col and David Graeber, 2011. For another study of African Pentecostalism that emphasizes motion and refrains from objectivizing its subject, see Premawardhana 2018.

8   Recall that I. M. Lewis (1971) placed possession under the rubric "ecstatic religion."

9   Whether in a given genre of possession the ambiguity between me and not-me is maintained in performance (as appears to be the case in Sudanese *zar*) and perhaps even highlighted, or whether disambiguation of the me and not-me is deemed critical to the felicity of the performance and indeed an aspect of the underlying structure that renders possession meaningful such that the collapse of the distinction can be a failure of performance (as appears to be the case in Mayotte), at some level, possession is everywhere both ambiguous and unambiguous, constituting both one entity and two, or one unified or continuous self and one double or multiple or discontinuous self, much as when we say we are of two minds about something (cf. Lambek 2010, 2013).

10 I owe this insight and comparison to discussions years ago with Paul Antze. We described this in an orally delivered and never published paper as a form of "privileged communication."

11 My first book was called *Human Spirits*, evidently a paradox. The point was that spirits are constituted as alter to humans yet, as human products, can only be refracted humans, and further that although the cure or initiation in Mayotte is to get spirits to behave more like humans, in order to maintain their identity as spirits they had to periodically violate those human practices and assumptions and remind everyone of their difference from humans.

12 On incommensurability, Lambek 1993; on irony, 2003.

13 See Lambek 2008 for the suggestion that some indigenous concepts of divinity may be deictic.

14 An additional way to respond to the ostensibly contradictory remarks on the part of our interlocutors would be to take up the concept of "partial belief," a concept that was applied by Frank Ramsey to probabilistic predictions in economics (Misak 2020) but strangely has had little impact in the anthropology of religion. Some recent work on doubt aside, we tend to assume that people hold their beliefs (e.g., concerning the existence of God, but equally concerning the non-existence of God) with certainty rather than degrees of uncertainty. Where is the anthropology of agnosticism?

15 The conversational metaphor of Gadamerian hermeneutics might obviate some of the problems Goldman identifies.

16 The Rest is not a homogeneous object; it is a cover term for infinite diversity. Whereas the problems that Goldman describes are inherent in ethnographic

practice in which a lone anthropologist confronts a more or less singular and more or less homogeneous other world, Goldman rightly recognizes (in the quote above) that anthropology is constituted by trying to think through the relations between and among multiple worlds, whether two or three that a given anthropologist has confronted in person over a lifetime (or even more: think of Fredrik Barth) or by reading and comparing the work of other ethnographers and drawing on an anthropological conceptual vocabulary. Additionally, the members of a given society are unlikely to be in full agreement with each other, even with respect to fundamental assumptions. And, to increase the scale, non-Western societies have compared themselves to each other, often in the complete absence of the West as a third.

17 Despite attachment to the term "possession," I do not think that most ethnographic accounts of the subject have seen it as analogous to chattel slavery or placed an emphasis on the host as property.

18 The term "power" in place of "spirit" is found also in Godfrey Lienhardt's magnificent account of the Dinka (1961).

19 Compare Simmel 2011. This might be seen as "experience," though it corresponds to neither *Erfahrung* nor *Erlebnis*.

20 Unfortunately, Ishii does not provide examples, whether in English or Japanese or in Twi or Tulu in which she worked, but it would be good to know how speakers make use of this verbal modality and specifically with reference to possession. In any case, it requires the ethnographer has sufficient linguistic ability to discern it. The middle voice, or something like it, is found in Malagasy, where, I would say, it forms an affinity with spirit possession rather than setting its manifestation or interpretation in any given direction.

21 Lambek 2002. In Malagasy transcription, these would be *menjiky, mianjaka,* and *manjaka.*

22 For my own attempts in this direction with respect to the mind/body problem, irony, and the forensic and mimetic dimensions of the person, see respectively Lambek 1998, 2003, 2013.

23 The term is Janet Malcom's (1982), used with respect to psychoanalysis.

Bibliography

Introduction

Abramson, Allen and Martin Holbraad. 2014. "Introduction: The Cosmological Frame in Anthropology." In Allen Abramson and Martin Holbraad (eds) *Framing Cosmologies: The Anthropology of Worlds*, 1–30. Manchester and New York: Manchester University Press.

Anchor, Robert. 1978. "History and Play: Johan Huizinga and His Critics." *History and Theory* 17 (1): 63–93.

Babcock-Abrahams, Barbara. 1975. "'A Tolerated Margin of Mess': The Trickster and His Tales Reconsidered." *Journal of the Folklore Institute* 11 (3): 147–86.

Bateson, Gregory. 2000 [1972]. *Steps to an Ecology of Mind*. Chicago: University of Chicago Press.

Beliso-de Jesús, Aisha. 2015. *Electric Santería: Racial and Sexual Assemblages of Transnational Religion*. New York: Columbia University Press.

Boddy, Janice. 1988. "Spirits and Selves in Northern Sudan: the Cultural Therapeutics of Possession and Trance." *American Ethnologist* 15 (1): 4–27.

Caillois, Roger 2001 [1961]. *Man, Play, and Games*. Urbana, IL: University of Illinois Press.

Carmeli, Yoram. 2001. "Circus Play, Circus Talk, and the Nostalgia for a Total Order." *Popular Culture* 35 (3): 157–64.

Clark, Andy and David Chalmers. 1998. "The Extended Mind." *Analysis* 58 (1): 7–19.

Cohen, Emma. 2007. *The Mind Possessed: The Cognition of Spirit Possession in an Afro-Brazilian Religious Tradition*. Oxford and New York: Oxford University Press.

Comaroff, Jean and John Comaroff (eds) 1993. *Modernity and Its Malcontents: Ritual and Power in Postcolonial Africa*. Chicago: University Press of Chicago.

Csikszentmihalyi, Mihaly. 1990. *Flow: The Psychology of Optimal Experience*. New York: Harper and Row.

Danforth, Loring. 1989. *Firewalking and Religious Healing: The Anastenaria of Greece and the American Firewalking Movement*. Princeton: Princeton University Press.

Espírito Santo, Diana. 2016. "Clothes for Spirits: Opening and Closing the Cosmos in Brazilian Umbanda." *HAU: Journal of Ethnographic Theory* 6 (3): 85–106. ISSN 2049-1115 (Online).

Espírito Santo, Diana. 2017. "Possession Consciousness, Religious Individualism, and Subjectivity in Brazilian Umbanda." *Religion* 47 (2): 179–202.

Forman, Milos. 1999. *Man on the Moon*. Written by Alexander Scott and Larry Karraszewski. Feature Film.

Geschiere, Peter. 1997. *The Modernity of Witchcraft: Politics and the Occult in Postcolonial Africa*. Charlottesville: University of Virginia Press.

Geschiere, Peter. 2013. *Witchcraft, Intimacy and Trust: Witchcraft in Comparison*. Chicago: University of Chicago Press.

Goldman, Marcio. 1985. "A construção ritual da pessoa: a possessão no Candomblé." *Religião e Sociedade* 12 (1): 22–54.

Goldman, Marcio. 2005. "Formas do Saber e Modos do Ser: Observacões Sobre Multiplicidade e Ontologia no Candomblé." *Religião e Sociedade* 25 (2): 102–20.

Goldman, Marcio. 2007. "How to Learn in an Afro-Brazilian Spirit Possession Religion, Ontology and Multiplicity in Candomble." In David Berliner and Ramon Sarró (eds) *Learning Religion: Anthropological Approaches*, 103–20. Oxford and New York: Berghahn.

Handelman, Don. 1967. "The Development of a Washo Shaman." *Ethnology* 6 (4): 444–64.

Handelman, Don. 1992. "Passages to Play: Paradox and Process." *Play and Culture* 5: 1–19.

Handelman, Don. 1998. *Models and Mirrors: Towards an Anthropology of Public Events.* New York: Berghahn.

Handelman, Don. 2004. "Introduction: Why Ritual in Its Own Right? How So?" *Social Analysis* 48 (2): 1–32.

Handelman, Don. 2008. "Afterword: Returning to Cosmology – Thoughts on the Positioning of Belief." *Social Analysis* 52 (1): 181–95.

Handelman, Don. 2021. *Mobius Anthropology: Essays on the Forming of Form.* Edited by Matan Shapiro and Jackie Feldman. New York and Oxford: Berghahn.

Holbraad, Martin. 2012. *Truth in Motion: The Recursive Anthropology of Cuban Divination.* Chicago: University of Chicago Press.

Huizinga, J. 1970 [1939]. *Homo Ludens: A Study of the Play Element in Culture.* London: Maurice Temple Smith Ltd.

Hutchins, Edwin. 1995. *Cognition in the Wild.* Cambridge, MA: MIT Press.

Hyde, Lewis. 1998. *Trickster Makes This World: Mischief, Myth and Art.* New York: Farrar, Strous & Giroux.

Jensen, Casper Bruun, Miho Ishii and Philip Swift. 2016. "Attuning to the Webs of *en*: Ontography, Japanese Spirit Worlds, and the 'Tact' of Minakata Kumagusu." *HAU: Journal of Ethnographic Theory* 6 (2): 149–72.

Johnson, Paul. 2014. "Spirits and Things in the Making of the Afro-Atlantic World." In Paul C. Johnson (ed.) S*pirited Things: The Work of "Possession" in Afro-Atlantic Religions*, 1–22. Chicago: University of Chicago.

Kapferer Bruce. 1997. *The Feast of the Sorcerer: Practices of Consciousness and Power.* Chicago: University of Chicago Press.

Kapferer Bruce. 2005. "Ritual Dynamics and Virtual Practice: Beyond Representation and Meaning." In Don Handelman and Galina Lindquist (eds) *Ritual in Its Own Right: Exploring the Dynamics of Transformation*, 35–54. New York: Berghahn Books.

Kreinath, J. 2012. "Naven, Moebius Strip, and Random Fractal Dynamics: Reframing Bateson's Play Frame and the Use of Mathematical Models for the Study of Ritual." *Journal of Ritual Studies* 26 (2): 39–64.

Lambek, Michael. 1980. "Spirits and Spouses: Possession as a System of Communication among the Malagasy Speakers of Mayotte." *American Ethnologist* 7 (2): 318–31.

Lambek, Michael. 1996. "Afterword: Spirits and Their History." In Jeannette Mageo and Alan Howard (eds) *Spirits in Culture, History and Mind*, 237–50. New York: Routledge.

Luhrmann, Tanya. 2012. "A Hyperreal God and Modern Belief: Toward an Anthropological Theory of Mind." *Current Anthropology* 53 (4): 371–95.

Malabou, Catherine. 2010. *Plasticity at the Dusk of Writing: Dialectic, Destruction, Deconstruction.* Translated by Carolyn Shread. New York: Columbia University Press.

Nachmanovitch, Stephen. 2009. "This Is Play." *New Literary History* 40: 1–24.

Neuman, Yair. 2003. "Mobius and Paradox: On the Abstract Structure of Boundary Events in Semiotic Systems." *Semiotica* 147 (1/4): 135–48.

Ochoa, Todd, Ramón. 2007. "Versions of the Dead: *Kalunga*, Cuban-Kongo Materiality, and Ethnography." *Cultural Anthropology* 22 (4): 473–50.

Ochoa, Todd, Ramón. 2010. *Society of the Dead: Quita Manaquita and Palo Praise in Cuba*. Berkeley: University of California Press.

Otero, Solimar. 2020. *Archives of Conjure: Stories of the Dead in Afrolatinx Cultures*. New York: Columbia University Press.

Sanders, Todd and Henrietta Moore (eds) 2001. *Magical Interpretations, Magical Realities: Modernity, Witchcraft and the Occult in Postcolonial Africa*. Abingdon: Routledge.

Shapiro, Matan. 2016. "Curving the Social, or, Why Antagonistic Rituals in Brazil Are Variations on a Theme." *Journal of Royal Anthropological Institute (JRAI)* 22 (1): 47–66.

Shapiro, Matan. 2021. "Introduction." In Matan Shapiro and Jackie Feldman (eds) *Mobius Anthropology: Essays on the Forming of Form*, 1–16. New York and Oxford: Berghahn.

Smith, Chris. 2017. *Jim & Andy: The Great Beyond*. Netflix Documentary.

Stoller, Paul. 1989. *Fusion of the Worlds: Ethnography of Possession among the Songhay of Niger*. Chicago: University of Chicago Press.

Wafer, Jim. 1991. *The Taste of Blood: Spirit Possession in Brazilian Candomblé*. Philadelphia: University of Pennsylvania Press.

Wagner, Roy. 1981. *The Invention of Culture*. 2nd ed. Chicago: University of Chicago Press.

Winnicott, D. 2005 [1971]. *Playing and Reality*. London, UK: Routledge Classic.

Chapter 1

Aspen, Harald. 2001. *Amhara Traditions of Knowledge: Spirit Mediums and Their Clients*. Wiesbaden: Harassowitz Verlag.

Boddy, Janice. 1993. "Subversive Kinship: The Role of Spirit Possession in Negotiating Social Place in Rural Northern Sudan." *POLAR: Political Legal Anthropology Review* 16 (2): 29–37.

Brown, Peter. 1981. *The Cult of the Saints: Its Rise and Function in Latin Christianity*. Chicago: University of Chicago Press.

Boylston, Tom. 2018. *The Stranger at the Feast: Prohibition and Mediation in an Ethiopian Orthodox Christian Community*. Berkeley: University of California Press.

Espírito Santo, Diana. 2013. "Fluid Divination: Movement, Chaos, and the Generation of 'Noise' in Afro-Cuban Spiritist Oracular Production." *Anthropology of Consciousness* 24 (1): 35–56.

Hacking, Ian. 1999. *The Social Construction of What?* Cambridge, MA: Harvard University Press.

Handelman, Don. 2004. "Introduction: Why Ritual in Its Own Right? How so?" *Social Analysis* 48 (2): 1–32.

Hermann, Yodit. 2010. "Le Rituel de l'Eau Bénite: Une Réponse Sociale et Symbolique à la Pandémie du Sida." *Annales d'Ethiopie* 25 (1): 229–45.

Josipovici, Gabriel. 1996. *Touch*. New Heaven: Yale University Press.

Lambek, Michael. 1988. "Spirit Possession/Spirit Succession: Aspects of Social Continuity among Malagasy Speakers in Mayotte." *American Ethnologist* 15 (4): 710–31.

Lambek, Michael. 2003. "Rheumatic Irony: Questions of Agency and Self-deception as Refracted through the Art of Living with Spirits." *Social Analysis* 47 (2): 40–59.

Lambek, Michael. 2013. "Kinship, Modernity and the Immodern." In Susan McKinnon and Fenella Cannell (eds) *Vital Relations: Modernity and the Persistent Life of Kinship*, 241–60. Santa Fe: School for Advanced Research Press.

Levine, Donald. N. 1965. *Wax & Gold: Tradition and Innovation in Ethiopian Culture.* Chicago: University of Chicago Press.

Lindhardt, Martin. 2017. "Pentecostalism and the Encounter with Traditional Religion in Tanzania: Combat, Congruence and Confusion." *PentecoStudies* 16 (1): 35–58.

Malara, Diego Maria. 2019. "Exorcizing the Spirit of Protestantism: Ambiguity and Spirit Possession in an Ethiopian Orthodox Ritual." *Ethnos*, Online First, https://doi.org/10.1 080/00141844.2019.1631871

Malara, Diego Maria. 2020. "Sympathy for the Devil: Secrecy, Magic and Transgression among Ethiopian Orthodox Debtera." *Ethnos, Online First*, https://doi. org/10.1080/00141844. 2019.1707255

Malara, Diego Maria and Tom Boylston. 2016. "Vertical Love: Forms of Submission and Top-Down Power in Orthodox Ethiopia." *Social Analysis* 60 (4): 40–57.

McKinnon, Susan and Fenella Cannell. 2013. "The Difference That Kinship Makes." In Susan McKinnon and Fenella Cannell (eds) *Vital Relations: Modernity and the Persistent Life of Kinship*, 3–38. Santa Fe: School for Advanced Research Press.

Pandolfo, Stefania. 2018. *Knots of the Soul: Madness, Psychoanalysis, Islam.* Chicago: Chicago University Press.

Quiroz, Sitna. 2013. "Relating as Children of God: Ruptures and Continuities in Kinship among Pentecostal Christians in the South-east of the Republic of Benin." Unpublished PhD thesis. LSE.

Reece, Koreen. 2019. "A Global Family: Kinship, Nations, and Transnational Organisations in Botswana's Time of Aids." In Sandra Bamford (ed.) *The Cambridge Handbook of Kinship*, 675–99. Cambridge: Cambridge University Press.

Seremetakis, Nadia. C. 1990. "The Ethics of Antiphony: The Social Construction of Pain, Gender, and Power in the Southern Peloponnese." *Ethos* 18 (4): 481–512.

Tsintjilonis, Dimitri. 2019. "The Past Is a Promise to the Future: Stories, Persons and the Devil in Greece." *Journal of the Royal Anthropological Institute* 25 (1): 148–65.

Vilaseca, David. 1999. "Juan Goytisolo's Queer (be)hindsight." *Modern Language Review* 94: 426–37.

Chapter 2

Bastide, Roger. 2007 [1978]. *The African Religions of Brazil: Toward a Sociology of the Interpenetration of Civilizations.* Baltimore and London: Johns Hopkins University Press.

Beliso-De Jesús, Aisha. 2015. *Electric Santería: Racial and Sexual Assemblages of Transnational Religion.* New York: Columbia University Press.

Boddy, Janice. 1994. "Spirit Possession Revisited: Beyond Instrumentality." *Annual Review of Anthropology* 23: 407–34.

Bonilla-Silva, Eduardo. 2003. *Racism without Racists: Color-blind Racism and the Persistence of Racial Inequality in the United States.* Lanham, MD: Rowman & Littlefield.

Bubandt, Nils. 2002. "Interview with an Ancestor: Spirits as Informants and the Politics of Possession in North Maluku." *Ethnography* 10 (3): 291–316.

Capone, Stefania. 2010. *Searching for Africa in Brazil: Power and tradition in Candomblé.* Durham and London: Duke University Press.

de la Fuente, Alejandro. 2001. *A Nation for All: Race, Inequality and Politics in Twentieth-century Cuba*. Chapel Hill: University of North Carolina Press.

Descola, Philippe. 2013. *Beyond Nature and Culture*. Chicago and London: The University of Chicago Press.

Eliade, Mircea. 1974 [1949]. *The Myth of the Eternal Return or, Cosmos and History*. Princeton: Princeton University Press.

Essed, Philomena and David Theo Goldberg (eds) 2002. *Race Critical Theories*. Malden, MA and Oxford: Blackwell Publishers.

Fanon, Frantz. 2008 [1952]. *Black Skin, White Masks*. New York: Grove Press.

Fraser, Carly. 2009. "Race, Post-black Politics, and the Democratic Presidential Candidacy of Barack Obama." *Souls: A Critical Journal of Black Politics, Culture, and Society* 11 (1): 17–40.

Frazier E. F. 1957. *Race and Cultural Contacts in the Modern World*. New York: Alfred A. Knopf.

Gans, Herbert J. 1999. "The Possibility of a New Racial Hierarchy in the Twenty-first Century United States." In M. Lamont (ed.) *The Cultural Territories of Race: Black and White Boundaries*, 371–90. Chicago and London: University of Chicago Press.

Gilroy, Paul. 2010. *Darker than Blue: On the Moral Economies of Black Atlantic Culture*. Cambridge, MA and London: The Belknap Press of Harvard University Press.

Glazer, Nathan and Daniel P. Moynihan 1970 [1963]. *Beyond the Melting Pot*. Cambridge, MA: MIT Press.

Halloy, Arnaud and Vlad Naumescu. 2012. "Learning Spirit Possession: An Introduction." *Ethnos: Journal of Anthropology* 77 (2): 155–76.

Herskovits, Melville J. 1941. *The Myth of the Negro Past*. New York: Harper.

Hill, Rickey. 2009. "The Race Problematic, the Narrative of Martin Luther King Jr., and the Election of Barack Obama." *Souls: A Critical Journal of Black Politics, Culture, and Society* 11 (1): 60–78.

Johnson, Paul Christopher. 2011. "An Atlantic Genealogy of 'Spirit Possession.'" *Comparative Studies in Society and History* 53 (2): 393–425.

Kramer, Fritz. 1993. *The Red Fez: Art and Spirit Possession in Africa*. London: Verso.

Lambek, Michael. 1998. "The Sakalava Poiesis of History: Realizing the Past through Spirit Possession in Madagascar." *American Ethnologist* 25 (2): 106–27.

Lambek, Michael. 1993. "Cultivating Critical Distance: Oracles and the Politics of Voice." *Political and Legal Anthropology Review* 16 (2): 9–18.

Marable, Manning. 1996. *Beyond Black and White*. New York: Verso.

Matory, J. Lorand. 2018. *The Fetish Revisited: Marx, Freud, and the Gods Black People Make*. Durham and London: Duke University Press.

Mintz, Sidney W. and Richard Price. 1992 [1976]. *The Birth of African-American Culture: An Anthropological Approach*. Boston: Beacon Press.

Ochoa, Todd Ramón. 2010. *Society of the Dead: Quita Manaquita and Palo Praise in Cuba*. Berkeley, Los Angeles and London: University of California Press.

Ortiz, Fernando. 2001 [1906]. *Los negros brujos: Apuntes para un estudio de etnología criminal*. Habana: Editorial de Cièncias Sociales.

Palmié, Stephan. 2013. *The Cooking of History: How Not to Study Afro-Cuban Religion*. Chicago and London: The University of Chicago Press.

Panagiotopoulos, Anastasios. 2011. "The Island of Crossed Destinies: Human and Other-than-Human Perspectives in Afro-Cuban Divination." (Unpublished doctoral dissertation). University of Edinburgh, UK.

Panagiotopoulos, Anastasios. 2017. "When Biographies Cross Necrographies: The Exchange of 'Affinity' in Cuba." *Ethnos: Journal of Anthropology* 82 (5): 946–70.

Panagiotopoulos, Anastasios. 2018. "Food-for-Words: Sacrificial *Counterpoint* and Oracular *Articulacy* in Cuba." *HAU: Journal of Ethnographic Theory* 8 (3): 474–87.

Park, Robert E. 1950. *Race and Culture*. New York: Free Press.

Piot, Charles and Anne Allison. 2013. "Editors' Note." *Cultural Anthropology* 28 (3): 369–71.

Steinberg, Stephen. 2014. "The Long View of the Melting Pot." *Ethnic and Racial Studies* 37 (5): 790–4.

Stoller, Paul. 1995. *Embodying Colonial Memories: Spirit Possession, Power and the Hauka in West Africa*. New York: Routledge.

Taussig, Michael. 1993. *Mimesis and Alterity: A Particular History of the Senses*. New York and London: Routledge.

Viveiros De Castro, Eduardo. 1998. "Cosmological Deixis and Amerindian Perspectivism." *Journal of the Royal Anthropological Institute* 4: 469–88.

Wagner, Roy. 1981 [1975]. *The Invention of Culture*. Chicago and London: University of Chicago Press.

Yelvington, Kevin A. 2001. "The Anthropology of Afro-Latin America and the Caribbean: Diasporic dimensions." *Annual Review of Anthropology* 30: 227–60.

Chapter 3

Adelugba, Dapo. 1976. "Trance and Theater: The Nigerian Experience." *Ufahamu: A Journal of African Studies*, 6 (2): 47–61.

Albers, Irene. 2008. "Mimesis and Alterity: Michel Leiris's Ethnography and Poetics of Spirit Possession." *French Studies* 62 (3) (July 1): 271–89.

Anderson, Mark. 2009. *Black and Indigenous: Garifuna Activism and Consumer Culture in Honduras*. Minneapolis: University of Minnesota Press.

Barad, Karen. 2007. *Meeting the Universe Halfway: Quantum Physics and the Entanglement of Matter and Meaning*. Durham, NC: Duke University Press.

Barrett, Justin and Emma Cohen. 2008. "Conceptualizing Spirit Possession: Ethnographic and Experimental Evidence." *Ethos* 36 (2): 246–67.

Bateson, Gregory. 1972. "A Theory of Play and Fantasy." In G. Bateon's (ed.) *Steps to an Ecology of Mind*, 177–93. New York: Ballantine.

Bateson, Gregory. 1988. "Play and Paradigm." *Play and Culture* 1: 20–7.

Becker, Judith. 2004. *Deep Listeners: Music, Emotion and Trancing*. Bloomington: Indiana University Press.

Birth, Kevin. 1997. "Most of Us Are Family Some of the Time: Interracial Unions and Transracial Kinship in Eastern Trinidad." *American Ethnologist* 24 (3) (August): 585–601.

Birth, Kevin. 1999. *Any Time Is Trinidad Time: Social Meanings and Temporal Consciousness*. Gainesville: University Press of Florida.

Boddy, Janice. 1989. *Wombs and Alien Spirits: Women, Men and the Zar Cult in Northern Sudan*. Madison: University of Wisconsin Press.

Boddy, Janice. 1994. "Spirit Possession Revisited: Beyond Instrumentality." *Annual Review of Anthropology* 23: 407–34.

Bourguignon, Erika. 1968. *A Cross-cultural Study of Dissociational States*. Columbus: Research Foundation, Ohio State University.

Bourguignon, Erika. 1976. *Possession. Chandler & Sharp Series in Cross-cultural Themes.* San Francisco, CA: Chandler & Sharp.

Bourguignon, Erika. 1989. "Multiple Personality, Possession Trance, and the Psychic Unity of Mankind." *Ethos* 17 (3): 371–84.

Brooks, David. 2010. "The Underlying Tragedy." *The New York Times*, January 14.

Caldwell, Sarah. 1999. *Oh Terrifying Mother: Sexuality, Violence, and Worship of the Goddess Kali.* New Delhi and New York: Oxford University Press.

Carnegie, C. V. 2006. "The Anthropology of Ourselves: An Interview with Sidney W. Mintz." *Small Axe: A Caribbean Journal of Criticism* 10 (1): 106–79.

Cohen, Peter F. 2002. "Orisha Journeys: The Role of Travel in the Birth of Yorùbá-Atlantic Religions." *Archives de Sciences Sociales des Religions* 47 (117) (March): 17–36.

Crosson, J. Brent. 2020a. *Experiments with Power: Obeah, Justice, and the Remaking of Religion in Trinidad.* Chicago: University of Chicago Press.

Crosson, J. Brent. 2020b. "Burdens of Proof: Obeah, Petroleum Geology, and Its Mediums in Trinidad." In Ehler Voss (ed.) *Mediality on Trial.* Berlin: De Gruyter.

Dayan, Joan. 1995. *Haiti, History, and the Gods.* Berkeley: University of California Press.

Deikman, Arthur. 1969. "Deautomization and the Mystic Experience." In *Altered States of Consciousness.* New York: Anchor Books.

Du Bois, W. 2009 [1903]. *The Souls of Black Folk.* Oxford University Press.

Duncan, Carol. 2008. *This Spot of Ground: Spiritual Baptists in Toronto.* Waterloo, Ontario: Wilfrid Laurier University Press.

Espírito Santo, Diana. 2017. "Possession Consciousness, Religious Individualism, and Subjectivity in Brazilian Umbanda." *Religion* 47 (2): 179–202.

Fanon, Frantz. 1967. *Black Skin, White Masks.* New York: Grove Press.

Fanon, Franz. 2004 [1961]. *The Wretched of the Earth.* New York: Grove Press.

Feinberg, Benjamin. 2003. *The Devil's Book of Culture: History, Mushrooms, and Caves in Southern Mexico.* Austin: University of Texas Press.

Foucault, Michel. 1991. *The Foucault Effect: Studies in Governmentality: With Two Lectures by and an Interview with Michel Foucault.* Chicago: University of Chicago Press.

Foucault, Michel. 1977. *Discipline and Punish: The Birth of the Prison.* 1st ed. New York: Pantheon Books.

Frazer, James G. 1958 [1890]. *The Golden Bough.* New York: Macmillan.

Gibson, Keane. 2001. *Comfa Religion and Creole Language in a Caribbean Community.* Albany: State University of New York Press.

Gibbal, Jean-Marie. 1982. *Tambours d'eau: journal et enquête sur un culte de possession au Mali occidental.* Paris: Le Sycomore.

Gilroy, Paul. 1993. *The Black Atlantic: Modernity and Double Consciousness.* Cambridge, MA: Harvard University Press.

Gordon, Edmund T. and Mark Anderson. 1999. "The African Diaspora: Toward an Ethnography of Diasporic Identification." *The Journal of American Folklore* 112 (445) (Summer): 282–96.

Halloy, Arnaud and Vlad Naumescu. 2012. "Learning Spirit Possession: An Introduction." *Ethnos* 77 (2): 155–76.

Handelman, Don. 1992. "Passages to Play: Paradox and Process." *Play and Culture* 5: 1–15.

Harrison, Lawrence. 2010. "Haiti and the Voodoo Curse." *The Wall Street Journal*, February 5. Accessed 4 December 2017. https://www.wsj.com/articles/SB10001424052 7487045332045750471634353484660

Harrison, Lawrence and Samuel Huntington (eds) 2000. *Culture Matters: How Values Shape Human Progress.* New York: Basic Books.

Hayes, Kelly. 2011. *Holy Harlots: Femininity, Sexuality, and Black Magic in Brazil*. Berkeley: University of California Press.

Heike, Behrend and Ute Luig (eds) 1999. *Spirit Possession, Modernity and Power in Africa*. Oxford: James Currey.

Henriques, Julian. 2008. "Sonic Diaspora, Vibrations, and Rhythm: Thinking through the Sounding of the Jamaican Dancehall Session." *African and Black Diaspora: An International Journal* 1 (July): 215–36.

Henry, Frances. 2003. *Reclaiming African Religions in Trinidad: The Socio-political Legitimation of the Orisha and Spiritual Baptist Faiths*. Barbados and London: University of the West Indies Press.

Herskovits, Melville. 1947. *Trinidad Village*. 1st ed. New York: A.A. Knopf.

Houk, James. 1995. *Spirits, Blood, and Drums: The Orisha Religion in Trinidad*. Philadelphia: Temple University Press.

Johnson, Paul Christopher. 2011a. "An Atlantic Genealogy of 'Spirit Possession.'" *Comparative Studies in Society and History* 53 (2): 393–425.

Johnson, Paul Christopher. 2011b. *Diaspora Conversions: Black Carib Religion and the Recovery of Africa*. Berkeley: University of California Press.

Johnson, Paul Christopher. 2014a. "Introduction: Spirits and Things in the Making of the Afro-Atlantic World." In Paul Christopher Johnson (ed.) *Spirited Things: The Work of "Possession" in Afro-Atlantic Religions*, 1–22. Chicago: University of Chicago Press.

Johnson, Paul Christopher. 2014b. "Towards an Atlantic Genealogy of Spirit Possession." In Paul Christopher Johnson (ed.) *Spirited Things: The Work of "Possession" in Afro-Atlantic Religions*, 23–46. Chicago: University of Chicago Press.

Johnson, Paul Christopher. 2019. "Possession's Native Land." *Ethnos* 84 (4): 660–77.

Keeney, Bradford (ed.) 2002. *The Shakers of St. Vincent*. Philadelphia: Ringing Rocks Press.

Kramer, Fritz. 1993. *The Red Fez: Art and Spirit Possession in Africa*. London and New York: Verso.

Lambek, Michael. 2014. "Afterword: Recognizing and Misrecognizing Spirit Possession." In Paul C. Johnson (ed.) *Spirited Things: The Work of "Possession" in Afro-Atlantic Religions*. Chicago: University of Chicago Press.

Leiris, Michel. 1958. *La Possession et ses Aspects Théâtreaux chez les Éthiopiens de Gondar*. Paris: Plon.

Ludwig, Arnold. 1968. "Altered States of Consciousness." In *Trnace and Possession States*. Montreal: R.M. Bucke Memorial Society.

Lum, Kenneth. 2000. *Praising His Name in the Dance: Spirit Possession in the Spiritual Baptist Faith and Orisha work in Trinidad, West Indies*. Australia: Harwood Academic Publishers.

Mathews, Andrew S. 2011. *Instituting Nature: Authority, Expertise, and Power in Mexican Forests*. Cambridge, MA: MIT Press.

Matory, James. 2005. *Black Atlantic Religion: Tradition, Transnationalism, and Matriarchy in the Afro-Brazilian Candomblé*. Princeton, NJ: Princeton University Press.

Matory, James. 2009. "The Many Who Dance in Me: Afro-Atlantic Ontology and the Problem with 'Transnationalism.'" In *Transnational Transcendence: Essays on Religion and Globalization*. Berkeley: University of California Press.

McNeal, Keith. 2003. "Doing the Mother's Caribbean Work." In Rachel Fell McDermott and Jeffrey J. Kripal (eds) *Encountering Kali: In the Margins, at the Center, in the West*. Berkeley: University of California Press.

McNeal, Keith. 2011. *Trance and Modernity: African and Hindu Popular Religions in Trinidad and Tobago*. Gainesville: University Press of Florida.

McNeal, Keith. N.d. "Pantheons as Mythistorical Archives: Pantheonization and Remodeled Iconographies in Two Southern Caribbean Possession Religions." (Author's Manuscript).

Miller, Daniel. 1994. *Modernity, an Ethnographic Approach: Dualism and Mass Consumption in Trinidad*. Oxford and Providence, RI: Berg.

Mintz, Sidney. 1985. *Sweetness and Power: The Place of Sugar in Modern History*. New York: Viking.

Morris, Rosalind. 2000. *In the Place of Origins: Modernity and Its Mediums in Northern Thailand*. Durham, NC: Duke University Press.

Morris, Rosalind. 2001. "Modernity's Media and the End of Mediumship?" In *Millenial Capitalism and the Culture of Neoliberalism*. Durham: Duke University Press.

Ochoa, Todd Ramón. 2010. "PRENDAS-NGANGAS-ENQUISOS: Turbulence and the Influence of the Dead in Cuban-Kongo Material Culture." *Cultural Anthropology* 25 (3): 387–420.

Ong, Aihwa. 1988. "The Production of Possession: Spirits and the Multinational Corporation in Malaysia." *American Ethnologist* 15 (1) (February): 28–42.

Ong, Aihwa. 1987. *Spirits of Resistance and Capitalist Discipline: Factory Women in Malaysia*. Albany: State University of New York Press.

Palmié, Stephan. 2002. *Wizards and Scientists: Explorations in Afro-Cuban Modernity and Tradition*. Durham, NC: Duke University Press.

Palmié, Stephan. 2006. "Creolization and Its Discontents." *Annual Review of Anthropology* 35: 433–520.

Palmié, Stephan. 2007. "Ecue's Atlantic: An Essay in Methodology." *Journal of Religion in Africa* 37 (April): 275–315.

Paton, Diana. 2009. "Obeah Acts: Producing and Policing the Boundaries of Religion in the Caribbean." *Small Axe* 13 (1) (January 1): 1–18.

Rouget, Gilbert. 1985. *Music and Trance*. Chicago: University of Chicago Press.

Routon, Kenneth. 2006. "Trance-Nationalism: Religious Imaginaries of Belonging in The Black Atlantic." *Identities: Global Studies in Culture and Power* 13 (3) (September 1): 483–502.

Schmidt, Leigh Eric. 2000. *Hearing Things: Religion, Illusion, and the American Enlightenment*. Cambridge, MA: Harvard University Press.

Sedgwick, Eve Kosofsky. 1994. "Epidemics of the Will." In *Tendencies*, 141–52. New York: Routledge.

Singh, Bhrigupati. 2012. "The Headless Horseman of Central India: Sovereignty at Varying Thresholds of Life." *Cultural Anthropology* 27 (2): 383–407.

Stoller, Paul. 1995. *Embodying Colonial Memories: Spirit Possession, Power, and the Hauka in West Africa*. New York: Routledge.

Taussig, Michael. 1993. *Mimesis and Alterity: A Particular History of the Senses*. New York: Routledge.

Thornton, John. 1992. *Africa and Africans in the Making of the Atlantic World: 1400–1680*, 1st ed. Cambridge: Cambridge University Press.

van der Walde, Peter. 1968. "Trance States and Ego Psychology." In *Trance and Possession States*. Montreal: R.M. Bucke Memorial Society.

Veal, Michael. 2007. *Dub: Soundscapes and Shattered Songs in Jamaican Reggae*. Middletown, CT: Wesleyan University Press.

Vertovec, Steven. 1998. "Ethnic Distance and Religious Convergence: Shango, Spiritual Baptist, and Kali Mai Traditions in Trinidad." *Social Compass* 45 (2) (June 1): 247–63.

Ward, Colleen and Michael Beaubrun. 1979. "Trance Induction and Hallucination in Spiritual Baptist Mourning." *The Journal of Psychological Anthropology* 2 (4).

Wilson, Peter J. 1967. "Status Ambiguity and Spirit Possession." *Man*, New Series 2 (3) (September): 366–78.

Wilson, Peter. 1969. "Reputation and Respectability: A Suggestion for Caribbean Ethnology." *Man* 4 (1): 70.

Wilson, Peter. 1973. *Crab Antics the Social Anthropology of English-speaking Negro Societies of the Caribbean*. New Haven: Yale University Press.

Wirtz, Kristina. 2014. "Spiritual Agency, Materiality, and Knowledge in Cuba." In Paul C. Johnson (ed.) *Spirited Things*, 99–130. Chicago: University of Chicago Press.

Zane, Wallace. 1999. *Journeys to the Spiritual Lands: The Natural History of a West Indian Religion*. New York: Oxford University Press.

Chapter 4

Andersen, Paul Kent. 1989. "Remarks on the Origin of the Term 'Passive'." *Lingua* 79: 1–16.

Beattie, John. 1969. "Spirit Mediumship in Bunyoro." In John Beattie and John Middleton (eds) *Spirit Mediumship and Society in Africa*, 159–70. London: Routledge and Kegan Paul.

Benveniste, Émile. 1966. *Problèmes de Linguistique Générale*. Paris: Editions Gallimard.

Boddy, Janice. 1994. "Spirit Possession Revisited: Beyond Instrumentality." *Annual Review of Anthropology* 23: 407–34.

Brückner, Heidrun. 2009. *On an Auspicious Day, at Dawn … : Studies in Tulu Culture and Oral Literature*. Wiesbaden: Harrassowitz Verlag.

Candea, Matei. 2011. "Endo/Exo." *Common Knowledge* 17 (1): 146–50. Accessed January 12, 2021. https://doi.org/10.1215/0961754X-2010-046

Claus, Peter J. 1978. "Oral Traditions, Royal Cults and Materials for a Reconsideration of the Caste System in South India." *Journal of Indian Folkloristics* 1 (1): 1–25.

Claus, Peter J. 1984. "Medical Anthropology and the Ethnography of Spirit Possession." *Contributions to Asian Studies* 18: 60–72.

Comaroff, Jean and John L. Comaroff. 1999. "Occult Economies and the Violence of Abstraction: Notes from the South African Postcolony." *American Ethnologist* 26 (2): 279–303.

Geschiere, Peter. 1997. *The Modernity of Witchcraft: Politics and the Occult in Postcolonial Africa*. Translated by Peter Geschiere and Janet Roitman. Charlottesville: The University Press of Virginia.

Graeber, David. 2015. "Radical Alterity Is Just Another Way of Saying 'Reality': A Reply to Eduardo Viveiros de Castro." *HAU: Journal of Ethnographic Theory* 5(2): 1–41.

Henare, Amiria, Martin Holbraad and Sari Wastell. 2007. "Introduction: Thinking through Things." In Amiria Henare, Martin Holbraad and Sari Wastell (eds) *Thinking through Things: Theorising Artefacts Ethnographically*, 1–31. London: Routledge.

Holbraad, Martin. 2009. "Ontography and Alterity: Defining Anthropological Truth." *Social Analysis* 53 (2): 80–93.

Ishii, Miho. 2005. "From Wombs to Farmland: The Transformation of *Suman* Shrines in Southern Ghana." *Journal of Religion in Africa* 35 (3): 266–95.

Ishii, Miho. 2013. "Playing with Perspectives: Spirit Possession, Mimesis, and Permeability in the *Buuta* Ritual in South India." *Journal of the Royal Anthropological Institute* 19 (4): 795–812.

Ishii, Miho. 2014. "Traces of Reflexive Imagination: Matriliny, Modern Law, and Spirit Worship in South India." *Asian Anthropology* 13 (2): 106–23.

Ishii, Miho. 2015. "Wild Sacredness and the Poiesis of Transactional Networks: Relational Divinity and Spirit Possession in the *Būta* Ritual of South India." *Asian Ethnology* 74 (1): 87–109.

Ishii, Miho. 2019. *Modernity and Spirit Worship in India: An Anthropology of the Umwelt.* London and New York: Routledge.

Johnson, Paul Christopher. 2011. "An Atlantic Genealogy of 'Spirit Possession.'" *Comparative Studies in Society and History* 53 (2): 393–425.

Kanaya, Takehiro. 2004. *Eigo nimo Shugo wa Nakatta* (There was no Subject in English too). Tokyo: Kōdan-sha.

Kemmer, Suzanne. 1993. *The Middle Voice.* Amsterdam and Philadelphia: John Benjamins Publishing Company.

Kokubun, Koichiro. 2017. *Chū-dō-tai no Sekai: Ishi to Sekinin no Kōkogaku* (The World of the Middle Voice: An Archaeology of Will and Responsibility). Tokyo: Igaku Shoin.

Kramer, Fritz. 1993. *The Red Fez: Art and Spirit Possession in Africa.* Translated by M. R. Green. London: Verso.

Lambek, Michael. 1993. *Knowledge and Practice in Mayotte: Local Discourses of Islam, Sorcery, and Spirit Possession.* Toronto: University of Toronto Press.

Lambek, Michael. 2010. "How to Make Up One's Mind: Reason, Passion, and Ethics in Spirit Possession." *University of Toronto Quarterly* 79 (2): 720–41.

Lewis, I. M. 1966. "Spirit Possession and Deprivation Cults." *Man* (N.S.) 1 (3): 307–29.

Lienhardt, Godfrey. 1961. *Divinity and Experience: The Religion of the Dinka.* Oxford: Oxford University Press.

Lord, Carol. 1993. *Historical Change in Serial Verb Constructions.* Amsterdam and Philadelphia: John Benjamins Publishing Company.

Macksey, Richard and Eugenio Donato (eds) 1972. *The Structuralist Controversy: The Languages of Criticism and the Sciences of Man.* Baltimore and London: The Johns Hopkins University Press.

Matsushima, Takeshi. 2014. *Psico-Nautica: Italia Seishin Iryō no Jinruigaku* (Psico-Nautica: An Anthropology of Mental Health in Italy). Kyoto: Sekaishisōsya.

Monier-Williams, Monier. 2008 [1899]. *A Sanskrit-English Dictionary: Etymologically and Philologically Arranged: With Special Reference to Cognate Indo-European Languages.* New Delhi and Chennai: Asian Educational Services.

Okazaki, Akira. 2003. "'Making Sense of the Foreign': Translating Gamk Notions of Dream, Self and Body." In T. Maranhão and B. Streck (eds) *Translation and Ethnography: The Anthropological Challenge of Intercultural Understanding*, 152–71. Tucson: University of Arizona Press.

Smith, Frederick M. 2006. *The Self Possessed: Deity and Spirit Possession in South Asian Literature and Civilization.* New York: Columbia University Press.

Taussig, Michael. 1980. *The Devil and Commodity Fetishism in South America.* Chapel Hill, NC: The University of North Carolina Press.

Upadhyaya, Uliyar Padmanabha (ed.) 1988–1997. *Tulu Lexicon*, vols. 1–6. Udupi: Rashtrakavi Govind Pai Samshodhana Kendra.

Vigh, Henrik E. and David B. Sausdal. 2014. "From Essence Back to Existence: Anthropology beyond the Ontological Turn." *Anthropological Theory* 14 (1): 49–73.

Viveiros de Castro, Eduardo B. 2014. "Who Is Afraid of the Ontological Wolf? Some Comments on an Ongoing Anthropological Debate." CUSAS Annual Marilyn Strathern Lecture, May 30. Accessed October 14, 2016. https://sisu.ut.ee/sites/default/files/biosemio/files/cusas_strathern_lecture_2014.pdf

von Uexküll, Jacob. 1921. *Umwelt und Innenwelt der Tiere*. Berlin: Verlag von Julius Springer.
von Weizsäcker, Victor. 1946. *Anonyma*. Bern: Verlag A. Francke AG.
von Weizsäcker, Victor. 1997 [1950]. *Der Gestaltkreis: Theorie der Einheit von Wahrnehmen und Bewegen*. Frankfurt am Main: Suhrkamp Verlag.

Chapter 5

Abramson, Allen and Martin Holbraad. 2014. "Introduction: The Cosmological Frame in Anthropology." In Allen Abramson and Martin Holbraad (eds) *Framing Cosmologies: The Anthropology of Worlds*, 1–30. Manchester: University of Manchester Press.
Beliso-De Jesús, Aisha M. 2015. *Electric Santería: Racial and Sexual Assemblages of Transna-tional Religion*. New York: Columbia University Press.
Bolívar Aróstegui, Natalia. 1990. *Los orishas en Cuba*. Havana: Editorial Ciencias Sociales.
Deleuze, Gilles and Félix Guattari. 1994. *What Is Philosophy?* Translated by Graham Burchell and Hugh Tomlinson. London: Verso.
Espírito Santo, Diana. 2013. "Materiality, Cosmogony and Presence among Cuban Spirits and Mediums." In Diana Espírito Santo and Nico Tassi (eds) *Making Spirits: Materiality and Transcendence in Contemporary Religions*, 33–56. London: I.B. Tauris.
Espírito Santo, Diana. 2014. "Plasticidade e pessoalidade no espiritismo crioulo cubano." *Mana* 20 (1): 63–93
Espírito Santo, Diana. 2015a. *Developing the Dead: Mediumship and Selfhood in Cuban Espiritismo*. Gainesville: University Press of Florida.
Espírito Santo, Diana. 2015b. "Liquid Sight, Thing-like Words, and the Precipitation of Knowledge Substances in Cuban Espiritismo." *Journal of the Royal Anthropological Institute* 21 (3): 579–96.
Figarola, Joel James. 2006. *La brujería cubana: El Palo Monte*. Santiago de Cuba: Editorial Oriente.
Handelman, Don. 1998 [1990]. *Models and Mirrors: Towards an Anthropology of Public Events*. London: Berghahn Books.
Handelman, Don. 2004. "Introduction: Why Ritual in Its Own Right? How so?" *Social Analysis* 48 (2): 1–32.
Handelman, Don. 2021. "Epilogue: Forming Form and Folding Time." In Matan Shapiro, Jackie Feldman and Don Handelman (eds) *Thinking Mobeously: The Logic of Forming of Form in the Anthropology of Don Handelman*, 289–345. New York and London: Berghahn Press.
Holbraad, Martin. 2008. "Definitive Evidence, from Cuban Gods." *Journal of the Royal Anthropological Institute* 14 (1): 93–109.
Jensen, Casper Bruun, Miho Ishii and Philip Swift. 2016. "Attuning to the Webs of *en*: Ontography, Japanese Spirit Worlds, and the 'Tact' of Minakata Kumagusu." *HAU: Journal of Ethnographic Theory* 6 (2): 149–72
Kapferer, Bruce. 1997. *The Feast of the Sorcerer: Practices of Consciousness and Power*. Chicago: University of Chicago Press.
Kapferer, Bruce. 2002. "Introduction: Outside All Reason – Magic, Sorcery and Epistemology in Anthropology." In Bruce Kapferer (ed.) *Beyond Rationalism: Rethinking Magic, Witchcraft and Sorcery*, 1–30. New York and London: Berghahn Press.

Keane, Webb. 2013. "On Spirit Writing: Materialities of Language and the Religious Work of Transduction." *Journal of the Royal Anthropological Institute* 19 (1): 1–17.

Malabou, Catherine. 2010. *Plasticity at the Dusk of Writing: Dialectic, Destruction, Deconstruction*. Translated by Carolyn Shread. New York: Columbia University Press.

Massumi, Brian. 2002. *Parables for the Virtual: Movement, Affect, Sensation*. Durham: Duke University Press.

Millet, José. 1996. *El Espiritismo: Variantes Cubanas*. Santiago de Cuba: Editorial Oriente.

Minakata, Kumagusu. 1971. *Minakata Kumagusu zenshū: 7. Shokan*. Tokyo: Heibonsha.

Nielsen, Morten. 2012. "Interior Swelling: On the Expansive Effects of Ancestral Interventions in Maputo, Mozambique." *Common Knowledge* 18 (3): 433–50.

Ochoa, Todd Ramón. 2010. "PRENDAS-NGANGAS-ENQUISOS: Turbulence and the Influence of the Dead in Cuban-Kongo Material Culture." *Cultural Anthropology* 25 (3): 387–420.

Palmié, Stephan. 2006. "Thinking with *Ngangas*: Reflections on Embodiment and the Limits of 'Objectively Necessary Appearances'." *Comparative Studies in History and Society* 48: 852–86.

Panagiotopoulos, Anastasios. 2017. "When Biographies Cross Necrographies: The Exchange of 'Affinity' in Cuba." *Ethnos* 82 (5): 946–70.

Pérez, Elizabeth. 2012. "Staging Transformation: Spiritist Liturgies as Theatres of Conversion in Afro-Cuban Religious Practice." *Culture and Religion* 13 (3): 361–89.

Román, Reinaldo. 2007. *Governing Spirits: Religion, Miracles, and Spectacles in Cuba and Puerto Rico*. Chapel Hill: University of North Carolina Press.

Shapiro, Matan. 2016. "Curving the Social, or, Why Antagonistic Rituals in Brazil Are Variations on a Theme." *Journal of the Royal Anthropological Institute* 22 (1): 47–66.

Sjørslev, Inger. 2013. "Boredom, Rhythm, and the Temporality of Ritual: Recurring Fieldwork in the Brazilian Candomblé." *Social Analysis* 57 (1): 95–109.

Wirtz, Kristina. 2007. *Ritual, Discourse, and Religious Community in Cuban Santería: Speaking a Sacred World*. Gainesville: University Press of Florida.

Wirtz, Kristina. 2016. "The Living, the Dead, and the Immanent: Dialogue across Chronotopes." *HAU: Journal of Ethnographic Theory* 6 (1): 343–69.

Chapter 6

Asad, Talal. 1986. "The Concept of Cultural Translation in British Social Anthropology." In J. Clifford and G. Marcus (eds) *Writing Culture: The Poetics and Politics of Ethnography*, 141–64. Berkeley: University of California Press.

Asad, Talal. 1997. "Remarks on the Anthropology of the Body." In Sarah Coakley (ed.) *Religion and the Body*, 42–52. Cambridge: Cambridge University Press.

Asamoah-Gyadu, J. Kwabena. 2005. *African Charismatics Current Developments within Independent Indigenous Pentecostalism in Ghana*. Leiden: Brill.

Bateson, Gregory. 1972. *Steps to an Ecology of Mind*. San Francisco: Chandler.

Beliso-De Jesús, Aisha. 2015. *Electric Santería: Racial and Sexual Assemblages of Transnational Religion*. New York: Columbia University Press.

Berliner, David and Ramon Sarró. 2007. *Learning Religion: Anthropological Approaches*. New York: Berghahn Books.

Bialecki, Jon. 2015. "Affect: Intensities and Energies in the Charismatic Language, Embodiment, and Genre of a North American Movement." In Simon Coleman,

Rosalind I. J. Hackett and Joel Robbins (eds) *The Anthropology of Global Pentecostalism and Evangelicalism*, 95–108. NYU Press.

Bialecki, Jon. 2017. *A Diagram for Fire: Miracles and Variation in an American Charismatic Movement*. Berkeley: University of California Press.

Blumenberg, Hans. 2016. *Paradigms for a Metaphorology*. Ithaca, NY: Cornell University Press.

Boddy, Janice. 1988. "Spirits and Selves in Northern Sudan: The Cultural Therapeutics of Possession and Trance." *American Ethnologist* 15 (1): 4–27.

Boddy, Janice. 1994. "Spirit Possession Revisited: Beyond Instrumentality." *Annual Review of Anthropology* 23: 407–34.

Brahinsky, Josh. 2013. "Cultivating Discontinuity: Pentecostal Pedagogies of Yielding and Control." *Anthropology & Education Quarterly* 44 (4): 399–422.

Bynum, Caroline W. 1991. *Fragmentation and Redemption: Essays on Gender and the Human Body in Medieval Religion*. New York: Zone Books.

Coleman, Simon. 2009. "Transgressing the Self: Making Charismatic Saints." *Critical Inquiry* 35 (3): 417–39.

Collu, Samuele. 2019. "Refracting Affects: Affect, Psychotherapy, and Spirit Dis-Possession." *Culture, Medicine, and Psychiatry* 43: 290–314.

Comaroff, Jean. 1985. *Body of Power Spirit of Resistance: The Culture and History of a South African People*. Chicago: Chicago University Press.

Crapanzano, Vincent. 1982. "The Self, the Third, and Desire." In B. Lee (ed.) *Psychosocial Theories of the Self*, 179–206. Boston: Springer.

Crapanzano, Vincent and Vivian Garrison. 1988. *Case Studies in Spirit Possession*. Ann Arbor, MI: University Microfilms International.

Csikszentmihalyi, Mihaly. 1990. *Flow: The Psychology of Optimal Experience*. New York: Harper & Row.

Csordas, Thomas. 1997. *The Sacred Self: A Cultural Phenomenology of Charismatic Healing*. Berkeley: University of California Press.

De Abreu, Maria José. 2008. "Goose Bumps All Over: Breath, Media, Tremor." *Social Text* 25 (3): 59–78.

Debaise, Didier. 2008. "Une métaphysique des possessions: Puissances et sociétés chez Gabriel Tarde." *Revue de Métaphysique et de Morale* 60 (4): 447–60.

Delanda, Manuel. 2005. "Space: Extensive and Intensive, Actual and Virtual." In Ian Buchanan and Gregg Lambert (eds) *Deleuze and Space*, 80–8. Edinburgh: Edinburgh University Press.

DeHeusch, Luc. 2007. *Why Marry Her? Society and Symbolic Structures*. Cambridge: Cambridge University Press.

Eisenlohr, Patrick. 2018. "Suggestions of Movement: Voice and Sonic Atmospheres in Mauritian Muslim Devotional Practices." *Cultural Anthropology* 33 (1): 32–57.

Engelke, Matthew Eric. 2007. *A Problem of Presence beyond Scripture in an African Church*. Berkeley: University of California Press.

Espírito Santo, Diana. 2018. "Assemblage Making, Materiality, and Self in Cuban Palo Monte." *Social Analysis* 62 (3): 67–87.

Faubion, James. 2011. *An Anthropology of Ethics*. New York: Cambridge University Press.

Foucault, Michel. 1997. "On the Genealogy of Ethics: An Overview of Work in Progress." In P. Rabinow (ed.) *Ethics: Subjectivity and Truth*, 253–80. New York: The New Press.

Foucault, Michel. 2006. *The Hermeneutics of the Subject: Lectures at the Collège de France, 1981–1982*. New York: Picador.

Gibson, James. 1979. *The Ecological Approach to Visual Perception*. Boston: Houghton Mifflin.

Goldman, Marcio. 2007. "How to Learn in an Afro-Brazilian Spirit Possession Religion: Ontology and Multiplicity in Candomblé." In D. Berliner and R. Sarró (eds) *Learning Religion: Anthropological Approaches*, 103–19. New York: Berghahn Books.

Halloy, Arnaud and Vlad Naumescu. 2012. "Learning Spirit Possession: An Introduction." *Ethnos* 77 (2): 155–76.

Holbraad, Martin and Morten Axel Pedersen. 2017. *The Ontological Turn*. West Nyack: Cambridge University Press.

Ingold, Tim. 2001. *The Perception of the Environment Essays on Livelihood, Dwelling and Skill*. New York: Routledge.

Ivakhiv, Adrian. 2003. "Orchestrating Sacred Space: Beyond the 'Social Construction' of Nature." *Ecotheology* 8 (1): 11–29.

Johnson, Christopher. 2011. "An Atlantic Genealogy of 'Spirit Possession'." *Comparative Studies in Society and History* 53 (2): 393–425.

Kirsch, Thomas. 2013. "Intangible Motion. Notes on the Morphology and Mobility of the Holy Spirit." In Ruy Llera Blanes and Diana Espírito Santo (eds) *The Social Life of Spirits*, 33–51. Chicago: University of Chicago Press.

Kramer, Fritz. 1993. *The Red Fez: Art and Spirit Possession in Africa*. London: Verso.

Lambek, Michael and Michael Lambek. 1981. *Human Spirits: A Cultural Account of Trance in Mayotte*. New York: Cambridge University Press.

Lambek, Michael. 1993. *Knowledge and Practice in Mayotte: Local Discourses of Islam, Sorcery and Spirit Possession*. Toronto: University of Toronto Press.

Lambek, Michael. 2016. "On Contradictions." *Hau: Journal of Ethnographic Theory* 6 (1): 6–13.

Lambek, Michael (ed.) 2011. *Ordinary Ethics: Anthropology, Language, and Action*. New York: Fordham University Press.

Latour, Bruno. 2002. "Gabriel Tarde and the End of the Social." In Patrick Joyce (ed.) *The Social in Question: New Bearings in History and the Social Sciences*, 117–32. Routledge: London.

Lempert, Michael. 2014. "Imitation." *Annual Review of Anthropology* 43: 379–95.

Lewis, Ioan. 2003. *Ecstatic Religion: A Study of Shamanism and Spirit Possession*. London: Routledge.

Luhrmann, Tanya. 2012. *When God Talks Back: Understanding the American Evangelical Relationship with God*. New York: Alfred A. Knopf.

MacIntyre, Alasdair. 1984. *After Virtue. A Study in Moral Theory*. Notre Dame, IN: University of Notre Dame Press.

Mahmood, Saba. 2001. "Rehearsed Spontaneity and the Conventionality of Ritual: Disciplines of Ṣalat." *American Ethnologist* 28 (4): 827–53.

Mahmood, Saba. 2005. *Politics of Piety: The Islamic Revival and the Feminist Subject*. Princeton, NJ: Princeton University Press.

Meyer, Birgit. 1998. "'Make a Complete Break with the Past' Memory and Post-Colonial Modernity in Ghanaian Pentecostalist Discourse." *Journal of Religion in Africa* 28 (3): 316–49.

Mittermaier, Amira. 2012. "Dreams from Elsewhere: Muslim Subjectivities beyond the Trope of Self-cultivation." *Journal of the Royal Anthropological Institute* 18 (2): 247–65.

Oduro-Frimpong, Joseph. 2014. "Sakawa Rituals and Cyberfraud in Ghanaian Popular Video Movies." *African Studies Review* 57 (2): 131–47.

Pálsson, Gísli. 1994. "Enskilment at Sea." *Man* 29: 901–27.

Reinhardt, Bruno. 2014. "Soaking in Tapes: The Haptic Voice of Global Pentecostal Pedagogy in Ghana." *Journal of the Royal Anthropological Institute* 20 (2): 315–36.

Reinhardt, Bruno. 2015. "A Christian Plane of Immanence? Contrapuntal Reflections on Deleuze and Pentecostal Spirituality." *HAU: Journal of Ethnographic Theory* 5 (1): 405.

Reinhardt, Bruno. 2016. "'Don't Make It a Doctrine' Material Religion, Transcendence, Critique." *Anthropological Theory* 16 (1): 75–97.

Reinhardt, Bruno. 2017a. "Praying Until Jesus Returns: Commitment and Prayerfulness Among Charismatic Christians in Ghana." *Religion* 47 (1): 51–72.

Reinhardt, Bruno. 2017b. "The Pedagogies of Preaching: Skill, Performance, and Charisma in a Pentecostal Bible School from Ghana." *Journal of Religion in Africa* 47: 72–107.

Reinhardt, Bruno. 2020. "Atmospheric Presence: Reflections on 'Mediation' in the Anthropology of Religion and Technology." *Anthropological Quarterly* 93 (1): 1523–53. In Press.

Robbins, Joel. 2004. *Becoming Sinners: Christianity and Moral Torment in a Papua New Guinea Society*. Berkeley: University of California Press.

Robbins, Joel. 2009. "Pentecostal Networks and the Spirit of Globalization: On the Social Productivity of Ritual Forms." *Social Analysis* 53 (1): 55–66.

Schechner, Richard. 2003. *Performance Studies: An Introduction*. London: Routledge.

Silverstein, Michael. 1993. "Metapragmatic Discourse and the Metapragmatic Function." In John Lucy (ed.) *Reflexive Language: Reported Speech and Metapragmatics*, 33–58. Cambridge: Cambridge University Press.

Stewart, Kathleen. 2011. "Atmospheric Attunements." *Environment and Planning D: Society and Space* 29: 445–53.

Stoller, Paul. 1989. *Fusion of the Worlds: An Ethnography of Possession among the Songhay of Niger*. Chicago: University of Chicago Press.

Tarde, Gabriel de. 2012. *Monadology and Sociology*. Melbourne: Re.press.

Taussig, Michael. 1987. *Shamanism, Colonialism, and the Wild Man A Study in Terror and Healing*. Chicago: University of Chicago Press.

Taussig, Michael. 1993. *Mimesis and Alterity: A Particular History of the Senses*. New York: Routledge.

Turner, Victor. 1974. "Liminal to Liminoid in Play, Flow and Ritual: An Essay in Comparative Symbology." *Rice University Studies* 60 (3): 53–92.

Wagner, Roy. 1981. *The Invention of Culture*. Chicago: University Of Chicago Press.

Chapter 7

Bastide, Roger. 1978. *The African Religions of Brazil: Toward a Sociology of the Interpenetration of Civilizations*. Baltimore: Johns Hopkins University Press.

Bateson, Gregory. 2000 [1972]. *Steps to an Ecology of Mind*. Chicago: University of Chicago Press.

Bilu, Yoram. 1985. "The Taming of the Deviants and beyond: An Analysis of Dybbuk Possession and Exorcism in Judaism." *Psychiatric Studies of Society* 11: 1–32.

Birman, Patrícia. 2009. "Feitiçarias, Territórios e Resistências Marginais." *Mana* 15 (2): 321–48.

Birman, Patrícia. 2012. "O Poder da Fé, o Milagre do Poder: Mediadores Evangélicos e Deslocamento de Fronteiras Sociais." *Horizontes Antropológicos* 18 (37): 133–53.

Boyer, Pascal. 2001. *Religion Explained: The Evolutionary Origins of Religious Thought*. New York: Basic Books.

Burdick, John. 1998. *Blessed Anastasia: Women, Race and Popular Christianity in Brazil.* Routledge: New York and London.

Butticci, Annalisa. 2016. *African Pentecostals in Catholic Europe: The Politics of Presence in the Twenty-First Century.* Cambridge, MA and London, UK: Harvard University Press.

Cohen, Emma and Justin Barrett. 2008. "Conceptualizing Spirit Possession: Ethnographic and Experimental Evidence." *Ethos* 36 (2): 246–67.

Chesnut, Andrew. 2003. "A Preferential Option for the Spirit: The Catholic Charismatic Renewal in Latin America's New Religious Economy." *Latin American Politics and Society* 45 (1): 55–85.

Chesnut, Andrew. 2007. *Competitive Spirits: Latin America's New Religious Economy.* New York: Oxford University Press.

Espírito Santo, Diana. 2016. "Clothes for Spirits: Opening and Closing the Cosmos in Brazilian Umbanda." *HAU: Journal of Ethnographic Theory* 6 (3): 85–106. ISSN 2049-1115 (Online).

Espírito Santo, Diana. 2017. "Possession Consciousness, Religious Individualism, and Subjectivity in Brazilian Umbanda." *Religion* 47 (2): 179–202.

Fry, Peter and Nigel Howe. 1975. "Duas respostas à aflição: umbanda e pentecostalismo." *Debate e Crítica* 6: 75–94.

Giumbelli, Emerson. 2013. "Cultura pública: evangélicos y su presencia en la sociedad brasileña." *Sociedad y Religión* XXIII (40): 13–43.

Halloy, Arnaud. 2012. "Gods in the Flesh: Learning Emotions in the Xangô Possession Cult (Brazil)." *Ethnos* 77 (2): 177–202.

Handelman, Don. 1992. "Passages to Play: Paradox and Process." *Play and Culture* 5: 1–19.

Handelman, Don. 1998. *Models and Mirrors: Towards an Anthropology of Public Events.* New York: Berghahn.

Handelman, Don. 2004. "Introduction: Why Ritual in Its Own Right? How so?" *Social Analysis* 48 (2): 1–32.

Harding, Susan. 2000. *The Book of Jerry Falwell: Fundamentalist Language and Politics.* Princeton: Princeton University Press.

Hayes, Kelly E. 2008. "Wicked Women and Femmes Fatales: Gender, Power and Pomba Gira in Brazil." *History of Religions* 48 (1): 1–21.

Holbraad, Martin. 2012. *Truth in Motion: The Recursive Anthropology of Cuban Divination.* Chicago: University of Chicago Press.

Kapferer, Bruce. 1983. *A Celebration of Demons: Exorcism and the Aesthetics of Healing in Sri Lanka.* Bloomington: Indiana University Press.

Kramer, Eric. 2002. "Making Global Faith Universal: Media and a Brazilian Prosperity Movement." *Culture and Religion* 3 (1): 21–47.

Kramer, Eric. 2005. "Spectacle and the Staging of Power in Brazilian Neo-Pentecostalism." *Latin American Perspectives* 32 (1): 95–120.

Lévi-Strauss, Claude. 1979 [1973]. "The Effectiveness of Symbols." In Lessa, William and Armand (eds) *Reader in Comparative Religion: An Anthropological Approach*, 318–27. New York: Harper and Row.

Luhrmann, Tanya. 2012. "A Hyperreal God and Modern Belief: Toward an Anthropological Theory of Mind." *Current Anthropology* 53 (4): 371–95.

Mafra, Clara, Swatowiski Claudia and Camila Sampaio. 2012. "O Projeto Pastoral de Edir Macedo: Uma Igreja Benevolente para Indivíduos Ambiciosos?" *Revista Brasileira de Ciências Sociais* 27 (78): 81–192.

Mayblin, Maya. 2010. *Gender, Catholicism, and Morality in Brazil: Virtuous Husbands, Powerful Wives*. London and New York: Palgrave Macmillan.

Meyer, Birgit. 2010. "Aesthetics of Persuasion: Global Christianity and Pentecostalism's Sensational Forms." *South Atlantic Quarterly* 109: 741–63.

Nachmanovitch, Stephen. 2009. "This Is Play." *New Literary History* 40: 1–24.

Oosterbaan, Martjin. 2011. "Virtually Global: Online Evangelical Cartography." *Social Anthropology/Anthropologie Sociale* 19 (1): 56–73.

Oro, Pedro, Ari. 2005. "O Pentecostelismo Macumbeiro." *REVISTA USP* (68): 319–32.

Pina-Cabral, João. 2007. "O Diabo e o Dilema Brasileiro: Uma Perspectiva Anticesurista II." São Paulo, USP: *Revista de Antropologia* 50 (2): 477–525.

Reinhardt, Bruno. 2007. *Espelho ante Espelho: A troca e a Guerra entre o Neopentecostalismo e os Cultos Afro-Brasileiros em Salvador*. São Paulo: Attar.

Robbins, Joel. 2004. *Becoming Sinners*. Berkeley: University of California Press.

Selka, Stephen. 2010. "Morality in the Religious Marketplace: Evangelical Christianity, Candomblé, and the Struggle for Moral Distinction in Brazil." *American Ethnologist* 37 (2): 291–307.

Shapiro, Matan. 2016a. "Curving the Social, or, Why Antagonistic Rituals in Brazil are Variations on a Theme." *Journal of Royal Anthropological Institute (JRAI)* 22 (1): 47–66.

Shapiro, Matan. 2016b. "Paradoxes of Intimacy: Play and the Ethic of Invisibility in Northeast Brazil." *Journal of Latin American Studies (JLAS)* 48 (4): 797–821.

Shapiro, Matan. 2019. "Moral Topology and the Making of Cosmological Boundaries: The Case of Neo-Pentecostal Exorcism in Brazil." *Social Analysis*, 63 (3), Autumn: 71–88. Doi:10.3167/sa.2019.630304

Shapiro, Matan. 2020. "Appropriating *Terra Santa*: Holy Land Tours, Awe, and the 'Judaization' of Brazilian neo-Pentecostalism." In Martijn Oosterbaan, Linda van de Kamp, and Joana Bahia (eds) *Lusospheres: Global Trajectories of Brazilian Religion*, 37–55. London, Oxford, New York, New Delhi and Sydney: Bloomsbury Publishing.

Silva, Vagner Gonçalves Da. 2007. "Neopentecostalismo e Religiões Afro-Brasileiras: Significados do Ataque aos Símbolos da Herança Religiosa Africana no Brasil Contemporâneo." *Mana* 13 (1): 207–36.

Sluhovsky, Moshe. 2007. *Believe Not Every Spirit: Possession, Mysticism, and Discernment in Early Modern Catholicism*. Chicago: University of Chicago Press.

Stewart, Charles. 1991. *Demons and the Devil: Moral Imagination in Modern Greek Culture*. Princeton: Princeton University Press.

Wellman, Henry M., David Cross and Julanne Watson. 2001. "Meta-analysis of Theory-of-Mind Development: The Truth about False Belief." *Child Development* 72: 655–84.

Chapter 8

Bender, Mark. 2008. "'Tribes of Snow': Animals and Plants in the Nuosu *Book of Origins*." *Asian Ethnology* 67 (1): 5–42.

Bender, Mark, Aku Wuwu, and Jjivot Zopqu trans. 2019. *The Nuosu Book of Origins: A Creation Epic from Southwest China*. Seattle: University of Washington Press.

Bloch, Maurice. 1992. *Prey into Hunter: The Politics of Religious Experience*. Cambridge: Cambridge University Press.

Deleuze, Gilles and Félix Guattari. 2004/1992. *A Thousand Plateaus: Capitalism and Schizophrenia*. London and New York: Continuum.

Espírito Santo, Diana. 2009. "Making Dreams; Spirits, Vision and the Ontological Effects of Dream Knowledge in Cuban *Espiritismo*." *Suomen Antropologi: Journal of the Finnish Anthropological Society* 34 (3): 6–24.

Espírito Santo, Diana. 2013. "Fluid Divination: Movement, Chaos, and the Generation of 'Noise' in Afro-Cuban Spiritist Oracular Production." *Anthropology of Consciousness* 24 (1): 32–56.

Espírito Santo, Diana. 2016. "Recursivity and the Self-Reflexive Cosmos: Tricksters in Cuban and Brazilian Spirit Mediumship Practices." *Social Analysis* 60 (1): 37–55.

Handelman, Don. 1992. "Passages to Play: Paradox and Process." *Play and Culture* 5: 1–19.

Handelman, Don. 1998. "*Symbolic Types—Clowns*" in *Models and Mirrors: Towards an Anthropology of Public Events*, 236–65. New York and Oxford: Berghahn.

Handelman, Don. 2006. "Framing." In Jens Kreinath, Jan Snoek and Michael Stausberg (eds) *Theorizing Rituals: Issues, Topics, Approaches, Concepts*, 571–82. Leiden: Brill.

Handelman, Don and David Shulman. 1997. *God Inside Out: Śiva's Game of Dice*. New York and Oxford: Oxford University Press.

Hill, Ann Maxwell and Eric Diehl. 2001. "A Comparative Approach to Lineages among the Xiao Liangshan Nuosu and Han." In Stevan Harrell (ed.) *Perspectives on the Yi of Southwest China*, 51–67. Berkeley, Los Angeles, and London: University of California Press.

Holbraad, Martin. 2012. *Truth in Motion: The Recursive Anthropology of Cuban Divination*. Chicago and London: University of Chicago Press.

Humphrey, Caroline. 1995. "Chiefly and Shamanist Landscapes in Mongolia." In Eric Hirsch and Michael O'Hanlon (eds) *The Anthropology of Landscape: Perspectives on Place and Space*, 135–62. Oxford: Clarendon Press.

Humphrey, Caroline and Hürelbaatar Ujeed. 2012. "Fortune in the Wind: An Impersonal Subjectivity." *Social Analysis* 56 (2): 152–67.

Kraef, Olivia. 2014. "Of Canons and Commodities: The Cultural Predicaments of Nuosu-Yi 'Bimo Culture'." *Journal of Current Chinese Affairs* 43 (2): 145–79.

Lash, Scott. 2012. "Deforming the Figure: Topology and the Social Imaginary." *Theory, Culture & Society* 29 (4/5): 261–87.

Oppitz, Michael. 1998. "Ritual Drums of the Naxi in the Light of Their Origin Stories." In Michael Oppitz and Elisabeth Hsu (eds) *Naxi and Moso Ethnography*, 311–42. Zürich: Völkerkundemuseum.

Pedersen, Morten Axel. 2007. "Multiplicity without Myth: Theorising Darhad Perspectivism." *Inner Asia* 9 (2): 311–28.

Swancutt, Katherine. 2007. "The Ontological Spiral: Virtuosity and Transparency in Mongolian Games." *Inner Asia* 9 (2): 237–59.

Swancutt, Katherine. 2012a. *Fortune and the Cursed: The Sliding Scale of Time in Mongolian Divination*. New York and Oxford: Berghahn.

Swancutt, Katherine. 2012b. "The Captive Guest: Spider Webs of Hospitality among the Nuosu of Southwest China." *Journal of the Royal Anthropological Institute* 18 (S1): S103–16.

Swancutt, Katherine. 2012c. "Fame, Fate-Fortune, and Tokens of Value among the Nuosu of Southwest China." *Social Analysis*, 56 (2): 56–72.

Swancutt, Katherine. 2015. "Imaginations at War: The Ephemeral and the Fullness of Life in Southwest China." In Øivind Fuglerud and Leon Wainwright (eds) *Objects and*

Imagination: Perspectives on Materialization and Meaning, 133–59. New York and Oxford: Berghahn.

Swancutt, Katherine. 2021. "The Chicken and the Egg: Cracking the Ontology of Divination in Southwest China." *Social Analysis* 65 (2): 19–40.

Thomassen, Bjørn. 2014. *Liminality and the Modern: Living through the in-between.* Farnham, Surrey and Burlington, VT: Ashgate.

Turner, Victor. 1967. *The Forest of Symbols: Aspects of Ndembu Ritual.* Ithaca and London: Cornell University Press.

Turner, Victor. 1969. *The Ritual Process: Structure and Anti-Structure.* Ithaca and London: Cornell University Press.

Turner, Victor. 1974. *Dramas, Fields, and Metaphors: Symbolic Action in Human Society.* Ithaca and London: Cornell University Press.

Turner, Victor. 1982. *From Ritual to Theatre: The Human Seriousness of Play.* New York: PAJ Publications.

Turner, Victor. 1986. *The Anthropology of Performance.* New York: PAJ Publications.

van Gennep, Arnold. 1960. *The Rites of Passage.* Monika B. Vizedom and Gabrielle L. Caffee (trans). Chicago and London: University of Chicago Press.

Chapter 9

Akenson, Donald Harmon. 2007. *Some Family: The Mormons and How Humanity Keeps Track of Itself.* Montréal: McGill-Queen's Press-MQUP.

Baugh, Alexander. 2002. "'For This Ordinance Belongeth to My House': The Practice of Baptism for the Dead Outside the Nauvoo Temple." *Mormon Historical Studies* 3 (1): 47–58.

Bennett, Richard. 2005. "'Line upon Line, Precept upon Precept': Reflections on the 1877 Commencement of the Performance of Endowments and Sealings for the Dead." *BYU Studies Quarterly* 44 (3): 39–77.

Bitton, Davis. 1974. "Mormonism's Encounter with Spiritualism." *Journal of Mormon History* 1 (1): 39–50.

Brooks, E. Marshall. 2018. *Disenchanted Lives: Apostasy and Ex-Mormonism among the Latter-day Saints.* Chicago: University of Chicago Press.

Brown, Samuel Morris. 2011. *In Heaven as It Is on Earth: Joseph Smith and the Early Mormon Conquest of Death.* Oxford: Oxford University Press.

Cannell, Fenella. 2005. "The Christianity of Anthropology." *Journal of the Royal Anthropological Institute* 11 (2): 335–56.

Cannell, Fenella. 2007. "How Does Ritual Matter?" In Astuti, Rita, Jonathan P. Parry and Charles Stafford (eds) *Questions of anthropology,* 105–36. Oxford, UK: Berg.

Cannell, Fenella. 2013. "The Blood of Abraham: Mormon Redemptive Physicality and American Idioms of Kinship." *Journal of the Royal Anthropological Association* 19 (S1): S77–94.

Colvin, Gina and Joanna Brooks (eds) 2018. *Decolonizing Mormonism: Approaching a Postcolonial Zion.* Salt Lake City, UT: University of Utah Press.

Evans, D.W. and John Grimshaw. 1871. *Journal of Discourses by President Brigham Young, His Two Counsellors, and the Twelve Apostles,* vol. 7. London: Horaace S. Eldredge.

Handman, Courtney. 2018. "The Language of Evangelism: Christian Cultures of Circulation beyond the Missionary Prologue." *Annual Review of Anthropology.* 47: 149–65.

Homer, Michael. W. 1994. "Spiritualism and Mormonism: Some Thoughts on the Similarities and Differences." *Le Défi magique* 1: 143–62.

Kramer, Bradley. 2014. "Keeping the Sacred: Structured Silence in the Enactment of Priesthood Authority, Gendered Worship, and Sacramental Kinship in Mormonism." Ph.D. dissertation, University of Michigan.

Lambek, Michael. 2003. "Rheumatic Irony: Questions of Agency and Self-deception as Refracted through the Art of Living with Spirits." *Social Analysis* 47 (2): 40–59.

Lambek, Michael. 2016. *The Weight of the Past: Living with History in Mahajanga, Madagascar*. New York City: Springer.

McConkie, Bruce. 1958. *Mormon Doctrine*. Salt Lake City, UT: Bookcraft, Inc.

Oppenheimer, Mark. 2012. "A Twist on Posthumous Baptisms Leaves Jews Miffed at Mormon Rite." *The New York Times*, March 2.

Otterstrom, Samuel. 2008. "Genealogy as Religious Ritual: The Doctrine and Practice of Family History in the Church of Jesus Christ of Latter-day Saints." In Dallen Timothy and Guelke Heanne Kay (eds) *Geography and Genealogy: Locating Personal Pasts*, 137–52. Aldershot, UK: Ashgate Press.

Stuy, Brian. 2000. "Wilford Woodruff's Vision of the Signers of the Declaration of Independence." *Journal of Mormon History* 26 (1): 64–90.

Watt, G.D. (ed.) 1851. *Journal of Discourses by Brigham Young, His Two Counsellors, the Twelve Apostles and Others*, vol. 2. London: Richards.

Woodruff, Wilford. 1855–86. *Journal of Discourses*, vol. 19. London and Liverpool: LDS Booksellers Depot.

Walker, Ronald Warren. 1998. *Wayward Saints: The Godbeites and Brigham Young*. Champaign, IL: University of Illinois Press.

Chapter 10

Asad, Talal. 1986. "The Concept of Cultural Translation in British Social Anthropology." In James Clifford and George Marcus (eds) *Writing Culture. The Poetics and Politics of Ethnography*, 141–64. Berkeley: University of California Press.

Barthes, Roland. 1961. "De Part et d'Autre." In *Essais Critiques*, 167–74. Paris: Seuil, 1964.

Bastide, Roger. 1958. *Le Candomblé de Bahia (Rite Nagô)*. París: Mouton.

Bateson, Gregory. 1956. "Toward a Theory of Schizophrenia." In *Steps to an Ecology of Mind: Collected Essays in Anthropology, Psychiatry, Evolution, and Epistemology*, 153–70. Chicago: University of Chicago Press, 1972.

Clastres, Pierre. 1968. "Entre Silence et Dialogue." In Raymond Bellour Et Cathérine Clément (orgs.). *Claude Lévi-Strauss*, 33–8. Paris: Gallimard, 1979.

Deleuze, Gilles. 1968. *Différence et Répétition*. Paris: PUF.

Deleuze, Gilles. 1993. *The Fold. Leibniz and the Baroque*. London and New Brunswick: The Athlone Press.

Deleuze, Gilles and Félix Guattari. 1994. *What Is Philosophy?* New York: Columbia University Press.

Detienne, Marcel. 1999. *The Masters of Truth in Archaic Greece*. New York: Zone Books.

Evans-Pritchard, Edward E. 1934. "Lévy-Bruhl's Theory of Primitive Mentality." *Bulletin of the Faculty of Arts, Egyptian University, Cairo (University of Egypt)* 2 (1): 1–36.

Evans-Pritchard, Edward E. 1937. *Witchcraft, Oracles and Magic among the Azande*. Oxford: Clarendon Press.

Evans-Pritchard, Edward E. 1956. *Nuer Religion*. Oxford: Oxford University Press.

Evans-Pritchard, Edward E. 1976. *Witchcraft, Oracles and Magic among the Azande* (abridged with an introduction by Eva Gillies). Oxford: Clarendon Press.

Foucault, Michel. 1976. "Cours du 7 janvier 1976." In *Dits et Écrits*, vol. 3, 160–75. Paris: Gallimard, 1994.

Geertz, Clifford. 1983. "'From the Native's Point of View': On the Nature of Anthropological Understanding." In *Local knowledge: Further Essays in Interpretive Anthropology*, 55–70. New York: Basic Books.

Goldman, Marcio. 1984. *A Possessão e a Construção Ritual da Pessoa no Candomblé*. Rio de Janeiro: UFRJ (Masters Thesis).

Goldman, Marcio. 2007. "How to Learn in an Afro-Brazilian Spirit Possession Religion. Ontology and Multiplicity in Candomblé." In Ramón Sarró and David Berliner (eds) *Learning Religion. Anthropological Approaches*, 103–19. Oxford: Berghahn Books.

Goldman, Marcio. 2009. "An Afro-Brazilian Theory of the Creative Process: An Essay in Anthropological Symmetrization." *Social Analysis* 53 (2): 108–29.

Goldman, Marcio. 2013. *How Democracy Works. An Ethnographic Theory of Politics*. London: Sean Kingston Publisher.

Goldman, Marcio. 2015. "Da Existência dos Bruxos (ou Como Funciona a Antropologia)." *R@U. Revista de Antropologia da UFSCar* 6 (1): 7–24.

Goldman, Marcio. 2016. "Cosmopolíticas, Etno-Ontologías y Otras Epistemologías." *Cuadernos de Antropología Social* 44: 27–35.

Goldman, Marcio. 2016. "Reading Roger Bastide: (Deutero) Learning the African Religions in Brazil." *Études Rurales* 196: 9–24.

Goldman, Marcio. 2017. "The Ontology of Possession in Bahian Candomblé." Working Papers Series #23: 1–6. Open Anthropology Cooperative (OAC) Press, February 23. http://openanthcoop.net/press/2017/02/23/the-ontology-of-possession-in-bahian-candomble/

Ingold, Tim. 1992. "Editorial." *Man* 27 (4): 693–6.

Latour, Bruno. 1993. *We Have Never Been Modern*. Essex: Pearson Education.

Latour, Bruno. 2003. *Un Monde Pluriel mais Commun. Entretiens avec François Ewald*. Paris: La Découverte.

Latour, Bruno. 2005. *Reassembling the Social*. Oxford: Oxford University Press.

Lévy-Bruhl. 1910. *Les Fonctions Mentales dans les Sociétés Inférieures*. Paris: PUF.

Lévy-Bruhl. 1938. *L'Expérience Mystique et les Symboles chez les Primitifs*. Paris: Félix Alcan.

Malinowski, Bronislaw. 1935. *Coral Gardens and Their Magic*. London: George Allen & Unwin.

Pignarre and Stengers. 2011. *Capitalist Sorcery. Breaking the Spell*. New York: Palgrave Macmillan.

Stengers, Isabelle. 2005. "The Cosmopolitical Proposal." In Bruno Latour and Peter Weibel (eds) *Making Things Public*, 994–1003. Cambridge, MA: MIT Press.

Stengers, Isabelle. 2011. *Cosmopolitics 7. The Curse of Tolerance*. Minneapolis: University of Minnesota Press.

Strathern, Marilyn. 1987. "Out of Context: The Persuasive Fictions of Anthropology." *Current Anthropology* 28 (3): 251–81.

Tylor, Edward Burnett. 1871. *Primitive Culture*. London: John Murray.

Viveiros De Castro, Eduardo. 2013. "The Relative Native." *HAU: Journal of Ethnographic Theory* 3 (3): 473–502.

Wagner, Roy. 1981. *The Invention of Culture*. Chicago: University of Chicago Press.

Weber, Max. 1967. *Ancient Judaism*. New York: Free Press.

Afterword

Anscombe, G. E. M. 1963. *Intention*. Ithaca: Cornell University Press.

Austin, J. L. 1965 [1955]. *How to Do Things with Words*. Oxford: Oxford University Press.

Bakhtin, Mikhail. 1984 [1965]. *Rabelais and His World*. Bloomington: Indiana University Press.

Boddy, Janice. 1989. *Wombs and Alien Spirits*. Madison: University of Wisconsin Press.

Brown, Peter. 1981. *The Cult of the Saints: Its Rise and Function in Latin Christianity*. Chicago: University of Chicago Press.

Cannell, Fenella. 2013. "The Re-enchantment of Kinship." In Susan McKinnon and Fenella Cannell (eds) *Vital Relations: Modernity and the Persistent Life of Kinship*, 217–40. Santa Fe: School for Advanced Research Press.

Crapanzano, Vincent. 1980. *Tuhami*. Chicago: University of Chicago Press.

Csikszentmihalyi, Mihaly. 1990. *Flow: The Psychology of Optimal Experience*. New York: Harper & Row.

Da Col, Giovanni and David Graeber. 2011. "Foreword: The Return of Ethnographic Theory." *Hau* 1 (1).

Daston, Lorraine. 2019. *Against Nature*. Cambridge MA: MIT Press.

Doniger, Wendy. 2014. *On Hinduism*. Oxford: Oxford University Press.

Douglas, Mary. 1966. *Purity and Danger*. London: Penguin.

Fernandez, James W. 1980 "Edification by Puzzlement." In Ivan Karp and Charles S. Bird (eds) *Explorations in African Systems of Thought*, 44–59. Bloomington: Indiana UP.

Gadamer, Hans-Georg. 1985. *Truth and Method*. New York: Crossroad.

Goffman, Erving. 1981. "Footing." In E. Goffman (ed.) *Forms of Talk*, 124–59. Philadelphia: University of Pennsylvania Press.

Handelman, Don and Galina Lindquist (eds) 2005. *Ritual in Its Own Right*. Oxford: Berghahn.

Handelman, Don, Matan Shapiro and Jackie Feldman (eds) forthcoming. *Thinking Mobeously: The Logic of Forming of Form in the Anthropology of Don Handelman*. New York and London: Berghahn Press.

Johnson, Paul Christopher. 2011. "An Atlantic Genealogy of 'Spirit Possession.'" *Comparative Studies in Society and History* 53 (2): 393–425.

Johnson, Paul Christopher (ed.) 2014. *Spirited Things: The Work of "Possession" in Afro-Atlantic Religions*. Chicago: University of Chicago Press.

Kapferer, Bruce. 1991. *A Celebration of Demons: Exorcism and the Aesthetics of Healing in Sri Lanka*. London: Berg.

Kapferer, Bruce. 1997. *The Feast of the Sorcerer: Practices of Consciousness and Power*. Chicago: University of Chicago Press.

Lambek, Michael. 1981. *Human Spirits: A Cultural Account of Trance in Mayotte*. Cambridge: Cambridge University Press.

Lambek, Michael. 1993. *Knowledge and Practice in Mayotte*. Toronto: University of Toronto Press.

Lambek, Michael. 1998. "Body and Mind in Mind, Body and Mind in Body." In M. Lambek and Andrew Strathern (eds) *Bodies and Persons: Comparative Perspectives from Africa and Melanesia*, 103–23. Cambridge: CUP.

Lambek, Michael. 2002. *The Weight of the Past: Living with History in Mahajanga, Madagascar*. New York: Palgrave Macmillan.

Lambek, Michael. 2003. "Rheumatic Irony: Questions of Agency and Self-Deception as Refracted through the Art of Living with Spirits." In M. Lambek and Paul Antze (eds) *Illness and Irony*, 40–59. New York: Berghahn. Reprinted in Lambek 2015, pp. 150–70.

Lambek, Michael. 2008. "Provincializing God? Provocations from an Anthropology of Religion." In Hent de Vries (ed.) *Religion: Beyond a Concept*, 120–38. New York: Fordham University Press.

Lambek, Michael. 2010. "How to Make Up One's Mind: Reason, Passion, and Ethics in Spirit Possession." *University of Toronto Quarterly* 79 (2) Special issue on Models of Mind, Marlene Goldman and Jill Matus, eds, 720–41.

Lambek, Michael. 2013. "The Continuous and Discontinuous Person: Two Dimensions of Ethical Life." *Journal of the Royal Anthropological Institute* 19: 837–58. Reprinted in Lambek 2015, pp. 302–28.

Lambek, Michael. 2015. *The Ethical Condition*. Chicago: University of Chicago Press.

Lambek, Michael. 2021. *Concepts and Persons*. The Tanner Lecture 2019. Toronto: University of Toronto Press.

Lévi-Strauss, Claude. 1966. *The Savage Mind*. Chicago: University of Chicago Press.

Lewis, I. M. 1971. *Ecstatic Religion*. Harmondsworth: Penguin.

Lienhardt, Godfrey. 1961. *Divinity and Experience*. Oxford: Clarendon.

Malcolm, Janet. 1982. *Psychoanalysis: The Impossible Profession*. New York: Vintage.

Masquelier, Adeline. 2001. *Prayer Has Spoiled Everything: Possession, Power, and Identity in an Islamic Town of Niger*. Durham, NC: Duke University Press.

Misak, Cheryl. 2020. *Frank Ramsey: A Sheer Excess of Powers*. Oxford: Oxford University Press.

Mulhall, Stephen. 2015. *The Great Riddle: Wittgenstein and Nonsense, Theology and Philosophy: The Stanton Lectures 2014*. Oxford: Oxford University Press.

Obeyesekere, Gananath. 1981. *Medusa's Hair*. Chicago: University of Chicago Press.

Pandolfo, Stephania. 2018. *Knot of the Soul: Madness, Psychoanalysis, Islam*. Chicago: University of Chicago Press.

Premawardhana, Devaka. 2018. *Faith in Flux: Pentecostalism and Mobility in Rural Mozambique*. Philadelphia: University of Pennsylvania Press.

Ram, Kalpana. 2013. *Fertile Disorder. Spirit Possession and Its Provocation of the Modern*. Honolulu: University of Hawaii Press.

Sahlins, Marshall. 2013. *What Kinship Is–And Is Not*. Chicago: University of Chicago Press.

Sahlins, Marshall. 2017. "The Original Political Society." *Hau: Journal of Ethnographic Theory* 7 (2): 91–128. Reprinted in Sahlins and Graeber, *On Kings*. Chicago: Hau Books.

Simmel, Georg. 2011 [1918]. *The View of Life: Four Metaphysical Essays*. Chicago: University of Chicago Press.

Stallybrass, Peter and Allon White. 1986. *The Politics and Poetics of Transgression*. Ithaca: Cornell University Press.

Stoller, Paul. 1989. *Fusion of the Worlds*. Chicago: University of Chicago Press.

Turner, Victor. 1969. *The Ritual Process: Structure and Anti-Structure*. Chicago: Aldine.

Index

www.ingramcontent.com/pod-product-compliance
Lightning Source LLC
Chambersburg PA
CBHW050428280326
41932CB00013BA/2038